MATCHING STUDENTS TO OPPORTUNITY

Expanding College Choice, Access, and Quality

Edited by

ANDREW P. KELLY
JESSICA S. HOWELL
CAROLYN SATTIN-BAJAJ

Harvard Education Press
Cambridge, Massachusetts

Paperback ISBN 978-1-61250-947-1
Library Edition ISBN 978-1-61250-948-8

Library of Congress Cataloging-in-Publication Data

Names: Kelly, Andrew P., editor. | Howell, Jessica S., editor. | Sattin-Bajaj, Carolyn, editor. |
Title: Matching students to opportunity : expanding college choice, access, and quality / edited by Andrew P. Kelly, Jessica S. Howell, Carolyn Sattin-Bajaj.
Description: Cambridge, Massachusetts : Harvard Education Press, [2016] | Includes bibliographical references and index.
Identifiers: LCCN 2016011696 | ISBN 9781612509471 (pbk.) | ISBN 9781612509488 (library edition)
Subjects: LCSH: College attendance--United States. | College choice--United States. | College students--Recruiting--United States. | College students--United States--Economic conditions. | College students--United States--Social conditions. | College costs--United States. | Academic achievement--United States.
Classification: LCC LC148.2 .M38 2016 | DDC 378.1/61--dc23 LC record available at https://lccn.loc.gov/2016011696

Published by Harvard Education Press,
an imprint of the Harvard Education Publishing Group

Harvard Education Press
8 Story Street
Cambridge, MA 02138

Cover Design: Saizon Design
Cover Photo: PeopleImages/Getty Images
The typefaces used in this book are Minion Pro and Myriad Pro

Contents

Introduction

Andrew P. Kelly, Jessica S. Howell, Carolyn Sattin-Bajaj

For a half-century, American higher education policy has been focused on providing access to postsecondary education. Federal grants, loans, and tax credits are designed to ensure that financial barriers do not keep qualified students from attending college. The access agenda has paid dividends: while 50 percent of recent high school graduates enrolled in college by age twenty-four in 1980, that proportion had climbed to nearly 70 percent by 2010.[1] Racial gaps in college enrollment have narrowed somewhat over time, reflecting an increase in the high school graduation rate of minority students.[2] College enrollment reached an all-time high in 2010 and remains higher than pre-recession levels.[3]

But degree completion rates have remained stubbornly stagnant; about 60 percent of students who start a degree finish one, and completion rates are far lower among low-income students.[4] Gaps in educational attainment between high- and low-income students have actually grown over time.[5] White students are more likely than their minority peers to earn a degree, and that gap has not changed markedly over the past two decades.[6] Though some studies find a payoff to earning some college credits, the real boost in economic opportunity comes from completing a degree or certificate.[7] Recently released data on postgraduation outcomes show that at hundreds of institutions, more than half of alumni earn no more than high school graduates.[8] Access without success often leaves students with debt and little else to show for it.

In light of these trends, higher education policy debates have shifted from a focus on access to a focus on student success, particularly for students from disadvantaged backgrounds. The discussion has examined a distinct set of questions about the correlates of student success in college, variation in student outcomes across institutions, and explanations of such variation: Can interventions meaningfully change the odds of degree completion? What can students, colleges, and policy makers do to increase the likelihood of completion? These questions have moved to the forefront of scholarly and policy conversations in higher education.

One theme gaining traction is the idea that student success is not entirely a function of demographics and high school preparation, but that it varies meaningfully across higher education institutions as well. Indeed, observational and quasi-experimental research shows that similarly qualified students are much more likely to complete a degree at some institutions than others. In other words, it's not only *whether* you go to college that matters, but *where* you go.

Researchers have therefore homed in on the college choice process as a potential lever to improve student postsecondary success. Do prospective students consider and choose colleges where they are likely to be successful? If we could only encourage more students to do so, the argument goes, we could increase college completion rates. This question has led analysts and policy makers to focus on how much students know about their postsecondary options, the application process, and financial aid; whether their eventual choices align with their aspirations; and whether efforts to provide additional information and assistance can improve these outcomes.

Over the past decade, researchers have identified the "match" between students' academic background and their choice of college as a key determinant of success in college. In particular, studies have shown that "undermatching"—that is, when students fail to apply to and enroll in the most selective institution they would be eligible to attend—decreases success rates. Undermatch has thus become a major issue in the emerging "completion agenda," so much so that it has reached the White House. In a January 2014 gathering of colleges, President Obama argued that ". . . to restore the essential promise of opportunity and upward mobility that's at the heart of America . . . young people, low-income students in particular, must have access to a college education."[9]

Over time, we have gained a better understanding of which students are most likely to undermatch (for example, low-income and first-generation students), the major bottlenecks in the college admissions process that lead to undermatching (for example, many qualified students do not even apply), and the types of interventions that might be able to assist students match to a college where they are likely to be successful (such as customized information about their options and college application fee waivers).[10]

Solving college match issues is intuitively appealing for a few reasons. First, the recent discussion from the White House on down has focused on a sympathetic group—low-income strivers in search of educational opportunity. Second, strategies for improving college match rates seem straightforward and inexpensive: evidence suggests that policy makers can improve educational attainment through low-cost informational interventions rather than costly new spending commitments or complicated school improvement policies.[11] Third, improving match would pay dividends for many students in the short term.

However, while researchers have made progress in understanding college match, existing research and current policy debates have been limited in three key respects. First, the most recent work has defined *match* narrowly as a comparison between students' academic qualifications and institutional selectivity and has focused on high-achieving, low-income students. There are likely other dimensions that are important to college match, like proximity to home, program offerings, and institutional size. Likewise, the focus on high-achieving, low-income students and elite colleges leaves out the vast majority of students. There is plenty of room for alternative conceptions of match that include a wider array of students, colleges, programs, and characteristics.

Second, existing work on undermatching tends to look at the question from the students' perspective: did they choose wisely? However, institutional behavior is equally important in shaping the opportunities available to students. Space and financial aid are finite, and competition for seats can be a zero-sum game. Focusing college match research on the demand side thus ignores important constraints on the supply side of higher education. For instance, we know very little about how selective colleges react when they get more applications from qualified low-income students. Do they expand? Or do those students displace others who might have gotten in? Capacity constraints, reinforced by rankings that reflect admissions selectivity, make it difficult for even the best-informed students to enroll in a good match. On the other side of the coin, existing research tells us almost nothing about the capacity of undersubscribed, less selective colleges to provide the type of supports and financial help that students need to stay on track to graduation. Informing students about their options is worthwhile, but if the number of quality seats is more or less fixed, better student choices won't necessarily lift attainment rates.[12]

Finally, these supply-side issues raise broader questions about institutional practice and the federal and state policies that shape it. Which practices, structures, and policies are in place at the most successful postsecondary institutions across the selectivity spectrum? How might existing policies reinforce the constraints discussed above? What reforms could increase the supply of quality seats by encouraging institutional expansion and improvement?

Thus, while there is convincing evidence that the match between students' abilities and their choice of college impacts their likelihood of success, there are still many unanswered questions when it comes to what to do about it.[13] Moving this discussion forward requires that we broaden our conception of college match to include the full spectrum of students and institutions, that we take supply-side constraints seriously, and that we acknowledge how institutional, state, and federal policies shape the behavior of students and institutions. Doing so will provide insight into how we can ensure that all students who are prepared for college—not just the top performers—have access to worthwhile postsecondary opportunities.

To that end, this volume uses new research from top higher education scholars to shed light on important, understudied college match questions. The chapters that follow consider how the research on college match has evolved over the past ten years and examine alternative definitions and measures of college match. They consider match across the range of academic qualifications and institution types and take a close look at the related supply-side issues; that is, how do the incentives facing colleges shape their capacity for growth and improvement? The final chapters look at how government policies—federal, state, and local—influence individual college choices and institutional behavior.

The goal here is to build on, add to, and synthesize the solid base of empirical research on college match and to fully explore the implications of that research for broader questions about college completion and educational attainment. To aid policy makers and institutional leaders, different chapters also lay out concrete, evidence-based policies and practices that can improve college match. Together, the book's chapters point out opportunities for improvement but acknowledge the limits of reforms to the demand side.

COLLEGE CHOICE AND COLLEGE MATCH

Students' choices of whether and where to attend college have a dramatic effect on the rest of their lives. It's logical, then, that the large body of research on college access focuses on the constraints—financial, geographic, academic, and informational—that shape student enrollment decisions. Using data from surveys and students' actual behavior, researchers have described college-going patterns and identified correlates of enrollment and student success: family income, academic background, high school quality, parents' education, and so on.

Researchers have also explored the ways in which college choice is not only a question of resources and background, but also the difficulties of decision making. Students must choose colleges based on imperfect information and navigate a tortuous series of procedural hurdles. Since college selection is generally a one-time event, students have few opportunities to learn from experience. The effect of this complexity varies predictably by socioeconomic status. Students with similar academic qualifications often make very different enrollment decisions. Low-income and minority students, in particular, are likely to lack the kind of information and social network support that more wealthy students rely on in searching for colleges, applying for financial aid, and matriculating. In other words, these differences are not only a function of their income and academic skills, but also their ability to navigate a complex, bureaucratic process.

Research has convincingly shown that similarly qualified students who attend different institutions often have very different rates of degree completion. Early work on the "community college penalty" argues that students who start at a two-year college actually reduce their chances of earning a degree compared with peers who start at a four-year college.[14] Observational studies have pointed out how schools with similar admissions selectivity often have very different completion rates.[15]

The college match discussion grows out of the behavioral research on college access and choice, particularly its emphasis on imperfect information and procedural hurdles, and the evidence that institutions influence student success. Together, those two bodies of work suggest that helping students identify "good" colleges and overcome behavioral obstacles to applying to and enrolling in one will increase college completion rates, which begs the question: What exactly qualifies as a "good college?"

College match research evaluates student choices according to a specific criterion: Do students choose colleges whose admissions standards match their academic skills? If not, why not? Is it because they apply and fail to get admitted? Or because they do not apply at all?

The contemporary discussion of college match started nearly a decade ago, when researchers at the Consortium on Chicago School Research released a study of college-going behavior in students in the Chicago Public Schools (CPS). In their landmark report "Potholes on the Road to College," Melissa Roderick and her colleagues set out to explain why so many students who aspired to a four-year degree ultimately enrolled in a two-year college or failed to attend at all. They found that roughly one-third of CPS students who aspired to complete a four-year degree enrolled in a college that matched their academic qualifications. The most highly qualified CPS students were as likely to not enroll or to undermatch (37 percent total) as they were to enroll in a very selective college (38 percent).[16] The article laid the groundwork for subsequent studies that would look at the mismatch between aspirations, academic qualifications, and enrollment across the country, confirming many of the basic patterns found in Chicago.

The following year, William Bowen, Matthew Chingos, and Michael McPherson tied undermatching to the emerging national conversation about bachelor's degree completion rates. In *Crossing the Finish Line*, they used data from four state higher education systems to examine college completion rates across racial and socioeconomic groups. They found compelling evidence that students were most likely to succeed when they attended institutions where the academic environment matched their own academic credentials. In addition, they found that matching rates varied by socioeconomic background, race/ethnicity, and student achievement.[17]

More recently, a study by Caroline M. Hoxby and Christopher Avery used data on SAT- and ACT-takers to show that the majority of high-achieving, low-income students do not apply to any selective college or university, while those who do apply are admitted to and enroll at comparable rates to their high-achieving, high-income counterparts. In the process, Hoxby and Avery put a spotlight on a small but important part of the college-going population that is particularly susceptible to undermatch.[18]

Taking a more expansive view, Jonathan Smith, Matea Pender, and Jessica Howell leveraged data from a nationally representative sample of students to examine undermatching among students across the achievement spectrum. They found that 41 percent of students undermatch in choosing a college, and that undermatch rates were 15 percentage points higher among students from the lower-half of the socioeconomic status distribution than the upper half of the distribution.[19] Another national study by Eleanor Dillon and Jeffrey Smith examined rates of over- and undermatch across a nationally representative sample of students. They found that a substantial proportion of students were mismatched, and, again, that undermatching was more prevalent among lower-income students (and vice versa for overmatching).[20]

The most recent wave of research has moved toward developing and testing interventions to eliminate undermatch. In 2013, Caroline Hoxby and Sarah Turner conducted a randomized control trial with nearly fifty thousand students to see if semi-customized information and college application fee waivers could improve college match rates among the high-achieving, low-income student population. The results showed that recipients of the low-cost ($6) intervention were more likely to apply and be admitted to more colleges, and to colleges with higher graduation rates, more academically able peers, and greater resources than students in the control group.[21] The College Board is now taking this intervention to scale in an effort to reduce the undermatch rates, particularly among disadvantaged student populations.[22]

THE LIMITS OF "UNDERMATCH"

The existing research on undermatch has made a significant contribution to our understanding of where students enroll and what happens after they do. Thanks to readily available data (from the College Board and ACT) and a dimension that is simple to measure with those data (the gap between a student's SAT score and the typical SAT scores at the colleges they apply to and an enroll in), the study of undermatch has made a significant contribution to our understanding of where students enroll and how they fare at different types of institutions. The research has also helped to identify simple, inexpensive solutions in the effort to raise college attainment among low-income students—a rarity in education research, where policy interventions tend to be complex and resource-intensive.

While progress has been made, major systemic questions remain: Is improving college match simply a question of increasing the flow of information to prospective students? Or are there other constraints on raising attainment that would apply even if more students successfully applied to more and better matched colleges? Likewise, the current conception of and narrative around undermatch—with its emphasis on high-achieving, low-income students—has felt far too narrow in the face of significant college dropout rates and mounting student debt. It also represents a departure from earlier work on college match, which focused on a broader swath of students.

In short, the existing work on college match has been limited in three key areas. First, recent research has relied on a narrow definition of match—the comparison between academic qualifications and institutional selectivity—for a narrow segment of students—high-achieving, low-income students. While certainly worthwhile, such a focus ignores the experiences of the largest share of college-going students and the institutions they attend: average achievers who choose from among less selective or open-access colleges. What does match mean for these students? Are there dimensions other than academic selectivity that matter for student outcomes?

For instance, we know that college graduation rates vary dramatically across institutions within the same selectivity categories, especially among less selective institutions.[23] Students could conceivably be better matched at a college with a track record of success than one with higher admissions standards but lackluster outcomes. Measuring match according to institutional selectivity also excludes other dimensions that are likely to influence student success, such as fit, choice of major, and the cost of tuition. At two-year colleges, choice of program arguably has a larger effect on student outcomes—completion and labor market success—than choice of institution. In other words, a focus on admissions selectivity and student test scores downplays other characteristics that are linked to student outcomes like on-time college completion and choice of a quality program.

Next, existing work on undermatching tends to look mainly at the demand side of college enrollment, overlooking the ways in which institutional behavior shapes the supply side of postsecondary opportunity. Implicit in the policy debates about undermatching is the notion that if we could only get qualified low-income students to apply to an institution where they are well matched, completion and attainment rates would rise. However, this conclusion ignores complex supply-side issues that affect the opportunities available to students. Selective colleges expand very slowly, if at all. At the other end of the spectrum, less selective colleges may have an ample supply of seats but insufficient financial, academic, and support services that students need to stay on track to graduation. For schools in the broad middle, the competition for prestige creates incentive to increase admissions standards and let fewer students in.

These constraints suggest that simply improving college match via the demand side may not automatically boost attainment rates. Even if more qualified students applied and enrolled at colleges that were a good match academically—or where student success rates were higher—they would likely displace others. Those displaced students might then wind up at institutions where student success rates are low, creating a zero-sum game. Though these supply-side constraints are central to drawing implications from existing research on undermatch, they have not received the attention they deserve.

Last, the questions surrounding the supply of quality postsecondary opportunities point to how little we know about both effective institutional practices and the ways in which federal and state policies affect the behavior of both students and institutions. The traditional measurement of match essentially treats institutions as a black box, using admissions selectivity as a proxy for "quality." But the variation in student outcomes and new evidence from randomized studies suggests that some colleges have adopted ideas that help students succeed in spite of their academic background.[24] Knowing more about the internal practices, structures, and policies in place at successful postsecondary institutions across the selectivity spectrum can help improve our understanding of how to improve both the supply and demand sides.

Colleges are creatures of the policy environment in which they operate, and the incentives to expand enrollments or adopt promising practices and the resources necessary to do so are often absent. Incentives and resources are, of course, a function of state and federal policy. How might existing policies reinforce the supply constraints discussed above, and what reforms could increase the supply of quality seats? The same question applies to the demand side: where do existing policies help or hinder students' ability to learn about their options? While some of the work on college match has placed state policy at the center of its analyses, a comprehensive look at how state and federal policy shape the supply and demand sides is still missing.[25]

Clearly, the match between a student's academic abilities and the admissions standards of her college is of critical importance. But that is true for all students, not just those at the top. That suggests a need to broaden the discussion of college match to include the full spectrum of students and institutions. Likewise, that students are free to choose an option that fits their needs and budgets does not imply that all students are able to; institutional behavior constrains the supply of seats. A closer examination of the institutional, state, and federal policies that shape these constraints is essential. A more complete picture will provide insight into how we can ensure that all qualified students, not just the top performers, can access educational opportunity. The goal of this volume is to bring new evidence, analysis, and policy recommendations to bear on these questions of growing national concern.

THE CHAPTERS AHEAD

The first two chapters of this volume examine the evolution of the college match concept and raise important questions about how best to define and measure it. In chapter 1, Jenny Nagaoka and her colleagues—some of the Chicago Consortium researchers who first developed the concept—revisit their original results and provide an update on the status of college match rates in CPS almost a decade later. The chapter then focuses on the use of college match as an indicator and considers how such indicators can function to effectively bridge research and practice in schools. In their conclusion, the authors set the stage for subsequent chapters by identifying some limitations of measuring match based solely on academic indicators and arguing that supply-side factors such as geographic constraints and insufficient quality must be included in analyses of the options available to students.

In chapter 2, Jessica Howell, Matea Pender, and Amal Kumar of the College Board extend the measurement discussion by evaluating the relative importance of nonacademic dimensions in college choice and postsecondary success. Drawing on data from seven cohorts of SAT-takers, they introduce the concept of "nonacademic fit" and examine the relationship between students' stated preferences for college attributes—proximity to home, size, the level of the institution (two- or four-year), and others—and their actual choice. Their results reveal that application and matriculation choices are influenced by financial, geographic, academic, and sociodemographic factors. The authors also find a positive relationship between several measures of student-college fit and collegiate outcomes. The chapter makes a strong case for considering nonacademic fit alongside traditional academic measures.

Chapters 3 and 4 expand the match concept to cover a broader array of students, institutions, and definitions. In chapter 3, Awilda Rodriguez and Christian Martell spotlight the characteristics, college application behaviors, and match rates of average-performing students who comprise the majority of the college-going population. Their analysis of a nationally representative data set finds significant evidence of mismatch between average-performing

students and the postsecondary educational institutions they attend on multiple dimensions. Their results illustrate the limitations of relying solely on
institutional selectivity and test scores to study match, particularly for this
student population. Rather, they suggest considering a combination of career
aspirations and academic interest; nearby college options; affordability; and
likelihood of completion to generate a richer measurement of match.

Chapter 4 argues that the selection of a major is an important and understudied element of matching at community colleges and broad-access
four-year institutions. Authors Thomas Bailey and his colleagues at the
Community College Research Center suggest that existing models of college (and major) match rely too heavily on static measures of students and
institutions and that major selection is actually a dynamic learning process,
though one that is severely constrained in many places by a lack of adequate
advising. Bailey and colleagues describe what some colleges and universities
are doing to improve the major selection process and draw out implications
for the college match discussion writ large.

The next pair of chapters shift away from the demand side of the college
match equation and center directly on questions of institutional supply, institutional quality, and the practices, policies, and incentive structures within
universities that shape the higher education landscape. In chapter 5, Andrew
Kelly paints an empirical picture of the supply side by examining where new
undergraduate enrollments have flowed over the past decade. He disaggre-
gates first-time, full-time enrollments by the institutional graduate rate to
illustrate that the majority of new enrollments are happening at colleges with
graduation rates below 60 percent. These results provide an empirical basis
for emerging discussions about the problem of limited supply of quality
seats. In chapter 6, Michael Bastedo examines the incentives that shape the
admissions policies of colleges and their enrollment managers. In particular,
he focuses on how those incentives affect the access of low-income, high-
achieving students. Drawing on extensive fieldwork and existing literature,
Bastedo describes how the mixture of institutional self-interest, prestige-
seeking behavior, and capacity constraints largely determine college match
on the institutional side, and presents a series of recommendations to revise
institutional, state, and federal funding mechanisms to incentivize high-performing colleges to admit more low-income students. Bastedo also suggests
additional experimental research that can help us better understand and
remedy admissions officers' biases against admitting low-income applicants.

Chapters 7, 8, and 9 examine the impacts of existing local, state, and federal policies on the supply and demand sides of college match factors. In chapter 7, Lindsay Page and Jennifer Iriti take a detailed look into a locally funded, philanthropic initiative, the Pittsburgh Promise program, which provides eligible graduates from Pittsburgh Public Schools with scholarship funds of up to $10,000 per year for up to four years of postsecondary education. Page and Iriti find that over time, students were more likely to attend college and less likely to undermatch, regardless of socioeconomic status. However, although students at the threshold of earning Promise funding (around 2.0 GPA) enrolled in college at higher rates than peers who just missed eligibility, the relative quality of their matches has not improved. Thus, this chapter points to the complexity of designing interventions that simultaneously address issues of college access, undermatching, and college success in the context of scarcity, particularly for students on the lower-performing end of the distribution.

Chapter 8 focuses on how four types of state-level policies might affect college quality and academic match: state funding of public colleges; need- and merit-based financial aid to students; mandates regarding college entrance exam taking; and state-imposed college admission criteria. Authors Joshua Goodman, Michael Hurwitz, and Jonathan Smith find that level, forms, and amounts of in-kind aid to students, as well as exam-taking policies, can have an important impact on the quality of college that students attend, and that geographic constraints and institutional capacity also factor into enrollment patterns. Goodman and colleagues argue that match quality itself matters relatively little for longer-run outcomes such as degree completion but that absolute college quality does matter, and they offer suggestions on state-level policies to maximize that quality.

In chapter 9, Robert Kelchen explores three potential policy mechanisms through which the federal government can strive to improve students' college choices. He argues that the federal government is uniquely positioned to disseminate information about colleges through venues such as the College Scorecard and emphasizes the tools of accountability and financial aid as possible avenues for increased federal government intervention. At the same time, Kelchen acknowledges a series of possible limitations to the power of the federal government to impact college match.

In the conclusion, we revisit the major themes, findings, and tensions that emerge from the chapters and discuss the implications of this volume for policy and future research. First, we discuss the benefits of adopting a more expansive definition of college match that captures the behaviors and experiences of the increasingly heterogeneous student populations choosing colleges each year. Next, we review a set of new, empirically tested measures that can be used in analyses of college matching to better explain students' multidimensional preferences and the dynamic process between student selection and institutional characteristics. Finally, we raise a number of unresolved issues in the field, and suggest a research agenda moving forward. We argue that if the problem of college matching is essentially a problem of institutional quality and insufficient supply of seats in high-performing colleges at all selectivity levels, then the current focus on providing better information to consumers will have, at best, limited impact on improving college completion rates. Instead, there is a need for greater understanding of what is happening at the most successful institutions across the selectivity spectrum and what can be done to expand their capacity and replicate their institutional structures, policies, practices, and culture at other less successful sites. In addition, we consider the ideas about improving match on multiple dimensions and begin to think through what it might take to provide more comprehensive guidance to students before and during college. We lay out an extensive research agenda that includes a combination of new empirical studies, experiments, and policy initiatives we believe may offer the greatest promise in increasing understanding of the roles that students, policy makers, and higher education institutions could play in addressing college match and, in turn, responding to stagnant college completion rates.

The College Match Indicator

Linking Research to Practice

Jenny Nagaoka, Matthew A. Holsapple, and Melissa Roderick

Young people are enrolling in college at unprecedented rates; 66.2 percent of high school graduates made an immediate transition to college in 2012.[1] Given these gains in college access, some recent research studies and interventions have started paying attention to not just whether students enroll in college, but also the *types* of colleges in which they enroll.[2] These studies have used the term *undermatching* to describe students who enroll in colleges with selectivity levels lower than their credentials would allow them to access. Getting students to enroll in "match" colleges has been viewed as a strategy for addressing the inequities in income-related postsecondary attainment rates by targeting an issue that is particularly relevant for low-income, first-generation college students.[3]

The college match indicator was originally developed by researchers at the University of Chicago Consortium on School Research (the Consortium) as a simple way to measure the extent to which Chicago Public School students were struggling on the path to college enrollment.[4] This allowed researchers to determine the magnitude of the undermatching phenomenon, observe patterns across types of students and schools, and evaluate progress over time. In the first report that used college match, almost two-thirds of the Chicago graduating class of 2005 undermatched. The indicator has since been used by researchers to evaluate the scope of the problem in other locations.[5] Nationally, 41 percent of the graduating class of 2004 undermatched, with the rates being higher among low-income and first-generation college students.[6]

The high rates of undermatching are not surprising; the phenomenon of low-income, first-generation college students struggling with the process leading up to college enrollment, when compared with their more advantaged peers, has been well documented.[7] Low-income students often lack the information and support they need to navigate the college search and application process and translate their qualifications into enrollment in four-year colleges.[8] Highly qualified low-income students, even when they are aware of their college options, often struggle with the complicated application processes of more elite colleges, and consequently make college choices that parallel those of their less qualified peers.[9] However, the critical issues identified by research findings were rarely translated into concrete changes in practice.

The contribution of college match has been to develop a means of easily quantifying the challenges that students face in the college search process and clarifying a specific point of intervention. Although it was originally developed to highlight the challenges faced by high-achieving, low-income, first-generation students, college match has applications to a broad range of students. It also serves as a framework for practitioners, students, and families to shift conversations from simply going to college to considering different college options. It also gives a clear, actionable way to clarify the type of guidance students and subgroups of students need in the process leading up to college choice. In addition, it has turned attention to not just the efforts of supporting students in the college enrollment process, but also supporting them in developing a list of potential colleges, applying to them, and ultimately making a choice about which college to attend. College match rates are also a way to track the progress of schools and districts in guiding their students.

In this chapter, we describe the origins of college match and use it as an example of how indicators can be used to shape practice. We first discuss the origins of the college match indicator, the role of the Consortium research project in its development, and related efforts in the Chicago Public Schools (CPS). We next turn to the role of indicator development more generally, and match specifically, as a critical mechanism for bridging research and practice. Finally, we discuss three limitations of the college match indicator: how match and its reliance on selectivity categories do not reflect many of the factors that matter for graduation; how efforts to improve match rates do not have an impact on degree attainment rates for students with lower academic qualifications; and how match rates in different locations depend on the availability of more selective colleges.

THE DEVELOPMENT OF THE COLLEGE MATCH FRAMEWORK AND INDICATOR: MAKING RESEARCH ACTIONABLE

In 2004, a team of Consortium researchers led by Melissa Roderick began a unique partnership with CPS to work on a common set of problems around college access and college completion. Before the start of the partnership, only 51 percent of CPS graduates enrolled in college, compared with 64 percent nationally. Among college enrollees, only 27 percent enrolled in a selective or very selective college.[10] In this project, Consortium researchers worked closely with CPS staff to set up a valid tracking system using the district's administrative data, National Student Clearinghouse data, and student surveys. This system allowed us to understand what students' post–high school plans were, compare those plans with actual enrollment, and track persistence and performance in college at the district and school level.

CPS based its efforts in its newly established Department of Postsecondary Education and Student Development ("the Department"), charged with ensuring that all CPS students would have access to the courses, opportunities and experiences that would prepare them for a viable postsecondary education or career. The Department was in charge of high school counseling and sought to strengthen the counseling program by using the standards developed by the American School Counselors Association.[11] College guidance became a core part of each counselor's role with students, and the emphasis shifted from serving students who came to a counselor's office requesting help to serving all students in a counselor's caseload. The Department partnered with community groups to provide extensive professional development opportunities and worked to ensure that counselors were freed from administrative duties such as test administration that took time away from serving students.[12] The Department also piloted a college coach program, later expanded to over half of all CPS high schools, that assigned a dedicated coach to provide the targeted support and monitoring that low-income, first-generation students needed as they progressed through steps in the college enrollment process.[13]

At the time of the Department's establishment in 2004, the aspirations of CPS seniors were high: 92 percent planned to attain a postsecondary degree or certificate, with 78 percent intending to get a four-year college degree.[14] However, the college readiness rates of graduates were very low; only 18 percent of graduates had over a 21 on the ACT and only 21 percent had at least a 3.0 GPA. Advanced coursework participation was slightly higher; 23 percent of all graduates had taken at least one AP course and 2 percent were enrolled in an International Baccalaureate program.[15] In 2007, 56 percent of graduates reported submitting at least three college applications, and 68 percent reported submitting the Free Application for Federal Student Aid (FAFSA).[16]

The role of the Consortium researchers was to develop indicators and frameworks to engage school practitioners and administrators in understanding the problems of college access and completion in ways that could help build schools' capacity to address them. It also highlighted key points at which school and district interventions would be most effective for students. In addition to the postsecondary tracking system developed with CPS, the Consortium embarked on a longitudinal qualitative study to examine the students' experiences in the college enrollment process, interviewing 105 students of varying achievement levels and backgrounds in three neighborhood high schools.

In 2006, the first report from the project, *From High School to the Future: A First Look at Chicago Public Schools Graduates' College Enrollment, College Preparation, and Graduation From Four-Year Colleges*, provided a baseline of where CPS stood as a school system, including the number of students enrolling in college, the types of colleges they attended, and the role of qualifications in shaping college access and graduation.[17] The second report in the series, *From High School to the Future: Potholes on the Road to College*, followed up on several important but unresolved issues identified in the first report. In particular, we sought to understand why there is such a large gap between students' educational aspirations and their college enrollment and why students tend to enroll in a limited number of colleges, many of which have very low institutional graduation rates.[18]

The qualitative component of the *Potholes* study played an instrumental role in provoking the question that led to the development of the college match indicator. We interviewed many high-achieving students who, despite their strong qualifications, were considering the same college options as their less qualified peers. When we talked to their teachers, many assumed that their brightest students were managing the college search process as adeptly as they managed their schoolwork, but this was far from the case. We asked the question: How can we identify whether students are effectively participating in college search?

Earlier research would suggest several markers of college search, such as the number of applications submitted, submitting the FAFSA, and application to out-of-state colleges. However, none of these indicators seemed to capture the pattern we saw in the students we interviewed. Highly qualified students in our study had a range of patterns—some applied to many colleges, others applied to the state flagship university—but very few had conducted an extensive college search that included colleges of higher selectivity levels. We needed a means of measuring the extent to which students, particularly students with strong qualifications, were conducting a college search that included a range of options and were receiving the guidance they needed to make a good college choice. We were looking for a simple measure to quantify the quality of college search and college choice that went beyond enrollment in college. To be able to determine the scope of the issues of college search and choice in CPS, we first classified students using a rubric that showed the level of selectivity of college to which the student would likely be able to gain admission to based on ACT scores and cumulative GPA (see figure 1.1).[19] We then compared that level of selectivity to the selectivity of the college they actually enrolled in and determined which students were enrolled in a "match" college and which were enrolled in an "undermatch" college. This framework formed the basis for the development of the college match indicator.

Through the match indicator, we were able to see a common pattern of undermatching: 62 percent of all CPS graduates enrolled in no college or an undermatch college. For students who had access to very selective colleges, 62 percent enrolled in an undermatch college. This is not surprising. Unless these students enrolled in a very selective college, they would be considered as undermatched, regardless of where they enrolled. We also found that Latino students were also more likely to undermatch, with 72 percent undermatching versus 55 percent for black graduates and 64 percent for white graduates. The match indicator allowed us to highlight the scope of the problem across the district, as well as which populations had particular struggles in the college search and choice process.

The match indicator and framework were of immediate use to practitioners. In Chicago, the district leadership had made increasing the number

FIGURE 1.1   Chicago college match framework

	Unweighted GPA in core courses				
	<2.0	2.0–2.4	2.5–2.9	3.0–3.4	3.5–4.0
Missing ACT	Two-year colleges	Nonselective four-year colleges	Somewhat selective four-year colleges	Selective colleges	Selective colleges
<18	Two-year colleges	Nonselective four-year colleges	Somewhat selective four-year colleges	Somewhat selective four-year colleges	Selective colleges
18–20	Nonselective four-year colleges	Somewhat selective four-year colleges	Somewhat selective four-year colleges	Selective colleges	Selective/ very colleges
21–23	Somewhat selective four-year colleges	Somewhat selective four-year colleges	Selective colleges	Selective/ very colleges	Selective/ very colleges
24+	Somewhat selective four-year colleges	Selective/ very colleges	Selective/ very colleges	Very selective colleges	Very selective colleges

(Left axis label: Composite ACT score)

Source: Melissa Roderick et al., *From High School to the Future: Potholes on the Road to College* (Chicago: Consortium on Chicago School Research at University of Chicago, 2008).

Note: Students in the "selective category" who are either in an IB program or have taken at least two AP and at least six honors courses are moved up to the "very selective" category.

of students who enrolled in college a priority, and the Department of Postsecondary Education partnered with local organizations to integrate college match into professional development activities. Organizations such as Chicago Scholars and the Network for College Success, a Consortium partner organization at the University of Chicago, worked with counselors around the college match framework to build their capacity to guide students in the college enrollment process. Counselors were trained in what colleges fell into which selectivity categories, the programs and characteristics of colleges that best supported students, financial aid packages, and how to advocate for students with colleges.

Counselors were then able to use the match framework to move beyond urging students to go to college to focusing on how to organize their discussions about college options with students in a clear and concise way. College choice discussions could focus on a shorter list of college options, rather than considering the entire universe of colleges. Counselors had a starting point to structure their guidance to students around their likelihood of gaining admission. Having a shorter, more manageable list of match colleges facilitated more effective discussions around fit, financial aid, and what kind of college could best serve a student's needs.

In 2010, the district developed an online match dashboard that allowed counselors to see which colleges, by level of selectivity, each of their eleventh- and twelfth-grade students would likely be able gain admission to based on their ACT scores and GPAs. The dashboard also provided resources that linked the actual postsecondary institutions with selectivity categories to which students had access. Counselors could move from having to ask students about their academic qualifications to having a baseline for what their college options were. Structuring these discussions required counselors to have a stronger knowledge base. Rather than recommending a standard list of colleges, they needed to customize the conversation to students' needs. The online match dashboard also established an expectation that counselors would be having discussions about postsecondary plans with *all* students. More students applied to three or more colleges; the percentage moved from 56 percent in 2007 to 63 percent in 2010. College match also became a part of that administration's performance management system, making match into an outcome measure that was used to evaluate the efforts of counselors and their schools.

The concept of college match and the accompanying rubric and indicator helped practitioners and students work on a problem that was meaningful to them in a way that was easily understood. Students could see how match applied to them and how to start a college search. Using match as a starting point for discussions about college options moved the process of college application and choice from what might have seemed an overwhelming set of options to a more manageable list. Match also provided counselors and students with language to start discussing the college search and college choice process.

Ultimately, finding the right college means more than enrolling in the most selective college possible. It is about finding a place that is a good "fit": a college that meets individual students' educational goals and social needs and will best support them in succeeding in college and furthering their intellectual and social development. Finding a good fit requires students to have both an understanding of their needs and preferences and guidance in finding colleges that meet that description. Fit can also encompass other critical factors such as institutional graduation rates and the availability of strong financial aid packages. Match is just one consideration of the larger process of engaging in an effective college search, but it is also an important indicator of whether students are engaged more broadly in a search that incorporates the larger question of fit.

The influence of the college match indicator was not just in being able to quantify a pattern that prior research had established as major issue for low-income students. It provided a framework for practitioners to engage in the questions of how to guide students in their college search and gave then a clear practical intervention point for making their students more likely to attain a college degree. It also moved from being a way of measuring participation in a process and illuminating specific problems to being used as a measure for evaluating progress. In the next section, we discuss the role of indicators in linking research to practice and how match moved from being an indicator of scope of the engagement issue in the college search process to a point of intervention and being treated as an outcome.

THE ROLE OF INDICATORS

Indicators can be the bridge that allows practitioners to apply research findings as a practical point of intervention with students. Indicator development requires conceptual clarity about what is being measured and the nature of the core problem being addressed. It can also link research across multiple studies, leading to a validation and replication of the work in different contexts as well as laying the basis for next steps in both research and practice. The concept of college match and the creation of the indicator provide an important example of how attention to measurement can have a critical impact on how researchers approach a problem and how practitioners structure their work with students.

In this section, we highlight three characteristics of the match indicator and its underlying rubric that facilitated its impact on research and practice. The indicator was linked to a relevant issue; schools could apply it through daily practice and other interventions; and it was meaningful and easily understood by practitioners and students.

The concept of using college selectivity as a way of organizing college search is not new. The categories of *safety schools, target schools,* and *reach schools* have long been used by students, parents, and counselors. In Chicago, the access framework had been developed by the Consortium in an earlier round of work. However, it was not until the framework was linked to college enrollment and developed as an indicator that practitioners began to use it around the issue of college search and choice. College match made a familiar concept measurable so practitioners could see what the patterns of college choice looked like for students with different qualifications and offered them greater clarity about how to support students in the college search process.

Practitioners quickly began to use the match indicator and framework because it was linked to issues they were working on: college access and success. We had sought to describe a problem using a framework based on college access and institutional selectivity and developed a simple indicator to use in our research. Because we were interested in understanding the scope and nature of the college search problem, we did not examine the relationship between enrolling in a match college and degree attainment. However, the concept of college match moved quickly from research to an intervention point for practice, well before there was research evidence supporting this approach. The pace of research does not always match the pace of the needs of practitioners. Fortunately, other researchers—including William Bowen, Matthew Chingos, and Michael McPherson, in *Crossing the Finish Line*—took the match indicator and applied it in another context in North Carolina.[20] While their comparisons are only suggestive of the relationship between enrolling in a match college and the likelihood of graduation, they provided initial evidence that college match could be a useful leverage point for increasing educational attainment.

The college match concept and rubric could be used by schools and through other interventions. In Chicago, spurred by the district and other organizations, practitioners began to incorporate college match in their work with students. Researchers have also developed interventions that have taken different approaches to using college match as a framework for supporting two different groups of low-income, highly qualified students. The MDRC College Match Program targeted urban high schools with concentrations of low-income, highly qualified students and provided intensive, direct intervention in the college application and choice process through "near-peer" match advisers.[21] Ultimately, the goal was to build a college-going culture so that all students would have a better understanding of the enrollment process. The Expanding College Opportunity Project took a lighter-touch approach and targeted high-achieving, low-income, geographically dispersed students who were not easily reached by traditional methods of imparting informing.[22] It provided students semi-customized information about their college options to influence their enrollment patterns. Both of these studies demonstrate how the development of college match indicator as a tool has helped bridge the gap between research and practice.

College match describes a concept that is meaningful and easily understood by practitioners and students. Low-income, first-generation students in particular often have high educational aspirations but lack information on what colleges suit their needs.[23] The familial and friendship networks that these students use to make college choices often only have limited information about colleges and the college enrollment process.[24] The college match framework gives students, their families, and counselors a way of engaging in college search that helps make sense of what can seem like an overwhelming set of options.

Indicator development makes important research findings more easily replicable and validated across different context and for different populations. But it is also important for practitioners to use an indicator and deepen the understanding of the underlying research through their experience using the indicator. Ultimately, research reports take time to read and absorb, no matter how much effort it put into making them accessible. The "window time" of a research report, or the time in which policy makers pay attention to a set of research findings before moving on to another strategy or policy focus, on the other hand, can be very short, while it requires considerable time for educators to grapple with the importance of the findings, incorporate the implications into their day-to-day work and have the time to see results.

This intentional engagement with schools by researchers can also go in unexpected directions. As practitioners began to use the match indicator, its role as a measure also changed. Consortium researchers had developed the match indicator as a way to examine the patterns of college search and college choice in different populations of students. It had not been intended as a normative measure of what constituted a good college choice for an individual student, nor had it been intended to imply that the optimal level of matching for a school was 100 percent. College match does not measure the appropriateness of college choices equally well for all students; a focus on college match is often most appropriate for students with strong qualifications that give them a broad range of options. For less qualified students, enrolling in any college may be considered a "match," and is thus not sufficient for determining if they made a college choice that maximized their likelihood for attaining a degree.

College match was used by practitioners to support students more effectively in the college search process, and CPS developed data systems with students' qualifications, corresponding match category, and potential college options to this end. However, as college match became a centerpiece for investments, college match rates were not being used to diagnose; rather, they were used to assess progress and hold schools accountable. While accountability can be a useful mechanism for improvement, it can also shift attention from helping students make appropriate college choices to ensuring that they enroll in match colleges, regardless of issues around fit. The process of moving an indicator developed for research to an indicator and intervention for practice changes the nature of measurement in ways that are not always anticipated. In the next section, we discuss some of the limitations of college match.

LIMITATIONS OF COLLEGE MATCH

Although college match is an important indicator that has allowed educators, policy makers, external service providers, and others to focus efforts in optimizing students' college choices, using the metric has limitations. These are especially pronounced when a single match indicator is used as a way of evaluating the college choice of individual students. As an indicator and an evaluation and accountability tool, college match is a blunt instrument that only tells a part of the college choice story.

In the final section of this paper, we discuss three limitations: match is related to college graduation, but does not include many of the student- and college-level factors that affect probability of graduation; college match is not an effective way of increasing degree attainment for students with lower high school academic qualifications; and students living in different locales have differing levels of access to selective and high-graduation rate colleges.

To demonstrate some of these limitations, we present data from five CPS graduation cohorts (2003–2007), which are collected and archived as part of the data-tracking system discussed earlier in this chapter.[25] These data include administrative data for all CPS graduates during the including course-taking patterns, ACT scores, cumulative GPA, predicted college access, and all high schools and colleges attended for graduates of traditional Chicago high schools.[26] These cohorts comprise 68,124 graduates, 34 percent of whom matriculated into a four-year college the following year. Unless otherwise noted, analyses and results presented in this section refer to these college-goers.

Matching for Graduation

Match is a relatively coarse way of grouping students. The Consortium uses a match framework that places students in just five categories: access to very selective, selective, somewhat selective, and nonselective four-year colleges; and access only to two-year colleges. These categories take into account only grade-point average; ACT scores; and, in some circumstances, the honors, AP, and IB courses students took. Because match was intended to frame patterns of college choice, it did not account for additional college fit factors that may also have an impact on students' likelihood of graduating, such as preference for attending a small college and availability of majors. College match also does not consider the range of other characteristics that can affect students' college outcomes, including individual and family background characteristics and a lack—or perceived lack—of financial resources.[27]

Perhaps more importantly for considering the practical implications of match as a tool for policy and practice, the college match framework is also an imprecise way of grouping colleges and universities. For the Chicago match framework, we used five selectivity categories that were based on *Barron's* college competitiveness ratings. Within each selectivity category, there are wide differences in institutional graduation rates. For example, two Chicago-area colleges, Dominican University and Chicago State University, are both categorized as somewhat selective colleges by that rubric; Dominican's four-year graduation rate, as reported to Integrated Postsecondary Education Data System (IPEDS), is 56 percent, while Chicago State's is 4 percent. Students who qualified for admission to a somewhat selective college would match by attending either, yet they would dramatically more likely to graduate from Dominican than Chicago State.[28]

In fact, there is wider variation in institutional graduation rates within these selectivity categories than there is in the averages across them. This variation can be demonstrated by considering the institutional four-year graduation rates of colleges attended by Chicago high school graduates who earned the academic credentials that, under the Chicago match framework, would be expected to qualify them for access to selective colleges.[29] Students who match in that group attend colleges with four-year graduation rates ranging from 14 to 74 percent. All of these students attended a match college, yet there is a sixty-point difference in the four-year graduation rates of colleges they attend. Further, there are wide differences in institutional graduation rates for all selectivity categories. These students with selective access attended very selective colleges with institutional four-year graduation rates as low as 12 percent and nonselective colleges with graduation rates as high as 80 percent. A college counseling strategy could be effective at helping students enroll in match colleges and still leave students attending colleges where students graduate at low rates.

It is beyond the scope of this paper to examine the multitude of reasons why students from Chicago who undermatch to one selective university graduate at much higher rates than similarly qualified students who match to other selective colleges. The important point for this discussion is that a college access strategy that relies on matching does not take into account these college-specific differences or explicitly focus on helping students attend the colleges from which they are most likely to earn a degree.

Students Left Behind

Other researchers represented in this volume have extended the definition of college match to consider new ways to apply the concept to four-year college-goers with lower academic qualifications and community college. However, these students do not benefit when the Chicago college match framework is used. By definition, students with low academic achievement who qualify only for two-year or the least selective four-year colleges do not undermatch as long as they attend one of these colleges. As a result, as long as they are matriculating at all, they do not see an additional benefit from a college match strategy. Much of the more recent research on college match has focused on the most highly qualified students, as has the national policy and practice conversation. These findings, however, point to a utility in college match for students with strong, but less than the highest, high school academic qualifications.

To understand the potential effects of attending a match college on students of differing academic qualifications, we simulated new estimated graduation rates that could be expected if all Chicago high school graduates who matriculated did so at least to a match college. To do this, we first estimated a hierarchical logistic model to estimate the effects of students' academic qualifications, demographic and socioeconomic characteristics, and high school type on their probability of earning a bachelor's degree in four years. This model was cross-classified, with students nested both in their high schools and their colleges; and it included random effects for the high schools and colleges that students attended. From this model, we were able to estimate the effects of pre-college student and high school characteristics on students' probability of graduating from college, when controlling for high school and college effects. Using the results of this model, we could also calculate college-level residuals, representing the difference in predicted and observed rates of graduation at each college, after accounting for individual and high school effects. We calculated new predicted probabilities of graduation for all students who had undermatched, assigning them a new college-level fixed effect based on a randomly selected match school. Students who were observed to have attended a match or overmatch college retained those original fixed effects under the simulation.

Figure 1.2 presents some of the results of these analyses. With no students attending an undermatch college, the overall college graduation rate for CPS college-goers was simulated to increase from 26 percent to 32 percent. This would close approximately half of the gap between Chicago's four-year graduation rate and the national rate, which fluctuated between 37 percent and 39 percent for the cohorts included in this analysis.[30]

This increase in the overall graduation rate, however, was almost completely due to improvements in graduation rates among more high-qualified students. CPS college-goers with access to very selective and selective colleges

FIGURE 1.2 Impact of shifting students' college choice to match colleges by selectivity level

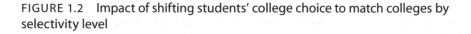

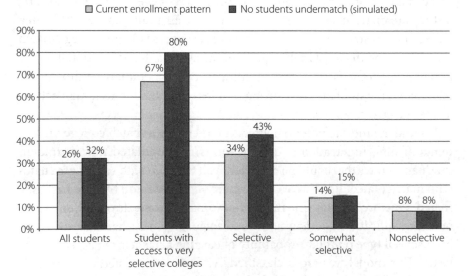

Source: Authors' analysis of CPS data

are simulated to have seen a thirteen-point and nine-point increase in their predicted college graduation rates, respectively, if they had all attended a match college. These students average, respectively, GPAs of 3.27 and 3.17 and ACT scores of 25 and 20. These qualifications place them above the qualifications of most of their CPS peers, but would not designate them as high-achieving students under the definitions used most frequently in research into college match.[31] This suggests a potential benefit to college match for a larger group of students than are often included in discourse.

This simulation is similar to one conducted by Matthew Chingos, in which he simulated a national higher education landscape that maximized matching for all students.[32] His findings suggest that this would do little to improve degree attainment rates nationally, largely because the improvements for students who currently undermatch would be offset by declines in degree attainment for students who currently overmatch. Similarly, Michael Bastedo and Ozan Jacquette suggest that perfect matching nationally would do little to alter institutional economic stratification.[33] Our analysis differs in that we approach the problem from a high school lens and are focused on how one school district could improve outcomes for its graduates rather than looking at changes nationwide. Therefore, we work with the assumption that there are available slots for all students at a match college without accounting for offsetting downward shifts for currently overmatching students. If every school district worked to eliminate undermatching in college choices, and colleges themselves did nothing to adjust for new application and enrollment patterns, the impact would be very different than if it were implemented, as in this simulation, by one district as a way to improve its outcomes relative to other districts. Our approach is similar to the one taken by Jessica Howell and Matea Pender, who estimate the effect of matching on low-income SAT-takers, allowing in the simulation for more selective colleges to absorb the additional students without displacing current matriculants.[34] Despite their different scope and focus, they find similar results, with attending a more selective college estimated to have large effects on students' probability of graduating.[35] The constraints placed on the benefits of matching as a national degree-attainment strategy—especially the constraints that arise from the lack of available high-quality college slots—are beyond the scope of this chapter. However, they are addressed more thoroughly in chapters 5 and 6.

Despite the predicted impacts of matching on students with above-average qualifications, these impacts do not extend to students with lower qualifications. As seen in figure 1.2, the predicted impact of matching on students with access to somewhat selective and nonselective colleges is virtually nonexistent. Students with access to somewhat selective colleges are estimated to see only a one-point increase in their graduation rates, while students with access to nonselective colleges (those who are matching simply by attending any four-year college, see no increase. A college access strategy focused only on getting all students into match colleges will provide no benefit to these students. Different strategies focused on improving students' abilities to do college-level work and guiding students to apply to and matriculate at colleges that are best equipped to support them, regardless of selectivity, are required.

The Geographic Lottery

College match also does not take into account the challenges and limitations of students' local higher education landscape. A large majority of four-year college-goers from CPS (83 percent in 2007) attend college within the state of Illinois, and other researchers have found that most students attend a college near to their home.[36] In chapter 3, Awilda Rodriguez and Christian Martell discuss some of the reasons for geographic constraints, particularly for those whom they term as "average-performing students."[37] Much of this research considers geographic proximity in terms of the distance between a college and a student's home; in this chapter, we consider students' access to colleges at the state level. Approximately 80 percent of college-goers attend an in-state college, and in many states there is a significant tuition discount for attending an in-state public college.[38] For many students, a college choice constrained by state boundaries would include a large number of selective colleges with high graduation rates, but for many others who want to stay close to home or take advantage of discounted tuition, there are few or no match options,

When the original match rubric was developed by the Consortium, there were no public colleges or universities in Illinois that were categorized as selective. The University of Illinois at Urbana-Champaign was the only public college classified as very selective; all other public options fell into the somewhat selectivity category. Thus there were no public, in-state options for students who qualified to attend selective colleges. Since that time, the University of Illinois at Chicago and Illinois State University have been reclassified as selective. But the original rankings still point to a national concern—that because of wide state-level variations in the higher education context, the state in which a high-achieving student resides can dramatically influence his or her ability to attend a match college.

While Illinois high school students were graduating into a higher education context that included no selective public colleges or universities, students in many other states were graduating with no in-state very selective options; sixteen states—not only states with small populations like Wyoming, Alaska, and Delaware, but also more populous states like Arizona and Alabama—and the District of Columbia have no very selective colleges at all. Staying in their home state is simply not an option for high-achieving students in these states who want to attend a match college. Further, only twenty states are home to very selective public colleges or universities. A small number of these states, like California, New York, and Virginia, have multiple public options for qualifying students. However, most, including New Mexico, Indiana, Pennsylvania, and South Carolina, offer only one such public option.

The geographic discrepancies do not stop at selectivity of four-year colleges; they extend to colleges' graduation rates. While some states, such as Massachusetts, Pennsylvania, and California, and Minnesota, have several colleges with four-year graduation rates in excess of 75 percent, other states are lacking in any option where students have a high chance of graduating in four years. Twenty-four states have no colleges with a four-year graduation rate of at least 75 percent, and twenty-eight states (plus the District of Columbia) have no public colleges where even half of enrolled students graduate within four years.

These differences form a sort of geographic lottery, with students in some states "winning" by having the opportunity to match with multiple high-quality, high graduation rate colleges while paying in-state tuition and/or staying relatively close to home. The "losers" in this lottery are the students graduating from high schools in states with no selective or high graduation rate colleges at all. The effect of those constrained choices on students' probabilities of degree attainment is an open question and beyond the scope of this paper. These state-by-state differences do, however, point to a limitation in using college match as a way of evaluating college choices of students or a high school's college counseling strategy. It is unfair to expect students in states with these constrained options to overcome these extreme weaknesses in their states' higher education systems.

CONCLUSION

The story of college match illustrates how research can influence practice and how this path can take unexpected turns. The development of college match as an indicator of the extent to which students were engaged in the college search process required having conceptual clarity around what this behavior might look like. It allowed researchers to build a deeper understanding of the scope of the problem and of which students were likely to undermatch and to develop interventions to support students in the college search process. In many ways, the movement of the college match indicator from research to practice is based in its origins; Consortium researchers grounded their work in understanding the needs and perspectives of practitioners through their partnership with the Chicago Public Schools. College match was not just an abstract indicator, it was meaningful and easily understood by practitioners and students alike and allowed for productive communications around the college search process. The college match framework had practical application in school practitioners' work with students with a limited amount of information about their academic qualifications. It was also linked to an outcome that was a priority for district leadership, practitioners, and students.

College match, however, is only a starting point in addressing issues around college search and college choice. Improving the college choices of students in ways that lead them to enroll in institutions with a higher likelihood of attaining a degree will require a much more nuanced discussion between students, their counselors and other adults. Other factors, particularly institutional graduation rates, should also be a part of the decision-making process. The regional higher education landscape also plays an important role; in many places, college options are limited. Improving students' college choices will require building the capacity of high schools to provide better guidance around college match and fit.

College match at its core is a strategy for guiding students to making good college choices. However, simply shifting the college choices of students to a match college does not improve the supply of higher education options that give students of all qualification levels a strong chance of attaining a degree. College match as a means for improving educational attainment rates at a national level will require an equivalent effort on the higher education supply side to improve the choices that high school students are given when they conduct their college searches.

2

Academic Match and Fit

What Can We Learn from Stated Preferences,
Student Actions, and Collegiate Outcomes?

Jessica S. Howell, Matea Pender, and Amal Kumar

Journalists and policy makers have become increasingly interested in the academic match between students and colleges.[1] Although the concept of match only recently emerged on the federal policy agenda, it is not a new topic among researchers; numerous studies over the past decade have presented compelling evidence on the importance of attending a more academically selective college, particularly a college that is well aligned to a student's own academic background. College selectivity and academic match are linked to better postsecondary outcomes like persistence, degree completion, and labor market experiences.[2] Many of these relationships have been established causally.[3]

Still, those conducting research in this area have faced disapproval about what critics see as an overemphasis on academic credentials in the growing literature on college match. This criticism is not without merit. From the student perspective, a good-*fit* college might mean an institution that is affordable, close to home, and culturally familiar. Given these student preferences, financial and geographic and program fit may be every bit as important to student success in college as academic match. Student surveys routinely reveal the importance of cost, geography, and available major programs as the most important facets of student college choice, and prioritization of the larger set of college factors that matter to students may vary substantially with student demographics.[4] From the colleges' perspective, a substantial proportion of admissions professionals remind us that they review applications holistically, so "presumptive eligibility" for admission is arguably tied up in much more than a student's academic credentials.[5] And just as the academic match literature has established a causal link between college selectivity and student outcomes, the social psychology literature has demonstrated that social belongingness and cultural fit matter for collegiate outcomes as well.[6]

Measuring these other dimensions of fit is admittedly more challenging than measuring college selectivity and student test scores (or GPA). Some concepts of fit are difficult to quantify using existing data sets (a challenge for researchers) and may also be difficult to predict before matriculation (a challenge for students); many students will have to actually experience life on a particular campus before they are able to assess whether it is a good fit or not. Still, other dimensions of fit *are* captured in available data and *are* observable to students during their college exploration and search phases. College exploration tools like College Navigator and Big Future certainly allow students to filter their college search results along a variety of dimensions related to campus size, location, sector, and cost in addition to academics—so, in theory, student users of these tools are receiving fairly clear signals that all of these facets of match and fit should be part of their college search process.[7]

So, to what should students pay attention (and in what order) as they conduct their college exploration and search? If geography is important, should students look only at colleges close to home? Certainly, the undermatch literature would indicate that geographically constrained students might enjoy improved college outcomes if they cast a wider geographic net and put more weight on academic match. But it is possible that good fit on geography, if a student expresses a preference for it, is every bit as important for college outcomes as is academic match. In this chapter, we present new empirical analyses to address the relative contribution of academic match and other measures of fit for bachelor's degree completion. The goal of these analyses is to determine whether education researchers and policy makers should be moving toward a more nuanced understanding and measure of student-college match that more explicitly incorporates broader measures of non-academic fit.

DATA AND DEFINITIONS

Our data set comes from the College Board's universe of SAT-takers from the high school graduating classes of 2006 through 2012.[8] Every year, approximately 1.6 million high school students take the SAT and roughly 1.3 million of them complete the SAT Questionnaire (SATQ) at the point of registration. Because many students take the SAT more than once, the SATQ survey responses reflect students' answers on their last attempt at the SAT. In two-thirds of a typical cohort, SATQ responses are last provided in the fall of the senior year, while the remaining one-third of the typical cohort is asked the SATQ survey questions for the last time in spring of the junior year.[9] SATQ survey questions cover high school coursework, grades, and extracurricular activities; student and family demographics; and preferences for different college attributes. In particular, students are asked about their preferences for (1) institutional level (such as two-year and four-year), (2) control (such as public and private), (3) campus size (enrollment), (4) urbanicity of a college's location, and (5) proximity to home.

We supplement the College Board data with data from the Integrated Postsecondary Education Data System (IPEDS) to further characterize each college by the same five attributes listed above and provide additional institution-level controls. The data on SAT-takers are also merged with National Student Clearinghouse (NSC) data that track postsecondary enrollment information for nearly all students enrolled in four-year and public two-year postsecondary institutions in the United States.[10] Data from the NSC allow us to observe which college, if any, a student enrolls in after high school graduation and whether and from which institution a student eventually obtains a degree.

Match and Fit Variable Construction

We define an academic match by comparing the percentile of a student's SAT score to the percentile associated with the average SAT score of students enrolled at their chosen college.[11] If a student's SAT percentile is no more than 15 percentile points above his or her college's average SAT percentile, we define the student to be academically matched.[12]

Student responses to the SATQ survey questions enable us to construct five binary measures of "fit" that reflect whether the colleges in which students enroll share the attributes for which they expressed a preference while still in high school. For example, if a student indicates a preference for public colleges and then enrolls in a public institution, he or she is assumed to fit on the dimension of institutional control. If a student selects multiple options (for example, checks both public and private), checks "undecided," or fails to respond, we control for these responses in our models, but such students are not classified as either "fitting" or "not fitting" in our analyses. We also create an alternate definition of "fit" that is agnostic to students' preferences on individual college attributes. This alternate definition of fit counts the number of college attributes on which a student fits; for each matched attribute, a student earns one "fit point" up to a maximum of five. Importantly, in this alternative definition of fit, students who select multiple options, check "undecided," or fail to respond earn zero fit points on those attributes and are included in the analysis.[13] An important caveat, to which we return in the conclusion, is that the SATQ does not include questions about all facets of fit that we would like to examine. There are no questions asked about financial, cultural, or social preferences. Although students are asked about their potential fields of study on the SATQ, it is challenging to ascertain whether they match on this dimension because nearly all colleges offer a broad set of majors and because we cannot observe whether and when students change their intended majors in our data, which is problematic because most students change their major multiple times.

STUDENT PREFERENCES FOR COLLEGE ATTRIBUTES

We examine students' stated preferences for college attributes across cohorts and across different student demographics. As measured on the SATQ, student preferences are remarkably stable over time, with yearly deviations from average preferences across the 2006–2012 cohorts rarely exceeding a few percentage points. Thus, figure 2.1 presents data on student preferences averaged across the seven cohorts that comprise our data set. SAT-takers report strong preferences for public and four-year institutions, tend to prefer cities over smaller and more rural locations, and prefer their home state over out-of-state postsecondary options. What is also quite obvious in figure 2.1 is that a substantial proportion of SAT-takers select "multiple" or "undecided" when filling out these questions on the SATQ. As we discuss in more detail below, it is challenging to disentangle whether these two groups are still expressing preferences through these responses.

The stability in preferences over time shown in figure 2.1 masks variation in preferences across different types of students. In results not shown, we find that some differences in stated preferences by student race/ethnicity and family income comport with public perception and evidence from other sources. For example, Latino SAT-takers are nearly twice as likely as black and white SAT-takers to express a preference for staying close to home.

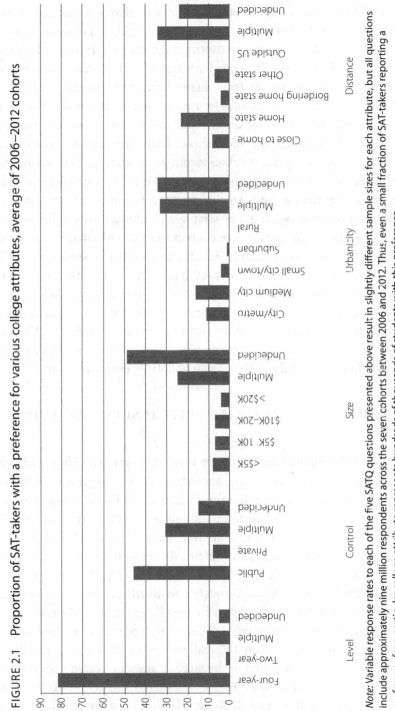

FIGURE 2.1   Proportion of SAT-takers with a preference for various college attributes, average of 2006–2012 cohorts

Note: Variable response rates to each of the five SATQ questions presented above result in slightly different sample sizes for each attribute, but all questions include approximately nine million respondents across the seven cohorts between 2006 and 2012. Thus, even a small fraction of SAT-takers reporting a preference for a particular college attribute represents hundreds of thousands of students with this preference.

Also, as self-reported family income rises, smaller shares of students express preferences for institutions that are two-year, public, and close to home.[14]

Figure 2.2 shows even clearer patterns in college preferences as they vary with students' SAT scores. Students with higher SAT scores are more likely to report weaker preferences for colleges that are two-year, public, with smaller student bodies, and close to home. Importantly, figure 2.2 also shows that, as student SAT score rises, more and more students select "multiple" or "undecided." Although the figure shows fairly dramatic declines in preferences for small colleges and urban locations as students' SAT scores rise, preferences for college size and urbanicity shift into the multiple/undecided categories rather than toward larger colleges and more rural locations. This may suggest open-mindedness or strategic thinking in the college search phase rather than truly no preference, a hypothesis to which we return when we discuss our regression results. Finally, in results not shown, we find a substantial amount of variation in preferences by geographic region of the country. SAT-takers from the Plains states are one-sixth as likely as SAT-takers from the Southern states to express a preference for staying in-state, for example. These geographic differences may be due simply to differences in the types of students who participate in the SAT in some regions of the country where ACT is the more prevalent college entrance exam.

ALIGNMENT BETWEEN STATED PREFERENCES AND STUDENT CHOICES

Given students' preferences for college attributes depicted in figures 2.1 and 2.2, to what extent do their college enrollment choices align with their preferences? Figure 2.3 indicates the proportion of SAT-takers who enroll in college, by fit along each of the five fit dimensions, as well as the proportion who enroll in a college that is an academic match.[15] As with trends in stated preferences over time, trends in our five dimensions of fit and academic match are also quite stable over time, so figure 2.3 reports averages across the 2006–2012 cohorts. Approximately two-thirds of enrolled SAT-takers fit on college level (two- or four-year) while 40 percent and 32 percent fit on control and distance, respectively. Students' preferences for college size and urbanicity are much less likely to be aligned with their actual enrollment choice. This may be a function of the larger number of categories available for size and urbanicity on the SATQ or it may reflect students' relative lack of knowledge about these two attributes of college campuses while they are

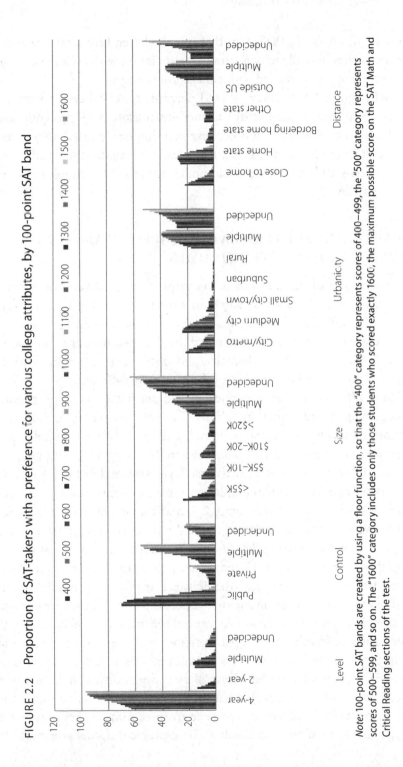

FIGURE 2.2 Proportion of SAT-takers with a preference for various college attributes, by 100-point SAT band

Note: 100-point SAT bands are created by using a floor function, so that the "400" category represents scores of 400–499, the "500" category represents scores of 500–599, and so on. The "1600" category includes only those students who scored exactly 1600, the maximum possible score on the SAT Math and Critical Reading sections of the test.

still in high school. To the extent that it is the latter, fitting on size and/or urbanicity may actually have a stronger association with college outcomes because it may be correlated with college knowledge.

Finally, figure 2.3 also shows that 81 percent of SAT-takers who enroll in college do so at an academically matched institution. A 19 percent under-match rate is consistent with other research that has focused on SAT-takers and college enrollees, but is a lower estimate than other studies that include non-enrollees or that would not consider safety schools to be academic matches.[16]

RELATIONSHIP BETWEEN MATCH AND FIT MEASURES AND STUDENTS' COLLEGIATE OUTCOMES

A primary goal of our analyses is to examine the relative importance of measures of fit and academic match for students' collegiate outcomes. We estimate the effect of academic match and fit measures on four- and six-year bachelor's degree completion using the five measures of fit mentioned above: level, control, size, urbanicity, and distance. (see appendix to this chapter for a detailed description of the model we estimate).

Our results suggest that academic match is associated with approximately a 7 percentage point higher probability of degree completion in four years and approximately a 5 percentage point higher probability of completion in six years, all else constant (see table A2.1 in the appendix to this chapter). Fit along three of the five fit dimensions (level, size, and distance) are positively associated with degree completion. Given students' strong preference for four-year institutions (see figure 2.1) and the potential for preferences for four-year institutions to be correlated with academic considerations, it is perhaps not surprising that fit on college level has the largest positive association with completion (5 percentage points) of all the measures of fit. Fit on institutional control and urbanicity are unrelated to completion. It is worth noting that the relationships between completion and academic match and completion and fit, individually, are not sensitive to the exclusion of the other variables. In other words, parameter estimates on the fit variables are similar between the models where academic match is included and excluded.

Beyond the associations between college completion and measures of fit, the estimates of the relationship between college completion and multiple preferences, undecided, and no response are intriguing, as they may be capturing some level of open-mindedness or strategic thinking going into the

FIGURE 2.3   Proportion of SAT-takers fitting on various college attributes, average of 2006–2012 cohorts

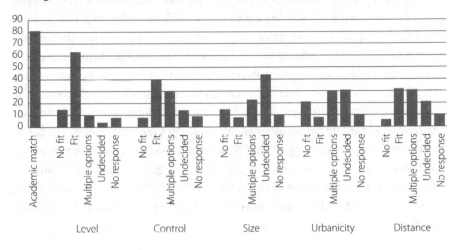

college search process. As depicted in figure 2.2, students with higher SAT scores are more likely than their lower-scoring peers to express a strong preference for college level and more likely to be explicitly undecided about college control, distance, size, and urbanicity. One hypothesis around this pattern is that academically stronger students may have more knowledge about their postsecondary options and be less likely to "foreclose" early on their options than their academically weaker peers.[17] Or it may simply represent the fact that academically stronger students are aware of their own appeal to admissions committees and that they will have more options.

While we are unable to explicitly test such hypotheses with our data, our findings suggest that having strong preferences about all aspects of one's postsecondary experience may not be optimal. Students who express early preferences for certain college attributes may be some of the same students who are prematurely ruling out colleges that could offer them a better shot at success.

For example, expressing *less* certainty about preferences for college control (that is, signaling an openness about both public and private institutions by checking both or undecided) is consistently associated with better completion outcomes than either fitting or not fitting on this dimension, all else equal. Similarly, our findings also suggest that students who express multiple preferences or who are undecided about college distance, all else equal, are nearly as likely to graduate in six years as students who fit on distance.

Uncertainty is not universally good for completion; students with multiple or uncertain preferences about college level and size are less likely to graduate than students who exhibit a clear preference (even if they do not fit), all else equal. Our findings may be evidence that during the college search phase, it is beneficial to have enough knowledge about colleges to have some preferences, while still being open-minded about other college attributes. Such partially formed preferences may provide students with an adequate starting point to engage in a productive college search without feeling overwhelmed by the number of available postsecondary options. If this is the case, our results suggest that there might be a natural order in which students could make decisions about their college options, and counselors and other advisers may have greater impact by focusing on solidifying knowledge about colleges and preferences for these attributes about which students still express uncertainty.

AN ALTERNATIVE CONCEPT OF FIT

One alternative explanation is that it matters less *how* students fit on individual dimensions of their preferences than the *number of dimensions* on which they fit. This alternative concept of fit allows for heterogeneity in preferences across students that results in students fitting first on those attributes that are the most important to them.(see appendix to this chapter for a detailed description of the model we estimate using this alternative definition of fit). Results from this model suggest that fitting on one, two, or three dimensions—regardless of which dimensions they are—is associated with a roughly 2–3 percentage point higher probability of completion (compared with fitting on no dimensions), while fitting on four or five dimensions is associated with a 4.0–4.6 percentage point boost (see table A2.2 in the appendix to this chapter). In practice, many students who fit on one dimension fit on college level (two- or four-year); given the strength of this fit measure, it is perhaps not surprising that there is a similar positive effect here. This alternative conception of fit does not alter the relationship between academic match and bachelor's completion, based on our estimates.

Collectively, our results suggest that measures of academic match and measures of non-academic fit capture different mechanisms that contribute to students' postsecondary success. Across all of our model specifications (as shown in the appendix to this chapter), the relationships between college completion, academic match, and fit are not affected by the inclusion of other variables. This clearly suggests that other measures of student-college fit—beyond the importance of academic match established in the literature and visible here—are also important predictors of successful bachelor's degree completion. Academically matched students in our sample fit on 18 percent more fit dimensions (about one-quarter of a dimension), on average, than undermatched students. Thus, match and fit may actually be complementary in the production of college degrees. There may be different mechanisms through which academic match and non-academic fit influence collegiate outcomes (possibly distinctly, possibly synergistically), which is a question perhaps best addressed by mixed-methods research or richer data on student preferences, choices, and outcomes.

Marginal Effects of Match and Fit on College Completion

Demonstrating the combined effects of academic match and non-academic fit on completion is an important contribution to our understanding of the factors within students' control during the college search and choice phases. This information could also be useful for those who are charged with advising and guiding students through the college search process. But there is an additional public policy angle that we can explore: the degree to which improved match and fit might be harnessed to close college completion gaps that exist between students who come from different family income and racial/ethnic groups.[18]

According to the *Digest of Education Statistics*, 59.2 percent of students in the 2006 starting cohort at all four-year institutions graduated with a bachelor's degree within six years at the institution at which they began.[19] This single completion rate statistic masks substantial variation by student characteristics (40.2 percent completion rate for black students compared with 62.5 percent for white students, for example) and by institutional attributes (32.8 percent completion rate at open admissions institutions, compared with 85.6 percent at very selective institutions). To what extent can improved match and fit within certain subgroups of students help close the gaps in college completion rates that we see in the data?[20]

To address this question, we compute the average predicted probability of completing a bachelor's degree associated with different amounts of academic match and non-academic fit, and present this information to demonstrate the marginal effects on graduation rates in figure 2.4. This figure includes predicted overall completion rates as well as by race/ethnicity and family income (for more information consult the appendix to this chapter).

One way to interpret the bars in figure 2.4 is as the predicted probabilities of graduation for perfectly "average" students within each subgroup who differ from each other only in whether, and how, they match or fit at their postsecondary institution.

Figure 2.4 suggests that academic match and non-academic fit may have the potential to close some of the completion gaps observed by family income. For SAT-takers in the lowest family income category (below $50,000), enrolling in an academically matched college where the student also fits on all five dimensions is associated with a 9.2 percentage point higher six-year completion rate, compared with no match or fit (from 40 to 49.2 percent). The resulting predicted completion rate—nearly 50 percent—is almost on par with students in the next income category of $50,000–$80,000 who do not match or fit. And for *those* students with modest family incomes, the 9.3 percentage point higher six-year completion rate associated with academic match and full fit actually brings their completion rate to 60.4 percent, which is *higher* than the completion rate of students in the next income category who do not match or fit. While academic match and full fit are not the great equalizers that we would perhaps like, the results suggest that guiding students to more intentionally match *and* fit in postsecondary education has the potential to substantially narrow some long-standing college completion gaps by family income.

The middle panel of figure 2.4, which focuses on differences by race/ethnicity, paints a less rosy picture for the potential of match and fit to substantially narrow completion gaps along racial/ethnic lines. Neither black nor Latino SAT-takers are predicted to complete bachelor's degrees at the same rate as their white peers, even when enrolled at colleges where they are academically matched and fit according to their preferences for non-academic dimensions. The predicted completion rates in figure 2.4 take into account all other measurable student attributes, which indicates that the differences in completion by race/ethnicity stem from differences in underlying factors like academic preparation or parental education. Importantly, this policy analysis is limited by our ability to capture the aspects of fit that matter for student outcomes. The five fit measures based on the SATQ may be particularly inadequate for certain students; fitting on factors related to socio-emotional, cultural, schedule flexibility, campus activities, and supports may be especially important for degree completion, in which case our estimate of the potential contribution of fit to completion outcomes is understated in these subgroups.

FIGURE 2.4 Predicted six-year graduation rates associated with academic match and fit, by race/ethnicity and family income

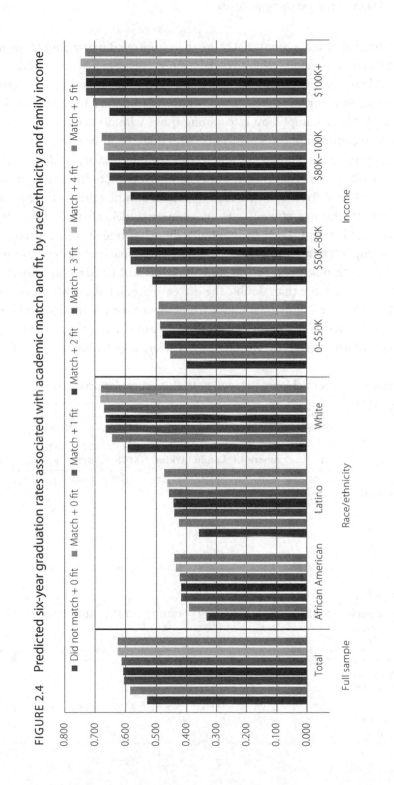

Although it is apparent that more than improved match and fit (as measured here) are needed to close racial/ethnic gaps in college completion, one should not dismiss the large potential for match and fit to improve completion outcomes for underrepresented minority students. Because of the lower predicted base completion rate among those who do not match or fit, the boost in completion rates associated with match and fit represents much a larger percentage increase for underrepresented minority students than for their white peers. That is, without existing differences in base completion rates that are driven by other factors, match and fit actually have stronger potential to improve student outcomes among students from historically disadvantaged groups. Table 2.1 highlights these findings: academic match and achieving full fit are associated with increases in bachelor's degree completion for both black and Latino students of 18 and 12 percent, respectively, rates that are more than double the increase predicted for white students.

Finally, table 2.1 also highlights the evidence for the fundamental question posed in this chapter: *What is the relative importance of academic match compared with other measures of fit for bachelor's degree completion?* In the full

TABLE 2.1   Potential for match and fit to close completion gaps

	Full sample	Race/ethnicity			Income			
	Total	African American	Latino	White	$0–$50K	$50–$80K	$80–$100K	$100K+
Maximum increase in six-year BA completion via match and full fit	0.097	0.109	0.114	0.087	0.092	0.093	0.094	0.079
Percentage point increase via match	0.054	0.061	0.065	0.049	0.055	0.054	0.044	0.053
Percentage point increase via full fit	0.042	0.048	0.049	0.038	0.037	0.039	0.050	0.026
% increase via match (as a % of base rate)	10.2%	18.3%	18.0%	8.2%	13.8%	10.6%	7.5%	8.1%
% increase via full fit (as a % of base rate)	7.2%	12.3%	11.6%	5.8%	8.2%	6.9%	7.9%	3.7%

sample and in every subgroup depicted in table 2.1, the predicted increase in six-year bachelor's completion rates associated with academic match is always larger—sometimes substantially so—than the predicted increase associated with fully fitting on other dimensions on which students express preferences. While this is certainly not definitive evidence that match is more important than fit, it does suggest that college counselors and policy makers are wise to emphasize the importance of academics in the college search process first and foremost—before considering the measures of fit described in this chapter.

CONCLUSION

We examine patterns in students' stated preferences for college attributes, the extent to which their college enrollment choices are consistent with those preferences, and whether consistency matters for students' college outcomes. Our analyses indicate that academic match and non-academic fit are important predictors of bachelor's degree completion. Yet high school juniors and seniors do not seem to know exactly what they want in a college, and that may not be detrimental to their collegiate outcomes. We find that uncertain preferences for some college attributes—at least during the college exploration and search phases in high school that we are able to observe—are more positively associated with degree completion than student preferences expressed with certainty. This suggests two ideas for consideration. First, an informed openness about what constitutes the right kind of college may actually be beneficial in that students might not "foreclose" on potentially good postsecondary options. Second, openness and uncertain preferences imply a clear role for information and guidance shortly after this point in the college search phase that can help students to more clearly articulate their preferences and refine their list of colleges under consideration. Thus, students may not respond well to early interventions that provide all information and advice at a single point in time, and perhaps it explains why we see growing evidence of the effectiveness of college counseling, coaching, and mentoring programs that engage students throughout the college choice process.[21]

Our empirical results also support the idea that academic match and non-academic fit are complementary constructs. Both match and fit are uniquely important for explaining variation in bachelor's degree completion rates and the sizes of the relationships are substantial enough that both have practical significance. We also provide evidence that the relationships between match and fit and degree completion vary with student demographics, so targeted interventions that provide information and counseling to those at greater risk of considering colleges that are poor matches and poor fits may be inexpensive and effective levers for narrowing persistent gaps in college completion.

All analyses come with caveats, and an important one here centers on the fact that the SATQ survey does not include questions about all facets of fit that we would like to examine. Most notably absent are any questions asking directly about students' financial preferences, although it is quite likely that these are somewhat reflected in their preferences for college level and control and the desire to stay close to home or in-state. We do not assert that the five measures of fit we examine are the *only* or *best* measures, only that these measures are available to inform the discussion of whether and how academic match could be broadened to include other concepts of fit. Second, our results are applicable to the population of SAT-takers, which is broadly reflective of college applicants, yet distinct in its representation of roughly half of students taking a college entrance exam. Finally, it is important to recognize that preferences—particularly those expressed by high school students—may be learned or inherited rather than a true reflection of informed consideration. For example, if it is the cultural norm for students in particular communities to choose only community colleges, then expressed preferences for two-year, public institutions close to home will be the observed pattern. We should exercise caution in taking as given these kinds of "adaptive preferences" that are formed by students in response to restrictive options. Such preferences may provide a poor baseline for assessing fit, yet attempts to challenge and favorably influence student preferences ought to be done carefully and respectfully. Our evidence is meant to push this conversation about match and fit forward and, ideally, drive the discovery or development of better measures of these fit constructs. Better measures of fit, perhaps combined with a mixed-methods approach to examining them, would shed additional light on the mechanisms by which improved match and fit help to drive student success in college. A better understanding of the importance of timing and mechanisms underlying the relationship between academic match, fit, and collegiate outcomes can then be more clearly communicated to students and families through the college search tools they employ and the counselors and mentors they consult.

Appendix (Chapter 2)

To examine the relative importance of measures of fit and academic match for students' collegiate outcomes, we specify a simple model where student i's outcome at college j (Y_{ij}) is a function of academic match (M_{ij}), K different measures of fit indexed by k (F_{ijk}), student characteristics (X_i), institutional attributes (Z_j), and state-by-year fixed effects (μ_{st}):

(1) $$Y_{ij} = \alpha + \beta M_{ij} + \Sigma_{k=1}^{K} \gamma_k F_{ijk} + \delta X_i + \omega Z_j + \mu_{st} + \varepsilon_{ij}$$

The collegiate outcomes (Y_{ij}) we examine are bachelor's degree completion in four years and six years. The SATQ survey permits the inclusion of five different dimensions of fit. The student level controls we include in X_i are race/ethnicity, gender, family income, and parental education; the institutional controls in Z_j include college level, control, urbanicity, location, annual tuition/fees, instructional expenditures per FTE, and the number and proportion of the student body receiving financial aid. In order to examine six-year bachelor's completion outcomes, we restrict the sample in these analyses to the 2006 and 2007 cohorts only, and we estimate equation (1) using Ordinary Least Squares.

Table A2.1 presents estimates of equation (1) based on three different specifications: academic match included without fit measures (specifications [1] and [4]), fit measures included without match (specifications [2] and [5]), and both academic match and fit variables (specifications [3] and [6]). Each of these specifications explains roughly 28 percent of the variation observed in four- and six-year bachelor's completion outcomes.

TABLE A2.1   Effect of academic match and fit measures on bachelor's degree completion

	BA completion in four years			BA completion in six years		
	(1)	(2)	(3)	(4)	(5)	(6)
Academic match	0.072***		0.068***	0.055***		0.052***
	(0.001)		(0.001)	(0.001)		(0.001)
Fit on level		0.056***	0.051***		0.051***	0.047***
		(0.001)	(0.001)		(0.001)	(0.001)
Multiple preferences on level		−0.023***	−0.024***		−0.036***	−0.037***
		(0.001)	(0.001)		(0.001)	(0.001)
Undecided on level		−0.021***	−0.023***		−0.038***	−0.039***
		(0.001)	(0.001)		(0.002)	(0.002)
No response on level		0.023***	0.019***		0.019***	0.017***
		(0.003)	(0.003)		(0.004)	(0.004)
Fit on control		−0.002*	−0.003***		−0.008***	−0.009***
		(0.001)	(0.001)		(0.001)	(0.001)
Multiple preferences on control		0.021***	0.020***		0.013***	0.012***
		(0.001)	(0.001)		(0.001)	(0.001)
Undecided on control		0.023***	0.023***		0.014***	0.013***
		(0.001)	(0.001)		(0.001)	(0.001)
No response on control		0.020***	0.019***		0.014***	0.013***
		(0.003)	(0.003)		(0.004)	(0.004)
Fit on size		0.014***	0.013***		0.011***	0.011***
		(0.001)	(0.001)		(0.001)	(0.001)
Multiple preferences on size		0.001	0.000		−0.004***	−0.005***
		(0.001)	(0.001)		(0.001)	(0.001)
Undecided on size		−0.018***	−0.018***		−0.015***	−0.014***
		(0.001)	(0.001)		(0.001)	(0.001)
No response on size		−0.030***	−0.029***		−0.040***	−0.040***
		(0.002)	(0.002)		(0.002)	(0.002)
Fit on urbanicity		0.000	0.001		−0.004***	−0.004***
		(0.001)	(0.001)		(0.001)	(0.001)

TABLE A2.1   *(Cont.)*

	BA completion in four years			BA completion in six years		
	(1)	**(2)**	**(3)**	**(4)**	**(5)**	**(6)**
Multiple preferences on urbanicity		−0.005***	−0.005***		−0.009***	−0.008***
		(0.001)	(0.001)		(0.001)	(0.001)
Undecided on urbanicity		0.001	0.001		0.001	0.001
		(0.001)	(0.001)		(0.001)	(0.001)
No response on urbanicity		0.006**	0.006*		0.014***	0.014***
		(0.003)	(0.003)		(0.004)	(0.004)
Fit on distance		0.004***	0.004***		0.020***	0.020***
		(0.001)	(0.001)		(0.001)	(0.001)
Multiple preferences on distance		0.003**	0.002**		0.016***	0.016***
		(0.001)	(0.001)		(0.001)	(0.001)
Undecided on distance		0.000	−0.000		0.011***	0.011***
		(0.001)	(0.001)		(0.001)	(0.001)
No response on distance		0.011***	0.011***		0.018***	0.017***
		(0.003)	(0.003)		(0.004)	(0.004)
Student demographics	Yes	Yes	Yes	Yes	Yes	Yes
Student academics	Yes	Yes	Yes	Yes	Yes	Yes
Postsecondary charactersitics	Yes	Yes	Yes	Yes	Yes	Yes
State × Year fixed effects	Yes	Yes	Yes	Yes	Yes	Yes
Constant	−0.425***	−0.300***	−0.430***	−0.090***	−0.004	−0.100***
	(0.007)	(0.008)	(0.008)	(0.007)	(0.008)	(0.008)
Observations	3,423,628	3,434,284	3,420,900	2,291,941	2,297,924	2,289,229
Adjusted R-squared	0.278	0.279	0.280	0.276	0.278	0.279

Note: Standard errors in parentheses. *** $p < 0.01$, ** $p < 0.05$, * $p < 0.1$. All regressions include a full set of student and college attributes, and state-by-year fixed effects.

We also estimate an alternative specification of equation (1) that redefines F_{ijk} as fitting on k dimensions where k indexes the *number* of dimensions. Results of this model are presented in table A2.2 below.

In order to compute each subgroup's predicted probabilities, we use the coefficient estimates from table A2.2 and multiply them by values for the appropriate subgroup and the colleges students within the subgroup attended. The average predicted probabilities of completing a bachelor's degree (overall and by race/ethnicity and family income) associated with different amounts of academic match and non-academic fit are presented in figure 2.4 in the chapter.

TABLE A2.2   Effect of academic match and alternate fit measures on bachelor's degree completion

	BA completion in four years			BA completion in six years		
	(1)	(2)	(3)	(4)	(5)	(6)
Academic match	0.072***		0.071***	0.055***		0.054***
	(0.001)		(0.001)	(0.001)		(0.001)
Fit on 1 measure		0.029***	0.027***		0.023***	0.021***
		(0.001)	(0.001)		(0.001)	(0.001)
Fit on 2 measures		0.025***	0.023***		0.025***	0.024***
		(0.001)	(0.001)		(0.001)	(0.001)
Fit on 3 measures		0.027***	0.025***		0.031***	0.030***
		(0.001)	(0.001)		(0.001)	(0.001)
Fit on 4 measures		0.039***	0.036***		0.044***	0.043***
		(0.001)	(0.001)		(0.001)	(0.001)
Fit on 5 measures		0.046***	0.043***		0.046***	0.044***
Observations	3,423,628	3,437,013	3,423,628	2,291,941	2,300,636	2,291,941
Adjusted R-squared	0.278	0.276	0.278	0.276	0.275	0.276

Note: Standard errors in parentheses. *** $p < 0.01$, ** $p < 0.05$, * $p < 0.1$. All regressions include a full set of student and college attributes, and state-by-year fixed effects.

3

Average Students and College Match

Looking Beyond the Elite

Awilda Rodriguez and Christian Martell

M ost of the recent literature addressing college match has centered on high-achieving, low-income high school seniors and whether they applied to and enrolled at the colleges deemed "most selective" and "highly selective" by *Barron's* Admissions Competitiveness Index.[1] The argument underpinning the study of college match is that if students enroll in more selective institutions, they will enjoy a host of resources positively associated with admissions selectivity and therefore be more likely to graduate.[2] Undermatch can thus be described as either an issue of stratification or inefficiency in our education system. Studies documenting the degree to which students undermatch, particularly low-income, high-achieving students, have touched off an avalanche of (quite accurate) headlines about the dearth of poor students at top colleges; shown that a $6 mailer about college options can dramatically change the likelihood that students will apply to college; and attracted the attention of the White House, as President Obama asked colleges to make a public pledge to increase low-income student enrollment.[3]

Low-income, high-achieving students are a natural place to focus our attention. Americans have long been enamored of bootstrapping "rags to riches" stories of social mobility for the deserving poor. In the spring, newspapers predictably print inspiring versions of the "homeless to Harvard" story, depicting students who overcome extreme financial circumstances to gain admission to one (or several) of the most selective colleges in the country.[4] Beyond our collective fascination with such (rare) tales of social mobility, this population of students is of particular research interest because submitting an application is seen as the main obstacle to their success. After all, high-achieving, low-income seniors are well positioned to be accepted by and enroll in a wide range of colleges—and to do so at little to no cost, as their academic credentials and financial circumstances often qualify them for generous need- and merit-based financial aid packages.[5] The fact that these students miss out because they do not apply—not because they are unprepared or lack financial resources—seems like an obvious and easy target for research. What's more, it is fairly simple for researchers to identify "high-achieving, low-income students," typically through the use of income cut-offs and academic criteria such as exam scores or GPA.[6] Lastly, enrollment at a selective institution is seen as preferable to enrollment at a less selective four-year or two-year college, given the greater resources available to students at selective institutions and the increased likelihood of graduating.[7]

But for all the deserved attention the traditional conceptualization of undermatch has received, there are limitations to the problems we can solve—improving equity or increasing the number of college graduates—if we focus solely on these students and institutions. First, relative to the number of graduating high school students who wish to earn a college degree, the share of high-achieving, low-income students is small. For example, the national population of twenty-five to thirty-five thousand high-achieving, low-income students in a recent undermatch study comprised only 4 percent of high school seniors.[8] Second, most selective institutions aren't increasing the size of their freshman classes.[9] Because the number of college applicants has doubled since the 1970s, the bar for admission to selective US institutions has continued to rise, while the incoming class sizes at these institutions have remained stagnant.[10] This means that more colleges are making their way into the higher selectivity brackets, but it does not mean that increasing numbers of students are gaining access to the resources traditionally available at selective institutions. By focusing the conversation on a small percentage of students gaining access to an even smaller percentage of highly selective institutions, we limit our understanding of the college match phenomenon—and our understanding of other forms of stratification across the higher education system.

In contrast, the "average-performing" student is both ubiquitous and obscure. Large shares of average-performing students enroll in college every year. In 2012, between half and two-thirds of college-age students who were enrolled in either four- or two-year colleges had a high school GPA between 2.0 and 3.5.[11] Average-performing students comprise a large segment of the college-going population, yet their college aspirations and outcomes have not been a focus of the college match literature. These students are less likely to be competitive in securing a spot at a selective college, and thus enroll in colleges that would be deemed undermatches for high-achieving students. But the probability of completion is no higher (and likely lower) at these institutions for average-performing students, and they therefore face the same risks of not graduating from the less selective colleges they choose.[12]

In addition to underrepresenting average-performing students in match research, the literature is not clear about the types of colleges that *would* be a good match for them. Identifying students by their chances of gaining admission to a college is not the same as identifying college options for students with a particular academic profile. Given the large number of college-bound, average-achieving students, a study of match for the average-achieving student is overdue. This chapter addresses the gap in our knowledge about average-performing students and their college choice process by answering the following questions:

1. What are the characteristics of average-performing students?
2. How well do average-performing students match on degree-level aspirations, affordability, and completion?

In addressing these questions, we expand the college match conversation to include a large share of college-bound students and institutions and challenge ourselves to broaden our definition of what constitutes a good "match." We start with an examination of what the match literature has told us thus far about average-performing students.

PREVIOUS LITERATURE ON AVERAGE-PERFORMING STUDENTS AND COLLEGE MATCH

As noted, the undermatch literature has primarily drawn our attention to the high-performing student. To date, only two studies have considered undermatch for students of various academic levels. A series of reports from the Chicago Consortium for School Research examined college match across the full range of ACT and GPA scores (for example, a Chicago Public School graduate with a GPA between a 2.0 and 2.4 and a composite ACT score between 21 and 23 was eligible to enroll in a "somewhat selective" college). This examination of match included an analysis of the college-going behaviors that increase the chances that average-performing students find a good match, including filling out the FAFSA, discussing their college options with their counselor, and applying to six or more colleges. In discussing their findings, Melissa Roderick and her colleagues underscored the challenges of match across the achievement spectrum. Half of students in the graduating class of 2005 were eligible for "somewhat selective" or "nonselective" colleges, but only a fraction of them enrolled in a college at or above their qualification level (43 percent and 17 percent, respectively).[13]

Jonathan Smith and his colleagues extended our understanding of match by providing a national picture of average-performing students. The authors used student information collected in two national data sets to predict the likelihood of admission to schools with various levels of selectivity. They found that about a quarter of seniors in 2004 were 90 percent likely to gain admission into "somewhat selective" or "nonselective" schools. They also found that 65 percent of these students enrolled in colleges that were as or more selective than their qualifications. In the discussion of their findings, the authors characterized undermatch for average-performing students with limited college options as "high stakes," as these students might enroll in a two-year college or not enroll in college at all.[14]

While these two studies have set the groundwork for our understanding of match, their findings elicit more questions than answers. For example, they have very disparate findings about who is eligible for "somewhat selective" and "nonselective" colleges (50 percent versus 26 percent), most likely the result of their differing approaches to identifying student qualifications and samples.[15] Moreover, it is not clear that a four-year nonselective college is a better option than a two-year institution for an average-performing student if, for example, a student is place-bound, has financial restrictions (four-year colleges often cost more), or actually wishes to obtain an associate's degree or certificate. Furthermore, in some cases, less selective four-year institutions have graduation rates that are indistinguishable from those of two-year colleges. In other words, these studies do not resolve the key question: How do we determine a "good" option for the mass of students in the middle?

There are a number of limitations to applying the notion of college match, as currently conceptualized, to the college application and enrollment behaviors of average-performing students. One of the common critiques of college match research has been the arbitrary delineation of the qualifications needed for admission to various groups of institutions.[16] This is particularly true for institutions that are outside the most selective rung, where the range of admissible academic profiles is much larger. For this reason, our ability to reliably predict admission to a somewhat selective college remains elusive.

Beyond issues of measurement, there are structural limitations of institutional proximity and supply that may make some of the assumptions about undermatch inapplicable to many average-performing students. The college choice process cannot be examined without giving consideration to geographical context.[17] Students who are high-achieving or who come from high socioeconomic backgrounds typically engage in national college searches.[18] However, for most students, the college choice set involves colleges that are predominantly close to home.[19] With so many students bound to or preferring colleges within relatively small geographic areas, scholars have noted that the availability (or dearth) of postsecondary options is subject to the "geography of opportunity."[20] Simply put, students' postsecondary opportunities are directly linked to (and potentially limited by) where they happen to live. Students in areas where there are few college options, as Wisconsin professor Nicholas Hillman argues, are precluded from "shop[ping] around."[21] Proximity is thus key in framing the college choice process for average-performing students, who may also face additional constraints in their choices given their academic performance. A related structural limitation to match is the availability of seats in colleges that may be a match and are nearby. Indeed, a dearth of nearby "matched" seats may limit the extent to which match is a useful tool for understanding equity and access for average-performing students.

Taken together, the current conceptualization of college match has not served average-performing college-bound high school students well. As a result, we know little about the average-performing student and their college aspirations. In the next section, we examine the characteristics of average-performing students and their college-going behaviors and preferences.

WHO IS THE AVERAGE-PERFORMING STUDENT?

As there is still no clear picture of the average-performing student and his or her college choices, we first set out to characterize the average-performing student using data from the Education Longitudinal Survey of 2002 (ELS:2002). ELS:2002 is a national longitudinal survey administered by the National Center for Education Statistics (NCES) that collected data on students who were high school sophomores in 2002 (and due to graduate high school in 2004).[22] While ELS:2002 is over a decade old, it is still the most recent national data set tracking students' complete college-application behavior. Also, its larger sample size minimizes self-reporting discrepancies found in sets with fewer respondents. The data were restricted to students who participated in the first three surveys and were not enrolled in vocational, alternative, or special education, because college preparation is not an explicit goal of those programs. Likewise, only students who expected to attend college at the onset of their high school career were included, so we could be certain of their interest in attending. The resultant weighted sample totaled 1,105,880 students.[23]

We used two criteria to define average performance. First, we used students' math score on an NCES-administered test. Much of the current literature uses SAT scores to identify undermatched students; however, we used students' scores on the NCES-administered math test because this measure was available for all students and did not bias our results in the direction of high-performing students, who are more likely to take a standardized college entrance exam. Recognizing that the NCES-administered math exam might be perceived as a low-stakes exam for survey participants, we also included unweighted high school GPAs between 2.0 and 3.5 for all courses as a second criterion. As we are proposing to broaden our attention from high performers to include those with average academic ability in future undermatch research, a comparison of these two groups is merited. In the following section, we compare average-performing students with their higher-performing peers by demographic characteristics and college-going behaviors.

Characteristics of Average-Performing Students

Demographic Composition

There are notable differences in demographic composition between average and high performers, as the high-performing group has noticeably fewer black, Latino, low-income, and first-generation students than the average-performing group (see table 3.1). Though the majority of students in both groups identified as white, the representation of black and Latino students is much greater in the average-performing group (for example, 12.4 percent of average-achieving students are black versus 1.2 percent of high-achieving students). This is consistent with a number of other well-documented educational achievement disparities between racial/ethnic groups that in most cases start in the early grades.[24] With higher percentages of black and Latino students in the average-performing category, we can expect these

TABLE 3.1   Comparison of average- and high-performing students by select characteristics[a]

Variable		Percentage	
		Average-performing[b]	High-performing[c]
N[d]		1,105,880	209,470
Demographic characteristics			
Gender*	Female	55.3%	60.9%
Race/ethnicity*	Asian, Pacific Islander	4.1%	6.0%
	Black	12.4%	1.2%
	Latino	12.4%	4.3%
	Other race/ethnicity[e]	5.0%	2.0%
	White	66.2%	86.5%
Income	$0–$25K	15.8%	4.3%
	$25–$50K	29.4%	22.6%
	$50–$75K	23.2%	24.0%
	$75–$100K	16.1%	17.6%
	>$100K	15.6%	31.5%
Parents' highest level of education	High school or less	21.8%	7.9%
	Some college, no degree[f]	22.6%	14.6%
	Two-year graduate	11.7%	7.4%
	Four-year graduate	43.8%	70.0%
College-going behaviors			
College entrance exam[g]	Took an exam	80.3%	96.3%
Minimal college course reqs	Took Algebra II	94.2%	99.4%
College preparatory courses	Took calculus	10.3%	57.9%
	Took an AP/IB course	32.0%	80.0%
College application	Average applications	2.45	3.53
		0.03	0.10
		Mean	
Importance of college characteristics	Price	2.15	2.00
	Standard deviation	0.01	0.03

(continues)

TABLE 3.1   *(Cont.)*

Variable		Percentage	
		Average-performing[b]	High-performing[c]
	Academic reputation	2.50	2.80
	Standard deviation	0.01	0.02
	Availability of program	2.73	2.71
	Standard deviation	0.01	0.02
	Staying home	1.67	1.17
	Standard deviation	0.01	0.02
College enrollment			
Distance	Average distance (miles)	135.1	244.24
	Standard deviation	6.8	16.41
Sector	Four-year	61.0%	93.1%
	Two-year	30.2%	5.8%
	Less than two-year	1.2%	0.1%
	None	7.6%	1.0%

Source: Education Longitudinal Survey (ELS: 2002).

Note: Results from t-test or chi-square tests are "n.s." if not significant, ***significant at $p < 0.001$. (a) Data were weighted using the F2F1WT; (b) The sample of average students was restricted to respondents with scores above or below one SD from the mean on the ELS mathematics test; who had available responses for all described attributes listed in the table at the time of the first follow up; who were not enrolled in special, vocational, or alternative education; and had a GPA between 2.0 and 3.5; (c) High-achieving students met the same criteria as average students, except they had IRT Math scores above one SD; (d) Total *N* were rounded to ensure students' anonymity; (e) Respondents who identified as Native American/American Indian and multiracial were combined into a single category; (f) "Some college, no degree" combines parents who attended either a two- or four-year institution, but did not graduate; (g) Students took the SAT, ACT, or both.

students to have fewer postsecondary options on average than their white and Asian peers.

The distribution of socioeconomic status (SES) and parental education is also distinct across the two groups. Approximately 45.2 percent of average-performing students come from families earning less than $50,000, whereas only about 26.9 percent of high-performing students belong to the same income bracket. Similarly, the data indicate that about three-quarters (77.4 percent) of all high performers have parents with a college or advanced degree, while only 55.5 percent of average-performing students' parents hold the same level of education. Needless to say, parental education and income are influential in the college choice process.[25] High-SES parents in particular are known to use their own college experiences to influence or support their children's college application process, leaving students from more modest backgrounds—who are also more likely to be average-performing—at a disadvantage.[26] When we couple this income stratification with the existing racial/ethnic stratification, we can assume that many average-performing students have limited options for college. As discussed below, their college application and college-going behaviors support this hypothesis.

College Application Behavior

For students interested in college, the extent to which they engage in their coursework, exams, and college applications is essential to their competitiveness in the college admission market. The majority of average- and high-achieving high school students take Algebra II (94.2 and 99.4 percent of students, respectively), a minimum requirement for many four-year colleges. There are large gaps, however, in advanced coursework participation rates. For example, only 10.3 percent of average-performing students took Calculus, compared with 57.9 percent of high-performing students. Similar gaps exist in AP and IB course-taking rates. In addition, taking college entrance exams sets students on a path toward four-year college enrollment, since many colleges require an SAT or ACT score for admission. However, only about 80 percent of average-performing students reported taking the SAT, the ACT, or both tests, compared with nearly all high-performing students (96.3 percent). Yet taking college preparatory courses and exams is only the first step—students' performance in those courses and tests further differentiates their future opportunities.

College-application behavior differed to a lesser extent between the groups. Both high-achieving and average-performing students applied to college at similar rates, although average-performing students applied to one less college on average. In considering colleges, average-performing students were slightly more concerned with costs ($\mu = 2.15$ versus 2.0, respectively) and staying close to home ($\mu = 1.67$ versus 1.17, respectively) than were high-performing students. Moreover, although average-performing students generally reported a college's academic reputation to be an important consideration, they were slightly less likely to do so than high-performers. Their greatest consideration, on average, was the availability of their chosen academic program at an institution, a consideration that was not statistically different from their higher-performing counterparts. Thus, while average-performing students generally might not demonstrate the requisite academic performance to compete for enrollment in highly selective institutions, most who indicated an interest in college took purposeful steps toward college enrollment.

Where do average-performing students enroll? The bottom portion of table 3.1 shows enrollment figures for the sample based on institutional level, sector, and selectivity. Thirty percent of average-performing students enrolled in two-year institutions—five times the number of high-performing students who did so. An additional 61 percent of average performers enrolled in four-year colleges, as did the overwhelming majority of high-performing students (93.1 percent). Finally, 7.6 percent of average performers were not enrolled in college two years after high school graduation and were not in the military, compared with only 1 percent of high-performing students.

Understanding the demographic and college-going characteristics of average-performing students is essential to our understanding of how they fit into the broader conversation around undermatch. In comparing average- and high-performing students, we find there are sizable demographic differences. This finding underscores the importance of considering college choice for average-performing students if we are to improve equitable access to a high-performing college. The level of academic preparation, and participation in college entrance exams in particular, are likely to shape students' college choices and outcomes. Given the demographics of the sample of average-performing students, we can expect that many of them will have limited college options—if they decide to enroll at all. In the following sections, we explore what "match" looks like for these students, as well as the attributes of their postsecondary options.

COLLEGE MATCH ALTERNATIVES FOR AVERAGE-PERFORMING STUDENTS

Match has previously been defined purely by academic standards. In other words, a match occurs when a high-performing student attends a college or university with a student body with similar levels of academic achievement. Therefore, a "good" match for a high-performing student is a top college, where admission is based in large part on standardized test scores and GPA. However, average-performing students complicate this definition of match.

So far, we have identified average-performing students using academic measures such as standardized test scores and GPA, and have compared them with their high-performing peers demographically and academically. We have also discussed the influence of geography on college choice for average-performing students, who are more likely than high-performing students to enroll at an institution near home. In this section, we propose four alternative ways to consider match for average-performing students: (1) their career aspirations and academic interests; (2) their nearby college options; (3) affordability of the institution; and (4) likelihood of completion.

College Match by Career Aspirations and Academic Interest

Absent clear admissions criteria, an institution's academic and career offerings can drive match for average performers. An acknowledged shortcoming of the current match literature is the extent to which students match to institutions by their intended degree program. Indeed, 77 percent of respondents in our sample noted degree program was an important consideration in their college choice. Students who are interested in studying a specific vocation or are committed to working in a particular field may consider only a subset of schools, irrespective of selectivity. Therefore, one way to reconceptualize college match is to examine whether students "match" their stated plans as seniors to actual enrollment based on degree level.

Ideally, we would contrast students' career and academic interests with the strength of particular programs offered by colleges. There are several challenges to defining match by career aspirations and academic interests, however. First, students enrolling in college immediately after high school may not have a solid understanding of what they would like to study or what profession they will choose. Indeed, a large share of students change majors once enrolled in college (35 percent).[27] Basing match for average-performing students on what is effectively a moving target for many of them would be difficult. Second, it is not always clear what academic programs are being offered at which institutions, and whether those programs are considered significantly better or more attractive to prospective students than others. On a more practical level, ELS:2002 did not ask about students' intended majors, nor is there widely available information about institutions at the program level. (For more on the major selection process in two-year and open-access four-year colleges, see chapter 4.)

There is still value in understanding the degree level students intend on pursuing, which is a less volatile measure. In addition to enrollment information, NCES collected information about the type of college in which students wanted to continue their studies. We subsequently compared students' intended degree level with the level of institution in which they enrolled immediately after college.

Average-performing high school seniors who enrolled in college generally followed through with their degree aspirations and enrolled in a college with corresponding degree offerings. Three out of every four seniors who indicated a plan to pursue a four-year degree enrolled in a four-year college, as did students wanting a two-year degree (see table 3.2). Match is less clear for students who wanted to pursue vocational or technical training, as they were most likely to enroll in two-year colleges (47.1 percent) or not at all (25.7 percent). Therefore, the majority of average-performing students planned on earning either a two- or four-year degree and enrolled in a college that fit that description.

College Match by Institutional Proximity

One aspect of college match discussed less frequently is institutional proximity. Some students prefer to stay at home to save on room and board costs, while other students want to leave home to establish their independence or live in a particular city or region. In some cases, students' preferences are bound by the intersection of colleges to which they are able to gain admission, that are affordable, and that are nearby.

To understand differences in the way students consider geographic proximity, we examined their responses to the question, "How important is the ability to attend school while living at home in choosing a school you would like to attend?" We compared their responses ("not important," "somewhat important," or "very important") with the proximity of the colleges in which they chose to enroll.[28] This approach has some limitations, as it does not consider geographic attributes (for example, urbanicity, rural areas, or mountainous terrain) or transit routes, and thus the difference between distance and actual commuting times may vary. Nonetheless, this approach allowed us to estimate proximity in the aggregate. Our analysis included students with valid residential zip codes who enrolled in colleges that also reported recognized zip codes ($N = 977,810$).

Average-performing students were somewhat evenly divided in their preference for living at home or away during college. Table 3.2 illustrates how the value students attach to geographic proximity shapes their college enrollment choices. Three out of ten students reported that living at home was important, and 77.8 percent of these students enrolled in a college within twenty-five miles of home. Of those seniors who thought it was not important to live at home, 41.5 percent enrolled in colleges over one hundred miles away. The majority of students (70 percent) enrolled in colleges within fifty miles of home. Although many students intend to go away for college, only a fraction of them were able to do so. As a result, the extent of match for average-performing students largely depends on the available postsecondary options nearby, which vary widely by region.[29]

Some may argue that indicators such as institutional level and geographic proximity may be too broad for discerning college match, since the implicit goals of match are to improve students' college choices, thereby increasing their chances of degree completion at a reasonable cost. Institutional level and geography do not really address either. Thus, we next attempt to measure match for average-performing students on the basis of college affordability and the probability of degree completion.

College Match by Affordability

As college tuition continues to climb, affordability is ever more important in determining where students enroll. For many families, tuition costs and the availability of financial aid are the leading considerations in college enrollment.[30] With their postsecondary options limited by their academic performance, average-performing students may consider an affordable college a "good" match, especially since they are less likely to qualify for merit-based aid and are more likely to lack financial resources than high-performing students (as seen in table 3.1). Average-performing students indicated that college costs and availability of aid were "very important" relative to their higher-performing peers.

Affordability, however, is not a straightforward concept to measure, as it is highly variable not only across, but also within, institutions and comprises cost of attendance as well as the availability of grants. For example, some colleges may have a combination of lower costs and/or more aid that makes them more affordable than other colleges. At the same time, the amount of aid student receives is directly related to family income, so students attending the same college pay different amounts. Therefore it is more advantageous to examine affordability at the individual rather than institutional level (that is, we ask "Was the student's choice affordable?" rather than "Did the student choose an affordable college?"). In addition to college costs and aid, the amounts students need to borrow are also considered an

TABLE 3.2 Average-performing student-college match by college type, affordability, and graduation rate[a]

Twelfth-grade plans by college type[b]	N	No college	Four-year college	Enrollment by level Two-year college	Less-than-two-year college	Total
Missing	5,330	25.7%	12.3%	62.0%	0.0%	100.0%
Four-year college or university	816,403	5.4%	73.7%	20.5%	0.5%	100.0%
Two-year community college	228,634	16.2%	8.1%	73.1%	2.5%	100.0%
Vocational, technical, or trade school	55,510	25.7%	16.1%	47.1%	11.2%	100.0%

Importance of costs and aid in twelfth grade[c]	N	No loans	1–25% of income	Affordability[d] 25–50% of income	Over 50% of income	Total
Missing	5,810	92.9%	6.9%	0.0%	0.3%	100.0%
Not important	88,660	80.4%	18.5%	0.2%	0.9%	100.0%
Somewhat important	368,010	64.7%	31.5%	2.8%	1.0%	100.0%
Very important	596,060	56.3%	37.2%	4.1%	2.4%	100.0%

How far students think they will go[e]	N	0–25% graduation rate	26–50% graduation rate	51–75% graduation rate	76–100% graduation rate	Total
				Graduation rate[f]		
Missing	2,720	16.2%	38.5%	42.7%	2.6%	100.0%
Don't know	34,540	39.3%	39.5%	15.7%	5.5%	100.0%
High school or less	3,470	40.7%	46.5%	4.7%	8.2%	100.0%
Attend or complete two-year degree	77,960	40.9%	34.5%	20.3%	4.3%	100.0%
Some four-year college, no degree	8,340	45.6%	38.4%	16.0%	0.0%	100.0%
Bachelor's or beyond	837,270	20.7%	41.3%	32.7%	5.4%	100.0%

Importance of living at home	N	0–10 miles	11–25 miles	26–50 miles	51–100 miles	100+ miles
				Proximity		
Not important	287,490	14.1%	13.8%	11.2%	19.4%	41.5%
Somewhat important	396,420	40.5%	26.8%	11.4%	7.7%	13.6%
Very important	293,900	49.3%	28.5%	12.2%	4.1%	5.9%

Source: Education Longitudinal Survey (ELS: 2002); IPEDS 2004 Survey Files.

Note: (a) The sample represents average-performing students who participated in the first three waves of data collection, expressed an interest in postsecondary education, enrolled in college, and were not in alternative or special education. Figures were weighted using the F2F1WT and rounded to the nearest 10; (b) Response to the question (F1S49): "Which of the following will you most likely attend?"; (c) Rounded average of two ordinal questions (F1S52B, F1S52A): "Availability of aid important to participant" and "Postsecondary school's low expenses important to respondent" where 1 = Not important, 2 = Somewhat important, 3 = Very important; (d) Affordability is the difference between the amount of loans borrowed (F2B26R) and the expected family contribution (PLEFC) as a percent of the expected family contribution per year. The affordability categories are divided by quartiles; (e) Response to the question (F1S52k): "As things stand now, how far in school do you think you will get?"; (f) Graduation rate is 150% of time for first-time full-time undergraduates.

indicator of affordability, as loans are typically used in the absence of financial aid, income, or assets.

In this analysis, we contrasted students' responses to the importance of college affordability with the extent to which their college choices were affordable. First, we averaged and rounded the level of agreement to two items in the student survey, (1) "Availability of aid important to participant" and (2) "Postsecondary school's low expenses important to respondent." We then calculated affordability as the amount of loans borrowed as a percentage of annual family income (to account for the variation across students' ability to pay). Because the data on cumulative amount borrowed was collected by NCES two years after graduation, we divided the amount borrowed by two to get an annual amount. This is not a perfect measure, as some students might have delayed enrollment or enrolled part-time. However, it is an annual measure that is relative to what students can afford (that is, annual family income).

NCES collected information on family income as a categorical variable, with each category corresponding to a range of incomes. We therefore assigned family income as the midpoint of the ranges indicated by NCES. We then organized students by the amount they borrowed as a percentage of family income. This is a conservative estimate of affordability, since it does not cover families' out-of-pocket expenses, which were not included in the ELS:2002 data set. Further, not all students enrolled in college had information about the amount they borrowed, which resulted in a reduced sample size ($N = 963,694$).

We found that unlike the rates of match found between degree aspiration and institutional level, similar patterns did not emerge for affordability (see table 3.2). First, a majority of average-performing students indicated that low costs and availability of aid were "very important" considerations when selecting a college. The majority of those students (93.5 percent) were able to enroll in colleges where they were not required to borrow or did not borrow more than 25 percent of their family income, but they fared worse than those who indicated that college affordability was "not important," where virtually all students did not borrow more than 25 percent of their family income.

If we are to measure match for average-performing students as the extent to which students who care about affordability are enrolling in affordable options, then there are high rates of mismatch. There are two potential reasons for these findings. First, students' enrollment patterns may be constrained at the application step, which is a large source of undermatch.[31]

For example, this scenario would occur if a student's college choice set only included colleges that offered unfavorable aid packages. Moreover, the biggest challenge to considering affordability in a choice set is that students do not know whether a college is affordable a priori, but rather after they are admitted.[32]

Second, there simply may be a dearth of affordable options available to average performers. On closer inspection, the rates of matching at "affordable options" are almost entirely driven by students enrolling in two-year colleges, as 74 percent of average-performing students who enrolled in two-year colleges did not take out loans. We also know that few four-year colleges have the financial capabilities to offer generous aid packages, leading many colleges to "gap" students—or not fully cover a student's demonstrated need.[33] Therefore, while students may intend to apply or enroll in an affordable college, those who would like to attend four-year colleges may simply be unable to do so.

College Match by Likelihood of Completion

The overwhelming majority of students who enroll in college do so expecting to receive a degree.[34] As authors of previous college match research note, the main benefit of enrolling in a more selective college is the greater likelihood of completion, relative to completion rates at a less selective college.[35] Implicitly, this suggests that a college's inputs (that is, average high school GPA, average entrance exams, percent of students admitted) are a proxy for its outcomes (such as graduation rates and employment). Because it is less obvious where average-performing students should enroll, given the odds of getting into the most selective institutions in the country, in this section we matched average-performing students directly to institutional outcomes—specifically, graduation rates.[36]

To examine whether students choose to enroll at institutions with high graduation rates, we compared their expectations of earning a degree as high school seniors with the institutional graduation rate of their chosen college. Based on their responses to the question, "As things stand now, how far in school do you think you will get?" we categorized students into "high school or less," "attend or complete two-year degree," "some four-year college, no degree," and "bachelor's or beyond." Because ELS posed the the choice for students who wanted a two-year degree as "attend or complete two-year college," there was no way to differentiate between attending two-year college and obtaining an associate's degree. We were therefore unable to analyze students who chose this answer and instead focused our discussion on students who wanted a bachelor's degree.

We then pulled graduation rate data from the IPEDS 2004 Graduation Rate Survey File. Graduation rates are calculated as the share of first-time, full-time students who complete in three years for two-year colleges and six years for four-year colleges. A total of 974,300 average-performing students were found to have enrolled in a college that reported graduation rates. Of course, there are well-known drawbacks to including data on three- and six-year college graduation rates, and many institutions—particularly two-year colleges—object to using graduation rates as a measure of quality.[37] Further, institutional graduation rates are only a proxy for an individual's likelihood of completion. Research also tells us that students from varying demographic and academic backgrounds have different chances of completion, even within the same institution.[38] Notwithstanding these limitations, institutional graduation rates are currently the best measure that is consistently and widely available.

We found a large gap between students' degree aspirations and the graduation rates at the institutions they chose. An overwhelming majority of average-performing students who enrolled in college wanted to obtain a four-year degree (86 percent), with an additional share not captured by the ELS:2002 survey aspiring to two-year degrees. However, fewer than two in every five average performers who wanted a four-year degree enrolled in a college where their likelihood of graduating was greater than 50 percent (38.1 percent).

A "Good" Match

Individually, the institutional characteristics examined above may not constitute a "good" match on their own; for instance, a college may have a high graduation rate but also be extremely expensive. So what share of average-performing students match on a combination of these measures? We aggregated whether students matched on degree-level (four-year, two-year, or vocational), affordability (borrowed less than 25 percent of their family income), and degree attainment (enrolled in college with at least a 50 percent graduation rate). We excluded proximity because it is a preference and not a necessary condition for completing college. We then aggregated the number of matches for every student, which ranged from zero (no matches) to three (matched on all characteristics: degree level, affordability, and degree attainment rates).

We found that 22 percent of average-performing students matched on only one of these characteristics, 51 percent matched on two of these characteristics, and one out of every four was able to enroll in a college that matched on all three. An additional 2 percent of students did not match on any characteristics. In comparison, 65 percent of high-performing students enrolled in an institution that matched all three dimensions.

Parity in College Matching

Given the complexities of the college choice process and the myriad reasons that average students might reasonably choose a less selective college, researchers concede that students will never match 100 percent. Yet the estimation of match is quite useful as a comparative tool (for the extent to which students of different backgrounds match).[39] Research has revealed that black, Latino, and low-income students are more likely to undermatch than their peers, and thus much of the discussion around match has been around equity. In this section, we continue our examination of match by considering average-performing underrepresented racial/ethnic groups and students of first-generation status.

We included additional dimensions of race/ethnicity and parental education in our analyses. In light of sample sizes and our ability to produce reliable estimates, we limited our racial/ethnic groups to non-underrepresented minority (white and Asian) and underrepresented minority (black, Latino, and "other" racial/ethnic groups). We also dichotomized first-generation status into those whose parents have earned college degrees (bachelor's or beyond) and those whose parents have not. This yielded a somewhat even split of the average-performing sample (see table 3.3). We did not examine students by income because we did not find a meaningful way to separate income distribution, and further categorization of students would make estimates unstable.

In some, but not all cases, we found stark contrasts in the rates at which students matched their preferences as seniors and in their actual college enrollments across groups. With regard to degree aspirations, table 3.3 shows that average-performing students of underrepresented racial/ethnic backgrounds had somewhat similar degree goals as their non-underrepresented counterparts (for example, 71.1 percent and 75.0 percent, respectively, planned on enrolling in a four-year institution), yet there were much larger differences when considering parental education. Not only are there differences in college plans, but table 3.4 shows underrepresented minority

TABLE 3.3   Comparison of college plans and preferences by racial/ethnic minority and first-generation status[a]

	URM[b]	Non-URM[c]	First-generation	Non-first-generation
Twelfth-grade plans by college type[d]				
Total	328,660	777,220	621,510	484,370
Missing	0.50%	0.5%	0.60%	0.30%
Four-year college or university	71.1%	75.0%	66.9%	82.8%
Two-year community college	22.5%	19.9%	25.3%	14.7%
Vocational, technical, or trade school	5.9%	4.6%	7.2%	2.3%
Importance of living away from home[e]				
Total	286,340	716,130	545,330	457,140
Not important	27.7%	30.0%	35.0%	22.6%
Somewhat important	41.1%	40.4%	39.7%	41.7%
Very important	31.2%	29.5%	25.3%	35.7%
Importance of costs and aid in twelfth grade[f]				
Total	289,100	721,930	551,070	459,960
Missing	0.70%	0.4%	0.50%	0.40%
Not important	4.0%	10.3%	5.6%	11.9%
Somewhat important	26.8%	38.7%	30.5%	41.0%
Very important	68.5%	50.7%	63.4%	46.7%
How far students think they will go[g]				
Total	289,100	721,930	551,070	459,960
Missing	0.20%	0.30%	0.30%	0.30%
Don't know	4.4%	3.1%	4.2%	2.6%
HS or less	0.40%	0.30%	0.40%	0.30%
Attend or complete two-year degree	8.4%	8.6%	11.8%	4.7%
Some four-year college, no degree	3.0%	1.6%	2.5%	1.4%
Bachelor's or beyond	83.6%	86.1%	80.9%	90.8%

Source: Education Longitudinal Survey (ELS:2002); IPEDS 2004 Survey Files.

Note: (a) The sample represents average-performing students who have participated in the first three waves of data collection, expressed an interest in postsecondary education, enrolled in college, and were not in alternative or special education. Figures were weighted using the F2F1WT and rounded to the nearest 10; (b) Underrepresented minority students (URM) selected the black, Latino, or "other" race/ethnicity category; (c) Non-URM students selected the white or Asian race/ethnicity category; (d) Response to the question (F1S49): "Which of the following will you most likely attend?"; (e) Rounded average of two ordinal questions (F1S52B, F1S52A): "Availability of aid important to participant" and "Postsecondary school's low expenses important to respondent" where 1 = Not important, 2 = Somewhat important, 3=Very important; affordability is the difference between the amount of loans borrowed (F2B26R) and the expected family contribution (PLEFC) as a percent of the expected family contribution per year. The affordability categories are divided by quartiles; (f) Unlike table 3.2, response to the question (F1S52G): Away from home while attending postsecondary important to respondent; (g) Response to the question (F1S52K): "As things stand now, how far in school do you think you will get?"; Graduation rate is 150 percent of time for first-time full-time undergraduates.

and first-generation students who were four-year degree aspirants were less likely to enroll in four-year colleges than their non-minority and non-first-generation peers (for example, 65.8 percent of first-generation versus 81.8 percent of non-first-generation students). Average-performing first-generation students were much more likely than their counterparts with college-educated parents to enroll in a two-year college despite planning to enroll in a four-year college (25.7 percent versus 15.0 percent). This finding may be due to low-income students' enrolling at a community college with the intent to transfer, although these intentions were not captured in ELS:2002. Further, one out of every five underrepresented minority students who wanted a two-year degree had yet to enroll in any college two years after graduating high school, compared with one of every seven white or Asian students.

There were also differences between groups and their outcomes by institutional proximity. Of students who thought it was very important to live away from home, 20.6 percent of underrepresented minority students enrolled in a college that was within ten miles of home, relative to 14.7 percent of their non-underrepresented counterparts. As seen in table 3.3, first-generation

TABLE 3.4　Comparison of match by degree aspirations, institutional proximity, affordability, and degree completion for select student characteristics[a]

Preference	Actual	URM[b]	Non-URM[c]	First-generation	Non-first-generation
Degree aspirations[d]					
Four-year college	Four-year college	70.4%	75.0%	65.8%	81.8%
Four-year college	Two-year college	20.2%	20.6%	25.7%	15.0%
Two-year college	Two- or four-year college	75.2%	84.2%	80.9%	82.0%
Two-year college	No college	20.3%	14.3%	16.7%	15.3%

(continues)

TABLE 3.4   *(Cont.)*

Preference	Actual	URM[b]	Non-URM[c]	First-generation	Non-first-generation
Institutional proximity[e]					
Living away from home	Within 10 miles	20.6%	14.7%	19.3%	14.0%
Living away from home	Over 100 miles	36.7%	43.6%	31.1%	50.4%
Affordability[fg]					
Affordable college important	No loans	53.7%	47.6%	50.7%	46.9%
Affordable college not important	Loans over 50% of income	2.9%	2.0%	3.2%	1.5%
Degree Attainment[hi]					
Bachelor's or beyond	College with > 75% grad rate	5.1%	5.3%	3.0%	7.6%
Bachelor's or beyond	College with < 25% grad rate	21.7%	19.4%	25.1%	14.6%
Don't know	College with < 25% grad rate	35.9%	40.3%	41.4%	33.7%
Number of matched characteristics					
0		1.5%	2.4%	2.8%	1.3%
1		25.5%	21.3%	25.7%	18.6%
2		54.5%	48.9%	52.5%	48.2%
3		18.4%	27.4%	19.0%	31.9%

Source: ELS:2002; IPEDS 2004 Survey Files.

Note: (a) The sample represents average-performing students who have participated in the first three waves of data collection, expressed an interest in postsecondary education, enrolled in college, and were not in alternative or special education. Figures were weighted using the F2F1WT and rounded to the nearest 10; (b) Underrepresented minority students (URM) selected the black, Latino, or "other" race/ethnicity category; (c) Non-URM students selected the white or Asian race/ethnicity category; (d) Response to the question (F1S49): "Which of the following will you most likely attend?"; (e) Unlike table 3.2, response to the question (F1S52G): "Away from home while attending postsecondary school important to respondent"; (f) Rounded average of two ordinal questions (F1S52B, F1S52A): "Availability of aid important to participant" and "Postsecondary school's low expenses important to respondent" where 1=Not important, 2=Somewhat important, 3=Very important; (g) Affordability is the difference between the amount of loans borrowed (F2B26R) and the expected family contribution (PLEFC) as a percentage of the expected family contribution per year. The affordability categories are divided by quartiles; (h) Response to the question (F1S52K): "As things stand now, how far in school do you think you will get?"; (i) Graduation rate is 150% of time for first-time full-time undergraduates.

students were less likely to report that living away from home was "very important" than non-first-generation students (25.3 percent versus 35.7 percent). The differences by first-generation status for those who wanted to go away for college are also drastic. Table 3.4 reveals that half of students who had college-educated parents and had a desire to go away for college enrolled in colleges over one hundred miles away, whereas only 31.1 percent of first-generation students were able to do the same. This difference may be due to first-generation students' greater need to work while in college, desire or need to save money by living at home, or parents who prefer their children stay close to home.[40]

The differences in matching on degree and proximity preferences mirror the discrepancies in matching by affordability and degree completion. If we consider a "good" match to be a college that is affordable or that has high graduation rates, the majority of students think affordability is somewhat or very important, irrespective of background, and plan on achieving a bachelor's degree (see table 3.3). Average-performing black and Latino students matched on affordability at slightly higher rates than their white and Asian peers (53.7 percent versus 47.6 percent, respectively, did not need to borrow), yet were on par on institutional graduation rates (5.1 percent versus 5.3 percent, respectively, aspired to a bachelor's and enrolled in a college with graduation rates above 75 percent) (see table 3.4). Those first-generation students aspiring to a bachelor's degree lagged behind their peers in enrolling in colleges with high graduation rates (above 75 percent) and were more likely than their non-first-generation counterparts to enroll in colleges with extremely low graduation rates (below 25 percent). Finally, black and Latino students were less likely than white or Asian students to enroll in colleges that were affordable, had graduation rates above chance (i.e., 50 percent), and matched their degree aspirations (18.4 percent versus 27.4 percent). We saw similar patterns in first-generation students (19.0 percent of first-generation versus 31.9 percent of non-first generation students matched on all three characteristics).

DISCUSSION

The purpose of this chapter is to advance our understanding of college match for students who have average academic performance and to expand the definition of match. Given the heterogeneity of institutional performance for colleges that are less selective, identifying a "good" match for average-performing students is challenging if we employ the selectivity paradigm previously used to study match. The implied benefit for a high-performing student attending a selective college—a match—is an increased likelihood of completion and generous financial aid that will make college affordable relative to the student's individual financial circumstances. By applying this same rationale to the college choice decisions of average-performing students, we attain a better understanding of college match for a large share of the college-going population. Furthermore, this rationale moves us away from a hierarchical structure that is based on student inputs and implies that "good" students should go to "good" colleges and "average" students should go to "average" colleges, as this approach does not assume that two-year institutions are inferior to four-year colleges.

Degree aspirations are a major driver in college match that has thus far gone largely unexplored in the research. The above analyses illustrate that average-performing students align their degree goals well with the level of institution in which they enroll and that they care about program offerings as much as high-performing students. Organizing institutions into a hierarchy of selectivity does not account for these considerations, as students' ideal choices based on program may be at a two-year or less selective college. Therefore, imposing a label of mismatch or undermatch on such a decision may unfairly disregard students' intentions. One potential critique of our approach is that it maps students who are traditionally underrepresented onto existing stratified enrollment patterns. For example, if students from low-income backgrounds are implicitly (or explicitly) encouraged to enroll in trade schools or two-year colleges, then matching on students' intentions and their enrollment would support stratification.[41] On the other hand, understanding the high degree to which students align their degree goals and college choices may also provide the opportunity for underscoring the practice of accurate and abundantly accessible college guidance and the importance of providing affordable postsecondary opportunities with high likelihood of completion at all selectivity levels.

Average-performing students are unlikely to enroll in a college that has their desired degree level, manageable debt amounts, and high graduation rates. Consistent with previous research, we found traditionally underrepresented students are even less likely to match on all three characteristics. Some of this mismatch is a function of student demand, as college choice is a complex process, and students may be applying to and enrolling in colleges that meet none of their stated preferences. As noted in previous chapters, research tells us that part of the issue is the abundance, timeliness, and accuracy of information that students possess about their college options. One common, and yet to be addressed, prescription is to improve college guidance at high schools by accounting for institutional performance. Another potential solution has already been tested and taken to scale for high-achieving students—an informational mailer. Students could receive information about area colleges with high graduation rates. Such information could include the average amounts of debt of their graduates, tailored to students' income and zip codes.

At the same time, however, the lack of available seats at colleges that might be considered "good" helps explain persistent levels of mismatch for average-performing students. Average-performing students were more likely to want to stay close to home than their higher-performing peers. Although a good share of average-performing students who cared most about enrolling at a college away from home were able to do so, the majority of students were still constrained to enroll at nearby institutions. Given this fact, policy makers need to be made aware of the inequitable distribution of colleges by completion rate and affordability. Improving match can be achieved only if colleges that serve large shares of average-ability students well are encouraged to increase capacity, while at the same time improvements are made to the colleges that have low or middling completion rates. As more students seek entry into and credentials from higher education institutions, the ability to attend an affordable college with a decent likelihood of completion should not be a luxury reserved only for the highest academic performers.

4

Matching Talents to Careers

From Self-Directed to Guided Pathways

Thomas R. Bailey, Davis Jenkins, Clive R. Belfield, and
Elizabeth Kopko

College plays an important role in connecting students with jobs and careers. Individuals with college degrees are on average able to secure higher-paying, higher-status jobs than those with no college credential or even some college experience. Students bring to college innate aptitudes, tastes, and temperaments that may make them better suited to certain careers than to others. Yet the experience of college is intended to help them not only build on their talents in ways that will enable them to advance in the labor market, but also explore options and develop interests that will help them determine career paths.

This chapter examines the matching process between students and college programs or majors. The discussion of matching has so far focused primarily on the matching between individuals and institutions, but students' experiences in college and their college outcomes can vary profoundly depending on their chosen program. Students' choice of major is fundamentally related to how much they will earn and what types of jobs they will secure.[1] Choosing the right major—and completing the requirements for that major—is therefore a critical element of a good match.

In this chapter, we focus primarily on community colleges. Even if efforts are made to ameliorate the problem of undermatching discussed in other chapters in this volume, the role of community colleges and broad-access four-year institutions in helping students connect to employment is still important. One reason is that there are simply not enough slots in selective institutions to meet the demand for higher education in the United

States—even among students who would be qualified for admission to such institutions. Community colleges enroll nearly 45 percent of undergraduates; broad-access four-year institutions enroll more than 15 percent. Together, these institutions enroll the majority of undergraduates who come from low-income families or are students of color. And while some of these students are well qualified for college, large shares of new students in both types of institutions—and the majority of students in community colleges—arrive poorly prepared for college and would be unlikely to gain direct admission into more selective institutions. Regardless of their academic readiness, lower-income students in particular are constrained in their choice of college. Specifically, they are much more likely than higher-income students to choose a college based on price and proximity to their homes.[2] So for millions of students, broad-access institutions are their only option for college.

The concept of "match" or the matching model as it has been used in the college undermatching discussion has focused on the correspondence (or lack thereof) between fixed student characteristics (such as SAT scores) and fixed college characteristics (admissions selectivity). The emerging literature on undermatching emphasizes the importance of providing information to students in order to bring their characteristics and colleges' characteristics into alignment. The corresponding perspective for the student/career/major match would be to provide information on careers and programs—program requirements, completion rates, job placement outcomes, earnings, and so forth—so that students can find programs that correspond to their interests, goals, and aptitudes.

But this informational approach is too limited to be the basis of an effective system to help students choose a suitable academic program and career. Research on the major-selection process suggests that while information is important, students also need opportunities to learn about themselves and their options, and college programs and support services need to be organized to promote such learning. This will require the rethinking and redesign of the majors themselves. Thus, to improve students' major selections, college educators and policy makers need to explore how to make the major-selection process a rich learning experience for students and—in the case of community colleges and other broad-access institutions—how to do so with limited available resources.

Currently, the major- and career-selection process at most community colleges—and likely many broad-access four-year institutions—is haphazard, leaving students to find their way mostly on their own. Community college students typically arrive without clear goals for majors and careers and with little awareness of their options. Colleges offer an often bewildering array of programs, but provide limited advising and supports to help students choose one. This is particularly problematic for students in community colleges, who, compared with students in selective colleges, tend to have less support for making college and career decisions from their families and other networks outside of school. Further, colleges often do not keep close track of students' major decisions. As Bailey, Leinbach, and Jenkins have observed, it is often difficult to determine community college students' majors, in some cases because students themselves are unsure.[3] If students are unclear about their major—or decide on one relatively late—they may take courses that do not count toward their degree. Thus, the problem is not merely one of finding programs that are appropriate for students, but of helping them find these programs early in their college experience, before they waste time and resources and become discouraged.

Within this context, the major-selection process is far from a straightforward calculation of costs and benefits. It is a chaotic, confusing, and often delayed process that can create barriers to successful college completion.[4] Given the importance of major selection for students' career outcomes, and the limited resources community college students generally have for making such decisions, the lack of a well-supported process for major selection in community colleges may impede students' long-term success and upward mobility.

This chapter is an effort to broaden the discussion of match to include major selection in community colleges and broad-access four-year institutions. In the process, we seek to move from a static model of matching students with fixed characteristics to the "right" college or major to one that sees matching as a dynamic learning process and recognizes that the organization and practices of colleges and major programs may have to change. First, we discuss the importance of major selection to student outcomes, particularly employment. Then, we examine the undermatching controversy and highlight how that discussion relates to our argument about major choice. Next, we review research on the determinants of major selection and discuss the process of major selection, reporting on how it takes place in community colleges and broad-access four-year institutions. We describe what some colleges are doing to help students choose majors, and then conclude by relating our findings on matching students to majors to the broader discussion of college match.

THE IMPORTANCE OF MAJOR SELECTION

Across higher education, there are big differences in earnings by college major.[5] At the baccalaureate level, majors with significant math content (such as engineering or accounting) carry substantial earnings advantages. Annual salaries of high-pay majors are 13 percent higher than those of low-pay majors.[6] Over a working lifetime, the earnings of science, technology, engineering, and mathematics (STEM) graduates can exceed those of arts and humanities graduates by $800,000.[7] However, many liberal arts degree holders attend graduate school in professional subjects (such as law or medicine). For this subgroup, it is difficult to attribute earnings gains to their undergraduate college majors, although in many cases their majors give them better access to graduate degrees associated with higher earnings.

Similarly, substantial earnings gaps by major are evident among graduates of community colleges.[8] For associate degree holders, the labor market returns are higher in career/technical subjects than in arts and humanities. At the same time, community college arts and humanities degrees are designed for students intending to transfer; the earnings of students with such degrees who do not transfer may thus not convey the full value of the degree. Returns are especially high for graduates in nursing programs and health fields.[9] For diploma and certificate holders, the pattern across subjects is mixed. In general, returns to these programs tend to be smaller and may not be as long-lasting as higher-level degrees.[10]

The potential earnings associated with a major are also determined by the chances that the student will get a job that requires the skills taught in that major. Thus, the characteristics of college majors should not be considered in isolation from the occupational choices graduates make.[11] When making major choices, students should be aware that earnings depend on what was studied, together with the types of jobs the graduates wound up getting. Gelblum found large earnings premiums for working in an occupation that corresponds to the college major.[12] Robst estimated an earnings penalty of 10–12 percent if a graduate has a job that is "somewhat" or "not" related to his or her field of study.[13]

UNDERMATCHING AND THE CHARACTERISTICS OF STUDENTS AND COLLEGES

The limitations of narrowly defining college match in terms of correspondence between student quality measured by SAT scores and college quality measured in terms of selectivity are discussed in previous chapters. To summarize, if the notion of "college quality" assumes that student outcomes are in effect caused by the college, and if college quality is closely related to a college's average SAT score, then in a perfectly matched system, college would be an institution that amplifies initial differences in academic achievement. Students who attended high-SAT colleges would by definition have high scores themselves, and they would get access to a higher quality, or at least better resourced, education than their lower-scoring peers. Better matching through enhanced information would help some low-income students to consider more selective colleges. But the fact that most low-income students do not have access to K–12 education that prepares them for more selective colleges is a much larger problem than the fact that some low-income students are prepared for such colleges but do not attend them.

This analysis of the undermatching discussion also reveals the limitations of focusing primarily on information as a means to match students and colleges based on characteristics that are assumed to be fixed. Matching does not help most low-income students because they are not "high performing." To reduce achievement gaps and improve opportunities for low-income students, educators must change the "characteristics" of students by improving their preparation for college. They must also improve the performance of the institutions, such as community colleges, where most of those students enroll, so that not only high-performing students will have access to high-quality institutions. Focusing primarily on providing information to improve the academic match between students and colleges may well distract attention from the need for these broader changes.

Similarly, facilitating a better match between students and programs or majors will require broader changes in the programs themselves. To optimize major selection, and thereby improve student outcomes, we must understand the process through which students choose majors so that we can provide students with the information, tools, and experiences necessary to navigate that process. In the following sections, we review what existing literature has uncovered about major selection.

WHAT DO WE KNOW ABOUT THE DETERMINANTS OF MAJOR SELECTION?

Despite the importance of choosing a major, there has been little research detailing how students make this choice. The research is almost entirely descriptive, based on student choices of major and their association with fixed characteristics rather than on the underlying dynamic process that might make it possible to predict choice. Most of this research has focused on four-year institutions—and often selective universities—rather than on community colleges or broad-access four-year institutions.

Student Characteristics

Much of the literature examines simple relationships between demographic factors and personal characteristics and major choice. For example, many studies have found differences between women and men in preferences toward occupational roles and major field of study.[14]

While methodologically challenging to conduct, research has overwhelmingly found that ability is important in explaining sorting across majors. Findings suggest that sorting across academic disciplines reflects general ability, and that the probability that a student will choose a specific major increases with major-specific ability as revealed by the student's previous achievements in that subject area.[15] For example, students with higher levels of mathematical achievement (as measured using high school math grades or math SAT scores) are more likely to choose scientific and technical majors.[16]

Particularly relevant to concerns about equity, some research has shown that family background has a strong influence on a student's major choice, though only a few studies have examined this question. Maple and Stage found that parents with higher occupational prestige can influence their children to choose more quantitative majors.[17] Leppel, Williams, and Waldauer found that men from high-socioeconomic-status families were more likely to major in business (although women from the same families were less likely to do so).[18] Further, while the status of their father's occupation had a larger impact on female students' choice of college major than did their mother's, the opposite held true for male students. In an analysis of program enrollment patterns of two-year college students in Washington State, Jenkins and Weiss found that low-socioeconomic-status community college students were overrepresented in fields such as education and child care, which have low completion rates and relatively low labor market returns.[19] However, they were also well represented compared with high-socioeconomic-status students in nursing and allied health fields, which tend to have high completion rates and higher labor market returns for graduates.

Other studies have examined the connection between major selection and personal preferences or tastes. Using an experimental design and students from New York University, Wiswall and Zafar found that while both perceived ability and expected earnings were significant determinants of college-major choice, the most dominant factor was what they defined as "tastes."[20] The importance of tastes in academic sorting across disciplines suggests that students are concerned with finding the right match, or an environment in which they expect to find enjoyment or fulfillment.[21]

Characteristics of Majors

The characteristics of majors also ought to influence student choices. Much of the analysis of major choice has focused on the economic returns to particular majors, which we reviewed earlier, and knowledge about potential earnings has been shown to shape student choices. Several studies have examined the impact of expected returns—both pecuniary and nonpecuniary—on major choice. For example, using data from second-year students at Northwestern University, Zafar found that expectations of future earnings accounted for up to 55 percent of the choice of major, although job satisfaction was also an important consideration.[22]

The economic benefit of a given major also reflects the costs that the student must incur to complete that major. Stater used student-level data from three large public universities to determine the effects of tuition and financial aid on the choice of first-year college major. He found that a higher net cost of college participation was associated with increased probabilities of choosing majors leading to higher expected wages (such as professional majors) and decreased probabilities of choosing majors with lower expected wages (such as humanities majors) and majors with more technical complexity (such as science majors).[23] Stange found that differential tuition for different majors altered the distribution of students across majors, and that already marginalized students in certain fields, such as women in engineering, were particularly sensitive to new pricing policies.[24]

Dynamics of the Major-Selection Process

Identifying the factors associated with major selection does not necessarily tell us that a student's choice of major was optimal in that it was a good fit for his or her preferences and abilities—nor does it reveal much about the matching process itself. But we can infer certain things about that process by observing student behavior. An emerging literature supports the idea that major selection is the result of a dynamic learning process. For example, Stinebrickner and Stinebrickner found that while, on average, students come to college equally willing to major in math or science as in any other field, experienced math and science self-efficacy affects major preferences as students see how well they do in those subjects. Students with lower-than-expected grades move away from math and science as their final major selection.[25] Arcidiacono found that college grades provide students with information that can affect final major choice: those who perform worse than expected are more likely to drop out or switch majors, while those who perform better are more likely to persist with their initial major choice.[26] Some studies have found that students who delay their choice of major are more likely to persist and take less time to graduate, presumably because they are better able to make a decision after having more time to explore and learn about the available alternatives.[27]

What is noteworthy about these examples is that they rely primarily on students' making choices based on experience, but without much guidance and with ad hoc information. The broader undermatching discussion has relied on a rather simple way to measure the student–college match: using the correspondence between SAT score (and other student characteristics) and the academic admissions standards of the college. We do not have a similar measure of the student–major match, but we can observe colleges' policies and practices and the services and information they make available to students who are choosing a major. The next section examines the sorts of major decision-making supports typically provided to students in community colleges.

MAJOR SELECTION IN COMMUNITY COLLEGES AND OTHER BROAD-ACCESS INSTITUTIONS

Most students, especially those recently out of high school, enroll in community colleges and other broad-access institutions without clear goals for college and careers.[28] Low-income students in particular are unlikely to have a clear idea of what opportunities are available to them.[29] This lack of clear goals could reflect a lack of self-awareness or a poor understanding of the characteristics of majors and associated careers—or perhaps both.

School websites are the most common source of information community colleges provide to help students choose a major. Students can find a list of programs and program requirements online. In the past, web-based information has not been easy to use. A study of web-based information use by students at a college in Michigan found that although information about program requirements was available, often students were not able to find

it or understand it, and there was no consistency in the format across programs, making comparison difficult. Information on transfer requirements
for different four-year institutions was particularly difficult to understand.[30]

This type of information can be more effective when combined with sys-
tematic advising; indeed, the advising system is perhaps the most important
service provided to students to help them choose programs and majors.[31]
But community colleges in particular have few resources to devote to advising.[32] Their counseling and advising centers often have few counselors compared with the number of students, with ratios as high as fifteen hundred
students for every counselor.[33]

The advising process should provide an opportunity for staff to help students understand their strengths and weaknesses, develop academic and
associated career goals, and learn about what majors might correspond to
those characteristics. But too few resources are devoted to advising and career
counseling in particular to allow for this type of developmental learning process. A 2009 survey of entering community college students found that while
most met with an adviser to make their first-term schedules, almost a third
said they were not helped to set goals or create a plan for achieving them.[34]
Rather than helping students form goals, advising is focused on providing
students with information—and that information is often fragmented and
not presented in a way that helps students with decisions.[35] Students report
lacking clear guidance on where to go with their questions.[36]

Most advising in community colleges focuses narrowly on academic
planning. Career counseling is provided separately, usually on a sporadic
and voluntary basis. Shaffer and Zalewski note that academic advising in
the absence of career advising "builds a bridge to nowhere."[37] Students often
do not understand how to relate their academic goals to the realities of the
labor market.[38] Academic advisers may refer students who are undecided
about their field of study to the career office, but there is often no follow-up
to see if students took advantage of career services.[39]

Studies of career and self-assessment inventories indicate that these tools
can help put students on a path toward identifying appropriate majors and
careers for their interests and strengths.[40] But their use is generally independent of formal academic planning and course scheduling. Similarly,
descriptive studies have suggested that online tools, such as Valencia College's LifeMap and the Virginia Education Wizard, might be helpful to students in exploring career options.[41] Yet these e-advising tools and career
inventories are less effective if used outside of formal advising structures,

since students do not necessarily know how to use the knowledge gained from these sources to inform their academic plans.[42]

Many community colleges offer "college success" courses for new students, another opportunity for students to explore their own characteristics, set goals, and learn about their options. Such courses often include an introduction to different degree programs and guidance on how to explore options for college and careers. But most college success courses cover a large number of topics, and some are not covered in much depth. A study of college success courses at three community colleges found that the career exploration component was covered in a perfunctory way.[43] So far, there have been no studies linking participation in such courses to choice of or entry into a program of study.[44]

The quality of career and academic advising varies by field of study. In career fields, there is a tradition of faculty advising students in their programs, educating them about careers in their fields, and even helping them with internship and job placement.[45] And the curriculum paths through community college career/technical programs are often well structured, with relatively clear connections to jobs.[46] In contrast, students who are seeking to transfer or who are undecided about a major are frequently steered toward a "general education" track, which consists of an often bewilderingly long list of liberal arts and sciences courses that they must choose from to fulfill distribution requirements.[47] Community college students often do not understand the value or utility of general education courses, which tend to be broad surveys of a field.[48] Taking these courses may do little to help students clarify their interests and explore options for college and careers.

In short, community colleges have not created advising processes to guide students through goal formation and academic planning in a systemized way, in part because they lack the resources to do so. Rather, they provide information in a superficial manner. Students are expected to learn about their preferences by being "exposed" to the courses and majors that are available at a college. While additional services are available to those who seek them out, many students end up self-advising. Thus the students most often in need of supplemental advising and support—first-generation college students and others who are poorly prepared for college—are often the least likely to be aware that specialized services are available.[49]

Community colleges could certainly do a better job of providing information about career and major options to students, but the problems go deeper than a lack of information. The process of choosing a major should ideally be a dynamic experience of exploration and goal formation. Yet community colleges provide an often overwhelmingly large set of program options, many of which are poorly defined and not clearly aligned with student end goals.[50] As noted above, this problem is particularly acute in associate of arts programs intended to prepare students to transfer to four-year institutions. Students who want to obtain a bachelor's degree but lack a clear program goal are typically placed by default into general education coursework, where they can choose from a large array of courses within broad subject-area distribution requirements. While such courses may be accepted for elective credit by four-year institutions, they may not be accepted toward junior standing in a particular major, as major requirements are often set by individual departments within transfer destination institutions. Thus, after transferring, students may have to take additional courses to satisfy bachelor's program requirements. Recent research indicates that the biggest barrier to community college students earning bachelor's degrees is the inefficiency of the transfer process.[51]

With so many choices and without a clear roadmap or anyone monitoring their progress, it is not surprising that many community college students indicate that they are confused and often frustrated in trying to find their way through college.[52] The lack of clear pathways and guidance can lead students to make costly mistakes.[53] Research on community college student course-taking patterns suggests that many community college students are pursuing suboptimal pathways.[54] When asked, students indicate that being in a program with a well-defined pathway would improve their chances of persisting, completing, and transferring.[55]

In this context, providing more information about overly complex and poorly organized programs might help, but reorganizing programs to make them more coherent and better aligned with employment and further education outcomes may be even more important. In the next section, we examine colleges that have undertaken program redesigns along these lines.

STRENGTHENING SUPPORT FOR MAJOR CHOICE

Enterprising broad-access institutions are experimenting with some promising strategies for improving the major-choice process. Some colleges are making significant improvements in the quality, organization, and usefulness of web-based information. For example, City Colleges of Chicago has developed an easy-to-use website that categorizes all programs into ten academic/

career focus areas. For each of those areas, there is a home page with a brief description of the area, sample career options, the City College program offerings in the area, recommended transfer options, and sample courses. Information is also available on additional career options and degree and program requirements within the focus area, as well as earnings ranges. For more specific jobs within an area, students can find a tailored semester-by-semester course schedule. Other colleges and universities, such as Arizona State University (ASU), have developed similar resources.

These resources represent significant improvements over the types of program information traditionally available online and provide a better foundation for improved matches between students and programs. But they also move beyond information provision aimed at matching fixed student characteristics to fixed program characteristics. In order to develop its program guides, City Colleges of Chicago reorganized its college-level programs by working with employers and four-year institutional partners to review all programs, and where necessary revamped them to improve their alignment with the requirements for employment and further education in the given fields. It created maps for each program with semester-by-semester course sequences, critical program courses, and other milestones. Rather than only providing information to help students navigate programs, City Colleges made its programs easier to understand, thus putting less burden on the advising process.

But providing students with information about careers and programs— even clearer, more useful information—is not sufficient. Another way some colleges are improving the match process is by providing opportunities for integrated career exploration and planning. The traditional matching model assumes students are aware of their underlying characteristics, which they should aim to match. However, most students do not know what those characteristics are, and discovering them requires a learning process. Students need opportunities to actively explore options for majors and careers in advising and in the classroom. They also need to interact with faculty, more advanced students, and others who can inspire and guide them. Given the limited resources most community colleges have for advising and career services, if colleges hope to give all of their degree-seeking students an opportunity to explore college and careers, they are going to have to take a different approach than they have in the past.

A growing number of two- and four-year institutions are redesigning their programs and support services in ways that provide career exploration and planning assistance to all students who need it, not just the few who seek it out. Institutions are adopting a variety of strategies to accomplish this with limited resources. Ideally, they take a multipronged approach that starts as soon as students enter college and continues throughout their enrollment. Notably, four-year institutions may be further along than community colleges in implementing these practices at scale.

Some of the most promising ideas are described below.

Default Program Maps

Traditionally, students face a complex set of choices surrounding programs and a large number of course options within programs. Even when students have an idea about what kind of career they might want to pursue, it is difficult to find a corresponding program when those programs are not well organized. To simplify options and take some of the difficulty out of decision making, some institutions have engaged faculty and advisers in developing academic maps that lay out the courses students should take in a program and the sequence in which they should take them. For example, ASU's "major maps," first designed in 2006, specify the sequence of courses students should take for a particular program, identifying "critical courses" that should be taken early in a student's program, since completing them successfully has been found to predict success in the major.

Maps become the default basis for students' academic plans. Students can modify their plans, but to do so, they need to consult an adviser. Clearly mapping out programs and making them the default reduces the chances that students will choose courses that do not help them toward their goal. As at City Colleges of Chicago, the maps should be part of program descriptions that provide detailed information about the career opportunities and further education students can pursue when they finish the program. Students exploring career and college options can use this information to clearly see the educational path they would have to follow to prepare for a career in a field of interest.

Exploratory Majors

Program redesign can also facilitate career and program exploration. New ASU students who are undecided about their major are now required to enter an "exploratory major" in one of a small set of program areas that together encompass the more than three hundred majors offered by the university. Areas include business, education, engineering, applied computing, mathematics and technology, health and life sciences, humanities, fine arts and design, math, physical sciences and engineering, and social and behavioral sciences. ASU students in exploratory majors are required to enroll in a sequence of major and career exploration workshops, which are designed to lead students through the process of choosing a specific major. According to ASU's vice provost, Maria Hesse, these courses were developed by counseling psychologists to provide "a clear plan for what students need to do each semester to move closer to deciding who they want to be and what they want to become."[56] From a behavioral economics standpoint, exploratory majors use "active choice" to help students navigate to a major, requiring them to choose an initial broad program area and default curricula within each stream. Scaffolding students' decisions in this way makes it easier for students to choose from what may otherwise be an overwhelming number of choices. Hesse said identifying students as "exploratory" also allows advisers to target information and other supports that help them choose a major.

Similarly, students at Queensborough Community College (QCC), which is part of the City University of New York (CUNY), are required to choose a "freshman academy" based on their interests and goals. QCC currently offers five academies clustered around related majors and programs: business, visual and performing arts, STEM, health-related science, and liberal arts. Students must choose an academy before they enroll. This requirement is based on the contention that while many new students may not be able to choose a specific major, most are able to choose a broad field of interest. The academies thus create a bridge between the unfocused course taking that characterizes the current experience of many students and the focused pursuit of a specific major. According to a dean and former faculty member who oversaw the Queensborough academies, "The idea is that students begin to see themselves as students in a particular field, pretty much from the start." The researcher who oversees evaluation of the academies explained, "Students say that being in an academy gives them a sense of identity as a student . . . It causes them to reflect on what they want to do and what it will take to move ahead in the field."[57] Each academy has at least one faculty coordinator who works with other faculty and student affairs staff to improve practice and build a community of students and faculty with similar interests.

Students at QCC can change academies if they change their minds about what they want to study and do; approximately 20 percent of students switch academies in the first year. Likewise, ASU students are permitted to switch from one exploratory major to another. Even at these colleges, the process of deciding on a major continues for many students long after they enroll. However, unlike at other colleges, at ASU and QCC, there is an established process and clear guidelines to help students do so.

Building Career Exploration into the Curriculum

In fall 2012, CUNY opened a new two-year college in Manhattan, Guttman Community College. Guttman embeds career exploration into the required curriculum. The college's design team was challenged to create a model that would substantially improve graduation rates, particularly among populations traditionally underserved in higher education. To this end, the team rethought virtually every aspect of the traditional community college experience, from the structure of coursework, to the delivery of developmental education, to the mechanisms for supporting students academically and in their lives outside of school. All students take a common core curriculum embedded within a learning community; courses include a City Seminar and an Ethnographies of Work course, which allow students to connect to issues that affect their community and explore their own career interests. One purpose of the common first-year curriculum is to guide students through the process of choosing an appropriate program of study. The first-year curriculum includes exposure to workplaces in related fields and visits to bachelor's programs at four-year CUNY colleges.[58]

Embedded Advisers

Some colleges embed advisers into particular program areas. This has a number of advantages. For one, it means that advisers have to become experts on careers and further education only in their specific field. It also enables advisers to work more closely with faculty. At Santa Fe College in Florida— the winner of the 2015 Aspen Prize for Community College Excellence— students are required to choose a program area from the start.[59] Advisers assigned to program areas manage a caseload of students in that program area, working closely with program faculty to help students stay on track. According to Santa Fe program advisers, the ratio of students to advisers is a manageable 400:1. They also say that focusing on one program area enables them to keep up with transfer program and employer requirements in their assigned fields. Moreover, advisers report being able to work more closely with academic departments and faculty in their area than when advising was organized centrally at the college.

Tapping Faculty Expertise and Contacts

Given the high ratio of students to advisers at most community colleges and broad-access four-year colleges and the importance of personal relationships in becoming engaged in college life and finding jobs, involving faculty in college and career advising is critical to the success of any effort. At Miami Dade College, academic advising is a not a formal faculty role as specified in the union contract. However, as part of their allotted time for service, Miami Dade faculty can agree to serve as student mentors. More than 150 faculty members, department chairs, and departmental advisers have volunteered to coach and mentor students from the time they complete 25 percent of their program requirements until they graduate. The college has invested in extensive training for mentors, part of which involves shadowing an academic adviser. Each academic coach and mentor is supported by a peer in student services. The idea is to build a strong network of support and guidance for students to help them choose and stay on a path to completion.

Regional Career Pathways

Ideally, the process of exploring careers and college should begin before students enter college. There have been many efforts to provide such opportunities to high school students, but generally these efforts are not well connected to postsecondary paths that lead to jobs, and they are not easily scaled or sustained. Since 2009, ASU has worked with community colleges throughout Arizona and even other states to create guaranteed transfer agreements based on the ASU major maps. The transfer maps show community college students which courses they need to take in what sequence to be accepted with junior standing in a particular major at ASU. More recently, ASU created a mobile phone app that enables high school students to explore careers and provides information on ASU majors related to those careers. The app connects students (and parents, high school counselors, and other interested parties) with the ASU major maps showing not only the sequence of courses that students should take at ASU, but also what lower-division courses students should take if they plan to first enroll at a community college to pursue degrees in their field of interest. The app also indicates what courses students should take each year of high school to prepare for employment in that field. The overall vision, according to Maria Hesse, is to build pathways to postsecondary education in fields of economic importance for the region, starting in high school or even middle school. This would help educators at the secondary and postsecondary levels and employers monitor how many students come through the pipeline in particular fields and guide students' decisions at key junctures along the way. This approach is different in that it starts with career fields and then builds programmatic pathways downward through the educational pipeline, from universities to community colleges and then to high schools and potentially middle schools.

We want to emphasize that the practices described here are relatively new and have not been evaluated rigorously. Still, in every case mentioned here, the institutions have seen improvements in student outcomes that could be attributed at least in part to reforms in how they help students choose programs of study. ASU officials report that the university's fall-to-spring retention rates for first-time freshmen increased from 77 percent in 2006, when the institution began putting in place academic program maps and exploratory majors, to 84 percent in 2010.[60] Since launching its Reinvention initiative in 2009, City Colleges of Chicago has doubled its three-year graduation rate from 7 percent to 14 percent and has recorded all-time highs in the number of degrees awarded for the past three years.[61] Kennedy-King College, one of seven colleges in the City Colleges of Chicago system, received the Rising Star Award from the 2015 Aspen Institute College Excellence Program for tripling its three-year graduation rate and exceeding by over ten percentage points the average rate at which underrepresented minority community college students either graduate or transfer to a four-year institution.[62] After instituting the freshman academies in 2009, Queensborough Community College's three-year graduation rate increased from 12 percent for the 2006 cohort to 16 percent for the 2009 cohort. When Guttman Community College's inaugural class started in fall 2012, the college set a goal of graduating 35 percent of the class within three years. By summer 2015, 45 percent of the students who entered in 2012 had earned an associate degree. In contrast, the median three-year graduation rate for community colleges in large cities is under 20 percent. To be clear, all of these institutions have implemented multiple reforms. None would claim that these improvements in student outcomes are due entirely to efforts to redesign programs and supports to help students choose and complete programs of study—but all would say that such reforms have been key factors in the results they have achieved.

CONCLUSION

Postsecondary education plays a crucial role in preparing students to secure career-path employment, but for colleges to do this effectively, students need to be able to choose majors and associated careers that align with their interests, abilities, and goals. The typical model of major selection emphasizes the role of information in matching students with particular characteristics to majors and careers with corresponding characteristics. Similarly, the college matching debate—with its concern for undermatching—focuses on the use of information to match students with colleges that fit students' characteristics. In both of these cases, the conventional concept of matching is too narrow, and even significantly improved provision and quality of information will not achieve optimal outcomes for students and society.

In both cases, matching takes the demand and supply sides as fixed and directs attention away from changes that need to be made in both domains if outcomes are to be improved. In reality, significant improvements in college opportunity and success would require both improving the preparation of high school students so that more of them are higher performing, and improving the quality of broad-access institutions so that all students, whether or not they are high performing, have access to high-quality higher education. In the case of major and program selection, students need to engage in an education process in which they explore their aptitudes and interests and develop relevant skills, but the majors and programs that they are choosing should ideally also be redesigned to be more coherent and easier to navigate, and better connected to subsequent education and employment.

We have described some of the policies and practices that colleges are implementing to improve the major- and program-selection process. Here, we summarize key approaches to improving the information students need to make a good match, but we also discuss potential changes in the supply and demand sides of the match.

Certainly, more well-presented information would help students make better major decisions. Colleges can do a better job of disseminating information about career opportunities, programs, program maps, transfer options, and jobs and earnings related to particular programs. We described the website developed by City Colleges of Chicago, but there are similar model websites created by other institutions, including Arizona State University.

Changes to advising structures can also help colleges better support students as they choose a program. Colleges that have built more structured pathways for students have often had to hire more advisers. But they have also reorganized advising to make it more effective. For example, some of the colleges that have mapped program pathways and organized programs into broad exploratory majors have also embedded advisers in particular program areas, so that they can develop deep knowledge of the requirements of their particular field and develop close relationships with students and faculty in that field.

Colleges need to be able to devote adequate time and resources to helping students choose programs and make concrete plans. Technology or online advising ("e-advising") can be an important part of this process. Many students probably also need college success courses or required group advising. Currently, college success courses are often limited, one-credit offerings that cover many topics superficially—they are primarily designed to provide information about many activities and processes at the college.

The many students who arrive in college without clear goals for college and careers—or even an awareness of the options—need substantial time to discover, develop, and reflect on goals and objectives. A one-credit student success course does not afford enough time for in-depth exploration, but many colleges are reluctant to devote more credit hours to this type of activity, because additional time would crowd out other courses. However, if better plans and goals can improve completion and reduce the number of excess credits students take, then devoting more time to these activities is worth it. Moreover, academic instruction can be incorporated into these courses so that students are both making plans and strengthening their skills. For instance, Guttmann Community College has developed a six-credit first-year course that combines career exploration and planning and academic instruction.

Choosing a major or program, developing plans to complete the requirements, and monitoring progress through those programs will be easier and more effective if programs are well designed and easy to understand. They should be educationally coherent, with clear learning outcomes that are tied to the requirements for further education and employment in related fields. Mapping out educational programs in coherent pathways not only makes them easier for students to negotiate, but it also enables faculty to ensure that students are mastering essential learning outcomes as they progress. Ideally, faculty should build into the curriculum in-class and out-of-school experiences, such as projects and internships, which enable students to continue the process of career exploration and development after they have chosen a major. Creating clearly structured and well-aligned program pathways requires colleges to encourage faculty to engage in this type of work and to consult both with employers and with colleagues at the next level of education. All of the institutions mentioned as examples in this chapter have engaged faculty and advisers in this sort of program mapping within and across two- and four-year institutions and with employers.

The process of career and major exploration should begin as early as possible, ideally starting in high school or even middle school. Institutions such as Arizona State University, the University of Central Florida, and Florida International University are working with employers on one end, and with local community colleges and K–12 schools on the other end, to build regional educational pipelines that help guide and prepare students for careers in fields of economic importance to their regions.

Creating more structured program pathways and building an integrated learning process through which students can explore career and major options requires colleges to make substantial changes to the way they organize and offer programs and support services. Admittedly, making these changes involves substantial costs and requires leadership and skill in managing large-scale change.[63] Yet despite the costs, many colleges, universities, and even state systems are implementing reforms along these lines, due to the incentives created by a number of converging forces. More than ever, a college education is a gateway to a family-supporting career, and for most students, the returns to a college degree remain high. Yet, particularly as a result of cuts in state funding, the cost to students and their families of even public higher education is rising. As students and their families have to pay more of their own money for a college education, they will want colleges to offer programs that lead as quickly and inexpensively as possible to career-path jobs and further education needed for career advancement.

These consumer pressures, combined with growing restrictions on financial aid eligibility and increasing pressure from policy makers for improved graduation rates and shorter time to degree, are putting pressure on institutions to create career-focused programs and to help students complete these programs in a timely fashion. This in turn is encouraging colleges to spend more time up front helping students to explore career and major options and to choose a program of study that is suited to their goals and talents— one that they will therefore be more likely to complete. As more colleges experiment with ways of supporting students in this learning process, our limited knowledge of how to match students with majors well suited to their talents and aspirations will be enriched to the benefit of students and society.

5

The Supply Side of College Match

Where Are the Seats?

Andrew P. Kelly

For too long qualified students, especially low-income students, have headed off to campuses where they have little chance of graduating, wasting time and resources that could be better spent elsewhere. The recent research into undermatch suggests that gains in attainment and a narrowing of stubborn class-based gaps can be achieved with simple, inexpensive interventions that would provide high school students with the information they need to make better college choices. These interventions can encourage high-achieving, low-income students to apply to and be admitted to more selective colleges, thereby increasing the chances that they earn a degree.

This new focus on the "demand side" of student success is a welcome change. Helping more students avoid making bad bets will help many more students succeed. But optimism about the effect of improving college match on educational attainment raises thorny questions about the "supply side" of American higher education. Are there seats available for these students at better-matched colleges? While many reform proposals to improve college match focus on redirecting students and funds from institutions with low graduation rates, there has been little discussion about whether colleges with higher rates of student success would be willing or able to absorb those students. Some observers seem to assume so. As one education reformer argued, in light of Caroline Hoxby and Christopher Avery's study of "the missing one-offs," "There's much less scarcity [at elite colleges] than anyone presumed—an untapped pool of talented low-income students, many of them black or Latino, waiting to be recruited."[1] Others have a less sanguine view of the supply-side constraints. A key question is whether better matches for some mean worse matches for others. To the extent the supply side of the equation is constrained, for each student who "matches," another does not. Such a zero-sum game would improve the prospects for some students but would do little to improve educational attainment overall. As the Urban Institute's Matthew Chingos has shown, even if we improved the match between students' academic background and the selectivity of their college, the fixed supply of college seats implies that the bachelor's degree attainment rate would "barely [budge]."[2] "The number of undermatched students simply isn't large enough in the context of the entire education system," he concludes, ". . . reshuffling students across colleges means that some gain but others lose."[3] Reducing undermatch would narrow gaps in attainment of degrees, but only marginally.

These supply-side questions raise serious policy questions not only about the effect of college match interventions, but about our broader approach to higher education reform. Does the system have sufficient capacity to provide access to quality opportunities not just to the highest achieving, but also to those in the middle of the achievement distribution? Do good colleges grow to accommodate more demand? Can less selective colleges, which often have greater capacity to expand, improve their rates of student success?

The goal of this chapter is to paint a descriptive picture of American higher education's supply-side challenge. Unlike other chapters, which primarily use admissions selectivity as a proxy for institutional quality, I use federal six-year graduation rates to categorize institutions' performance. The two dimensions are, of course, tightly correlated, but the correlation is not exact. I begin by decomposing the growth in first-time enrollment over the past decade according to college graduation rates and other measures of institutional productivity. Where did first-time enrollees go during the boom of the early 2000s? I go on to examine why the distribution of seats in different categories has changed over time. Did existing colleges improve their performance? Or did particular types of schools grow larger? Finally, I consider the viability of common assumptions that undergird existing policy recommendations. How common was it for high-performing colleges to accommodate more students over the past decade? Did colleges improve over time, thereby adding to the supply of quality seats?

DATA SOURCES AND ANALYSIS

To get a sense of where the supply of seats expanded over the past decade, I used data from the Integrated Postsecondary Education Data System

(IPEDS) and data derived from IPEDS by the Delta Cost Project. IPEDS is a series of annual surveys administered by the National Center for Education Statistics (NCES). Colleges report data on institutional characteristics, tuition prices, graduation rates, enrollment, and a host of other information.[4] The Delta Cost Project has used raw IPEDS data to create a longitudinal dataset that includes measures of costs and productivity.

I relied primarily on two variables. First, the number of first-time degree-seeking students between 2002 to 2012 characterizes the supply of seats at each individual college, and changes in that number from year to year capture the addition (or subtraction) of new seats over the baseline year.[5] I recognize that schools enroll more than just first-time degree-seeking students, but I chose to focus on this group as it is in keeping with most of the existing work on college match.

Second, I used the federal Student Right-to-Know (SRTK) graduation rate data to sort schools into five discrete tiers according to their graduation rate. The federal completion rate measure calculates the proportion of first-time, full-time, degree-seeking students who complete a degree in 150 percent of "normal time." For students at four-year colleges, this is the share of students who graduate in six years; for students who go to two-year colleges, three years. The flaws in this rate are well established, and I do not claim that it perfectly captures the performance of different types of colleges—particularly those with a transfer mission.[6] However, the SRTK rate is the only consistent student outcome variable available from 2002 to 2012. To provide another look at the distribution of new enrollments by college performance, I also use the number of credentials awarded per full-time equivalent student (FTE) from the Delta Cost Project and disaggregate two- and four-year colleges.

In general, I divide enrollments into five tiers. For graduation rates, I simply categorized institutions into five 20-point tiers: average graduation rates below 20 percent, between 20 percent and 40 percent, between 40 and 60 percent, between 60 and 80 percent, and between 80 and 100 percent.[7] For the analysis of completions and degrees per one hundred full-time undergraduates—which essentially measures how many graduates an institution produces per student they enroll—I categorized two-year and four-year colleges separately into performance quintiles (labeled as tiers as well).

Given this volume's focus on traditional-age students, I chose to analyze the institutions where the vast majority of those students attend: public and nonprofit four-year and two-year colleges. I excluded for-profit institutions and less-than-two-year schools (federal data suggest that just 5 or

6 percent of first-time students under the age of twenty-three attend for-profit institutions).[8]

To be included in the sample, institutions also had to be located in the United States, be predominately postsecondary, and participate in federal student aid programs. In order to be included in a given year, an institution had to have ten or more degree-seeking students in its incoming class. Schools that did not report graduation rates in a given year were not included in the analysis for that year. I included institutions that opened after 2002 in order to account for increase or decrease of supply due to new college creation or existing college mergers or closures.

From there, the analysis is a simple, descriptive exercise: I illustrate the number of first-time students in each category in each year and examine how the distributions changed over time. I look mainly at raw numbers, though I also report changes in proportion to capture growth.

WHERE DO FIRST-TIME STUDENTS ENROLL?

In this section, I examine trends in first-time, degree-seeking undergraduate enrollments across different institutional categories. The first subsection examines enrollment trends by sector, the second by graduation rates, and the third by completions per full-time student at the two-year level.

Enrollment by Sector

Figure 5.1 plots the distribution of first-time enrollments from 2002 through 2012, broken down by institutional sector.[9] Overall, the number of first-time degree-seeking enrollments per year increased from just under 2.4 million early in the 2000s to 2.9 million in the recession and its aftermath. First-time enrollments peaked in 2009 and 2010 before falling slightly in 2012. In 2002, more than half of first-time enrollments were in four-year colleges; 36 percent enrolled in a public four-year college and 18 percent in a private four-year college. Forty-four percent of first-time undergraduates were in two-year public colleges. By the peak enrollment years (2009–2010), those proportions had tipped slightly in favor of public two-year colleges, which accounted for 48 to 49 percent of first-time students, compared with just over one-third at public four-year colleges. Figure 5.1 illustrates how college enrollment tends to be countercyclical—it goes up when the economy goes down—and that most of that additional enrollment flows to community colleges.

FIGURE 5.1   First-time degree-seeking undergraduate enrollments by sector and year

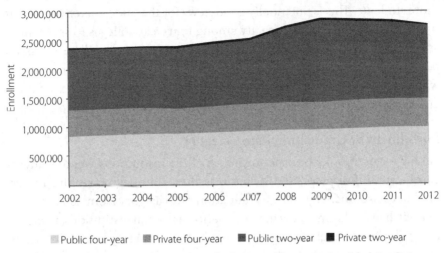

Source: Author's calculations using data from the Integrated Postsecondary Education Data System (IPEDS). Sample includes 3,589 four-year and two-year public and nonprofit colleges active over the eleven-year period.

Overall, first-time enrollments at public two-year colleges grew 22 percent over the period—a 1.8 percent annual rate—compared with 12 percent growth in public four-year colleges and 8 percent at private nonprofit colleges. Public two-year colleges added 13 million first-time students over the period, compared with 10.3 million at four-year public colleges and 5.1 million at four-year private colleges. Private two-year colleges grew over their 2002 levels (21 percent) but still enrolled only about 1 percent of students by 2012. Four-year colleges accounted for a larger chunk of total undergraduate enrollments than first-time enrollments—about 60 percent (not pictured)—which is to be expected, given lengthier programs.

However, the proportion of undergraduate enrollments at four-year colleges had actually declined by 2012 (to 55 percent); not because enrollment levels in four-year colleges declined, but because enrollment in two-year public colleges grew by 36 percent over the same period, adding 1.9 million students. In 2002, the 4.45 million students in two-year colleges made up 39 percent of the total. By 2010, that number had grown to 6.6 million, or 45 percent of the total.

These trends suggest a couple of things. First, enrollment in all sectors grew over the period, and four-year colleges did expand to accommodate more students. This is potentially good news for the undermatch story, as it implies that there is some capacity among four-year colleges to serve more students. But not all four-year colleges are created equal, as will be discussed below. Second, two-year colleges expanded more rapidly over the period, which suggests that the colleges with the greatest capacity to expand are also those where undermatched low-income students are likely to attend.[10]

Enrollment by Graduation Rate Category

Taking a closer look at the performance of the institutions where students enroll, table 5.1 displays the distribution of first-time degree-seeking undergraduate enrollment by college graduation rate category from 2002 to 2012. The left-hand columns show the distribution across all institutions, while the two right-hand panels disaggregate across four- and two-year institutions. One thing is immediately clear: in any given year, most first-time degree-seeking students enroll in an institution where the graduation rate is lower than 40 percent. Together, institutions in tiers 1 and 2 accounted for about 52 percent of all first-time enrollments across each of the years. Over the eleven-year period, colleges that graduated fewer than four in ten students enrolled a total of 15.1 million first-time degree-seeking students. Institutions in tiers 4 and 5 (with the highest graduation rates) accounted for just over one-quarter of first-time enrollments in 2012, up from just 22 percent in 2002. In total, though, these top performers enrolled less than half as many students (6.8 million) over the time period as those in the bottom two tiers.

As a proportion of enrollments, the top tier grew more than the bottom tiers, which indicates that the number of first-time students in this tier grew faster than in other tiers. In 2002, just 5 percent of enrollments flowed to the 132 institutions in the top tier; by 2012, 169 institutions qualified for the top tier, enrolling 9 percent of first-time students. The number of first-time students in that category more than doubled. In contrast, enrollments in the bottom two tiers made up about the same share of the total in 2012 as they did in 2002.

When four- and two-year colleges are disaggregated, two different patterns emerge. Among four-year colleges, the number and proportion of students attending schools with graduation rates better than 60 percent grew considerably over the period. The incoming undergraduate class at these institutions was 1.4 times as large in 2012 as it was in 2002—moving from about 500,000 to almost 700,000. At the very top (tier 5), the size of the incoming class more than doubled, from 114,000 in to just under 240,000. In total, the proportion of first-time, four-year enrollments in the top two tiers increased from 38 percent in 2002 to 47 percent by 2012. Meanwhile, the proportion of first-time enrollments in the bottom two tiers decreased from 23 percent to 15 percent over that time. These trends stand in contrast to some of the existing work on undermatch, which assumes that capacity at the top is more or less fixed.

In contrast, at two-year colleges, the vast majority of first-time students went to colleges with graduation rates of 40 percent or less. The 949 institutions in the bottom two tiers accounted for 88 percent of first-time enrollments in 2002. By 2012, there were 997 instituitons in those two tiers, accounting for 94 percent of two-year enrollments. Over the eleven-year period, colleges in these two tiers enrolled a total of 12.3 million first-time students. That's *sixty-three times* as many as the 195,600 first-time students who went to schools where 60 percent or more of students graduate.

I also examined the percentage of first-time students attending institutions where the graduation rate was under 50 percent in each year (not pictured). In any given year, more than 60 percent of first-time enrollments flowed to colleges where fewer than half of students finish in 150 percent time. The proportion varied a bit depending on the year, but was remarkably consistent, hovering between 66 and 63 percent. The story for two-year colleges is straightforward and discouraging: 94–97 percent of student enrollments flowed to schools where the chances of success were worse than 50 percent. At four-year schools, the proportion declined over time from 42 percent in 2002 to about one-third by 2012; and first-time enrollments grew faster at schools where more than half of students finished in six years.

The differences between two-year and four-year institutions are not entirely surprising—two-year colleges typically enroll students who are less academically prepared and from more disadvantaged backgrounds. But the apparent increases in availability of first-time slots at the top should encourage college match proponents. That more students were enrolled in the top two graduation rate categories suggests that high-performing institutions expanded their enrollments, that previously average-performing colleges improved their performance, or (most likely) some mix of both.

At the same time, though, despite increases in the supply of seats at the top of the performance distribution, it was still the case in 2012 that more than half of four-year students enrolled in one of the 986 institutions where

TABLE 5.1 First-time degree-seeking undergraduate enrollments by graduation rates, 2002–2012*

	All colleges				Four-year colleges				Two-year colleges			
	2002	2007	2012	Total, 2002–2012	2002	2007	2012	Total, 2002–2012	2002	2007	2012	Total, 2002–2012
Tier 1 (<20%)												
Number of enrollments	504,295	598,166	712,983	6,908,701	30,632	11,758	12,627	194,286	473,663	586,408	700,356	6,714,415
Share	21.2%	23.6%	25.7%		2.4%	0.8%	0.9%		44.0%	51.7%	54.0%	
Colleges	489	532	521		52	32	48		437	500	473	
Tier 2 (20%–39%)												
Number of enrollments	738,972	695,728	729,996	8,194,272	269,030	228,693	206,208	2,609,427	469,942	467,035	523,788	5,584,845
Share	31.1%	27.5%	26.3%		20.7%	16.4%	14.0%		43.6%	41.2%	40.4%	
Colleges	901	865	838		389	321	314		512	544	524	
Tier 3 (40%–59%)												
Number of enrollments	610,642	626,494	611,838	6,756,802	507,357	558,447	557,797	5,901,765	103,285	68,047	54,041	855,037
Share	25.7%	24.8%	22.1%		39.0%	40.0%	37.8%		9.6%	6.0%	4.2%	

Colleges	802	790	741		625	647	624		177	143	121	
Tier 4 (60%–79%)												
Number of enrollments	407,923	433,339	478,428	4,892,373	380,506	422,652	460,154	4,723,913	27,417	10,687	18,274	168,460
Share	17.1%	17.1%	17.2%		29.2%	30.3%	31.2%		2.5%	0.9%	1.4%	
Colleges	449	451	463		378	389	396		71	62	67	
Tier 5 (≥80%)												
Number of enrollments	116,785	176,717	241,184	1,926,300	114,043	174,961	239,664	1,899,173	2,742	1,756	1,520	27,127
Share	4.9%	7.0%	8.7%		8.8%	12.5%	16.2%		0.3%	0.2%	0.1%	
Colleges	132	143	169		114	126	154		18	17	15	
Total enrollments	2,378,617	2,530,444	2,774,429		1,301,568	1,396,511	1,476,450		1,077,049	1,133,933	1,297,979	

Source: Author's calculations using data from the Integrated Postsecondary Education Data System (IPEDS).

*In the interest of space, years between 2002 and 2007 and years between 2007 and 2012 were left out of the table. Totals in the right-most columns include enrollments from those years as well.

fewer than six in ten students graduated in six years. Meanwhile, the flow of students into two-year colleges in the bottom two tiers—12.3 million over eleven years—far outstripped the 6.6 million enrollments in higher-performing four-year colleges. These patterns suggest that while enrollments grew at above-average four-year colleges in response to demand, the effect of this expansion on graduation rates overall is likely swamped by the boom at the two-year level.

To be clear, these enrollment trends are not entirely—or even mostly—a function of institutional decisions about how many students to enroll and whom to admit. Instead, they obviously have much to do with the supply of eligible students and the effects of the economic recession. Put simply, there are far more students who are eligible to attend a two-year community college than a four-year college, let alone a selective one. This was especially true during the recession; difficult economic times pushed many adults back into the system, most of whom were looking for the kind of readily available short-term opportunities offered by two-year colleges. Indeed, the National Student Clearinghouse estimates that the number of students over the age of twenty-one increased 20 percent between 2007 and 2008 alone.[11] It is this trend, rather than a lack of seats at the four-year level, that helps explain much of the expansion in two-year college enrollments. This is not to say that the status quo of student success at two-year colleges is acceptable (I discuss the need to improve institutional performance below).

The obvious question is whether the modest increase in four-year enrollments at the top two tiers was sufficient to keep up with demand from qualified students. If so, the supply of seats may not be as fixed as some have assumed, and improving match may not be a zero-sum game. This is a more difficult question to answer. It is true that application rates have risen and that enrollments at selective colleges grew during this period.[12] At the same time, though, the growth in applications outstripped growth in admissions, and researchers have pointed out how few qualified minority students find a slot in an elite college. (Of course, many of those applications likely came from students who were not qualified to attend the institution in question.) Would colleges be able to expand even further to accommodate students who could be nudged away from undermatching? Again, if above-average four-year colleges are willing to expand, improving college match may not be a zero-sum game. One question for future research, therefore, is: What would be the optimal growth in seats, given the distribution of student ability? I return to this topic below.

Undergraduate Enrollments by Productivity Rating

Critics rightly argue that six-year graduation rates exclude a significant number of students and potential positive outcomes—returning students, part-time students, those who transfer in or out, and so on. Likewise, measuring only first-time enrollments leaves out a good number of students who choose to return to college. These measures are particularly narrow when it comes to two-year colleges, where many students are returning adults and many transfer out before finishing a credential.

Therefore, to take a different look at the distribution of enrollments by institutional performance in the two-year sector, I used data from the Delta Cost Project on the number of completions per hundred full-time equivalent (FTE) students. This measure is not perfect, but it at least counts more students than the SRTK graduation rate. Many other researchers have used this measure to assess institutional performance.[13]

I also used a slightly different enrollment variable to capture more of the students entering two-year colleges: undergraduate enrollments according to how many degrees and certificates they produced.[14] As noted above, at the two-year level, I excluded certificates of less than one-year and lumped "Primarily Associate's" colleges in with the other two-year colleges.

Table 5.2 shows the results. It is important to keep in mind that because the ratings are norm-referenced, two-year college enrollments will be more evenly distributed here than they were in the previous graduation rate analysis, where they were clustered in the bottom two quintiles (tiers 1 and 2). The general pattern for two-year colleges is only slightly more encouraging than what table 5.1 displays: the proportion of students going to the least productive institutions actually decreased over time, while the number and proportion of students in the top two quintiles (tiers 4 and 5) grew modestly. Still, 59 percent of entering students remained in the bottom two quintiles in 2012, down from 62 percent in 2002, in comparison with 21 percent in the top two quintiles in 2012 (up from 18 percent in 2002). In total, 8.7 million entering undergraduates enrolled in schools in the bottom quintile over the period, compared with 4.5 million in the top two.

Summary

The story of postsecondary enrollments from 2002 to 2012 is at times discouraging, at times optimistic. On the discouraging side, even after significant enrollment growth over the decade, the share of first-time students enrolling in a college where more than 60 percent of students graduate was

TABLE 5.2   Entering undergraduate enrollments by productivity rating (two-year colleges, completions per 100 full-time equivalent)

	2002	2004	2006	2008	2010	2012	Total 2002–2012
Tier 1							
Number of enrollments	792,845	742,007	730,129	778,765	846,921	755,637	8,658,328
Share	42%	38%	38%	37%	35%	33%	
Colleges	222	230	223	219	216	212	
Tier 2							
Number of enrollments	392,699	445,082	441,837	503,374	602,839	606,215	5,475,304
Share	21%	23%	23%	24%	25%	26%	
Colleges	220	230	227	226	222	222	
Tier 3							
Number of enrollments	365,326	366,862	368,956	441,221	501,516	455,371	4,669,612
Share	19%	19%	19%	21%	21%	20%	
Colleges	212	231	226	224	221	217	
Tier 4							
Number of enrollments	274,370	284,824	272,019	288,294	341,254	357,428	3,370,170
Share	14%	15%	14%	14%	14%	16%	
Colleges	212	229	218	223	211	212	
Tier 5							
Number of enrollments	76,501	93,070	93,497	101,085	116,278	125,415	1,118,243
Share	4%	5%	5%	5%	5%	5%	
Colleges	190	227	157	151	119	124	
Total enrollments	1,901,741	1,931,845	1,906,438	2,112,739	2,408,808	2,300,066	

Source: Author's calculations using data from the Integrated Postsecondary Education Data System (IPEDS) and the Delta Cost Project.

Note: Sample includes 1,556 public and private nonprofit two-year colleges. Not all colleges had valid data in each year, and the Delta Cost Project groups some institutions operating within the same system and reports aggregated completion and FTE data for the system. Institutions categorized on the basis of a rolling weighted average of the completions per 100 full-time equivalent students, where each year's completions per 100 FTE was weighted by the size of the undergraduate FTE. Certificates of less than one year were excluded from the completion count. Cells represent the sum of entering undergraduates enrolled in that tier, the share of entering undergraduate enrollments in that tier in that year, and the number of institutions in that tier in that year.

just over 25 percent. The share enrolling in colleges where graduation rates were lower than 40 percent was twice as large. The proportion of enrollments in the colleges with the worst graduation rates grew by nearly five percentage points over that period. The overall trend hides two distinct patterns, however. At the two-year level, the number and proportion of first-time students enrolling in the lowest-performing institutions increased by ten percentage points. At the four-year level, the number of first-time students enrolling in struggling colleges declined markedly while the number headed to above average and top-performing colleges grew faster than the sector as a whole.

WHAT EXPLAINS CHANGES IN THE DISTRIBUTION OF ENROLLMENTS? INSTITUTIONAL CHANGE OVER TIME

There are various potential explanations for shifts in the distribution of enrollments shown above. Colleges in a given performance category may have grown larger at a faster rate than enrollments as a whole, thereby accounting for more of the enrollments overall. Meanwhile, some types of institutions may not have grown quickly enough to keep up with enrollment growth in the rest of the system. This tends to be the criticism of elite colleges at the heart of the undermatch discussion—that most grow only a little and do so very slowly. Meanwhile, evidence in this volume and elsewhere suggests that colleges in the middle of the selectivity distribution have increased their capacity. Some public colleges—University of Central Florida, Arizona State University, and Miami Dade College, to name a few—have grown significantly over the past decade. They have done so by building online and hybrid courses that can serve greater numbers of students, fostering partnerships with community colleges, and, in some cases, relaxing admissions criteria. Whether policy reforms can encourage other institutions to follow suit is an open question I return to in the conclusion.

At the same time, colleges may improve (or struggle) over time, shifting seats from one performance category to another. Some colleges have been able to make significant gains in their retention and graduation rates over time. Georgia State University, for instance, instituted peer tutoring and data-driven counseling and advising, and has increased its graduation rate 22 percentage points since 2003.[15] The City University of New York (CUNY) has designed a comprehensive intervention—the Accelerated Study in Associate's Programs (ASAP)—that provides additional advising to developmental education students, groups them in cohorts, and provides tuition waivers and Metrocards in exchange for full-time enrollment. A randomized study of the program found that it doubled three-year graduation rates.[16] At the same time, other schools may have struggled under the burden of increased demand and declining per-pupil revenue from the state, resulting in lower completion rates overall.

The truth is likely a mix of each of these explanations. In this section, I provide a first look at each of them. Further work should consider these trends in more detail.

Do Colleges with High Graduation Rates Get Bigger?

For this analysis, I limited the sample to those colleges that had a complete set of data for all eleven years. I look first at how the first-time enrollments of institutions that started out at the top and bottom of the performance scale changed over time, then at how schools may have improved (or declined) over time.

The results suggest that while the average college in the top-performing group in 2002 did grow over this period, lower-performing colleges grew more. I first took the difference in first-time degree-seeking enrollment between 2002 and 2012 and looked at the average gain or loss by gradua-tion rate category. Colleges in tiers 4 and 5 grew by an average of 109 and 123 first-time students, respectively (median differences of 41 and 34 first-time students, respectively). At the other end of the spectrum, colleges with graduation rates between 20 and 40 percent (tier 2) grew by 147 first-time undergraduates on average, and those with graduation rates below 20 per-cent (tier 1) grew by more than 294 students (median difference of 50 and 114, respectively).

Figures 5.2 and 5.3 plot the trend in the average number of first-time degree-seeking undergrads for institutions that started in one of the five graduation rate categories in 2002, disaggregated by level. In figure 5.2, the data show that most four-year institutions grew roughly in parallel over the period by between 125 and 140 first-time students. The exception was in tier 1, where the colleges grew only slightly before declining. In other words, high-performing four-year colleges did grow, though no faster than lower-performing institutions. Figure 5.3 reveals almost a mirror image in the two-year sector: bottom performers grew steeply while the small num-ber of high-performing two-year colleges shrank.

These findings provide mildly good news for college match advocates, as they suggest that top-performing four-year institutions have the ability and/

FIGURE 5.2   Trends in average full-time enrollment by graduation rate tier and level, four-year colleges

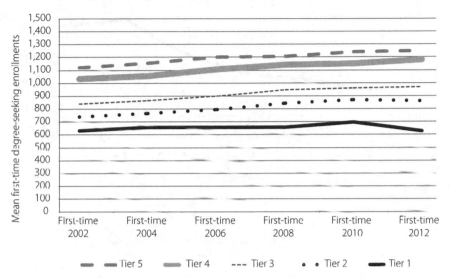

Source: Author's calculations using data from the Integrated Postsecondary Education Data System (IPEDS).

Note: Sample includes 1,467 public and nonprofit four-year colleges with complete data from 2002 to 2012. Colleges were divided by their average graduation rate over 2002 and 2003, and the lines track the average first-time, degree-seeking undergraduate enrollment in colleges in that category in that year.

or incentive to expand their capacity. The average increases were not particularly large among these schools (about 130 additional incoming students by the end of the eleven-year period), but they did grow. However, the data also show that lower-performing two-year institutions readily expanded to accommodate many more students, especially during the recession.

Do Colleges Improve Their Graduation Rates over Time?

To get some purchase on this question, I simply looked at how individual colleges' graduation rates changed over the period. This is somewhat difficult to assess, given year-over-year variation; a one-year blip should not be mistaken for a lasting trend. To account for that variation, I compared the three-year weighted average in 2003 (based on 2002–2004 data) to the three-year weighted average in 2011 (based on 2010–2012 data). Results from 2002 to 2012 do not show much change.

FIGURE 5.3   Trends in average full-time enrollment by graduation rate category and level, two-year colleges

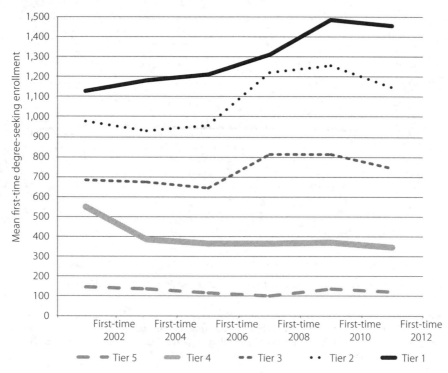

Source: Author's calculations using data from the Integrated Postsecondary Education Data System (IPEDS).

Note: Sample includes 1,062 public and nonprofit two-year colleges with complete data from 2002 to 2012. Colleges were divided by their average graduation rate over 2002 and 2003, and the lines track the average first-time, degree-seeking undergraduate enrollment in colleges in that category in that year.

Table 5.3 categorizes institutions according to how their graduation rate changed over time. The left-hand column corresponds to that change, running from a drop of 25 percentage points or more to an increase of 25 percentage points or more. The neutral category corresponds to schools whose graduation rates remained relatively constant; they were within 2.5 percentage points (increase or decrease) of their initial rolling average. The table also displays the size of first-time enrollments in these institutions, both the total enrollment across institutions in the category and the median first-time enrollment.

TABLE 5.3   Change in graduation rates, 2003–2011

Percentage point change in graduation rate	All colleges			
	Number	Percentage of colleges	Total first-time enrollment	Median first-time enrollment (2012)
(–) 25 or more	37	1.5%	50,202	182
(–) 10–25	211	8.3%	736,265	473
(–) 2.5–10	529	20.9%	1,750,714	521
(–) 2.5–(+) 2.5	746	29.5%	3,446,194	680.5
(+) 2.5–10	778	30.8%	4,606,539	677.5
(+) 10–25	209	8.3%	1,212,767	553
(+) 25	19	0.8%	16,179	61

Percentage point change in graduation rate	Four-year colleges			
	Number	Percentage of colleges	Total first-time enrollment	Median first-time enrollment (2012)
(–) 25 or more	14	1.0%	14,379	235
(–) 10–25	68	4.6%	153,598	396
(–) 2.5–10	217	14.8%	506,177	479
(–) 2.5–(+) 2.5	435	29.7%	1,911,827	913
(+) 2.5–10	575	39.2%	3,684,784	1,289
(+) 10–25	149	10.2%	1,061,382	1,325
(+) 25	9	0.6%	12,655	214

Percentage point change in graduation rate	Two-year colleges			
	Number	Percentage of colleges	Total first-time enrollment	Median first-time enrollment (2012)
(–) 25 or more	23	2.2%	35,823	498
(–) 10–25	143	13.5%	582,667	1,148
(–) 2.5–10	312	29.4%	1,244,537	1,122
(–) 2.5–(+) 2.5	311	29.3%	1,534,368	1,371
(+) 2.5–10	203	19.1%	921,755	1,237
(+) 10–25	60	5.7%	151,385	685
(+) 25	10	0.9%	3,524	136

Source: Author's calculations using data from the Integrated Postsecondary Education Data System (IPEDS).

Note: Sample includes 2,529 public and nonprofit, two- and four-year colleges (1,062 two-year colleges and 1,467 four-year colleges) with complete data in every year over the time period. The percentage corresponds to the proportion of colleges in the entire category made up by the colleges in that row. The enrollment figures measure enrollment across all colleges in the row and the median first-time degree-seeking undergraduate enrollment in those colleges.

The results show that many colleges do increase their graduation rates by more than 2.5 percentage points over time. The mean change in the average graduation rate across the 2,529 institutions was about 3 percentage points. In all, 1,006 institutions enrolling more than 5.8 million full-time students saw an increase in their graduation rate, with 228 institutions seeing increases of 10 percentage points or higher. In general, the institutions that gained 25 percentage points or more were quite small—enrolling just 16,000 students in 2012. Most of the institutions with complete data (60 percent) either exhibited no change (+/– 2.5 percentage points) or a decline in their success rates. But the institutions on the positive side of the ledger accounted for twice as many full-time equivalent students in 2012 than those that experienced declines.

Disaggregating across two- and four-year institutions reveals the familiar differences: exactly half of the four-year institutions experienced gains in their graduation rate, enrolling more than 4.7 million FTE in 2012. Most of these enrollments were in instituitons that made modest gains—between 2.5 and 10 percentage points. These gainers also had larger incoming classes in 2012 than those that experienced declines. In comparison, the 299 four-year institutions with complete records that experienced declines enrolled just under 675,000 students. These trends align with increases in the number of four-year institutions that had graduation rates of 60 percent or above between 2002 and 2012 (62 more institutions fell into those categories in 2012 than did in 2002).

At the two-year level, success rates were again lower. Just over a quarter of the two-year institutions (273), enrolling about 1 million full-time equivalent students, experienced graduation rate gains. The 478 institutions whose graduation rates declined enrolled 1.8 million students and had much larger incoming freshman classes in 2012 than their peers who made gains.

These results suggest that improvements in graduation rates are possible, particularly at four-year institutions. This likely helps explain some of the positive enrollment shifts shown above at the four-year level. How some colleges improve and why they do so are critical questions that deserve further research. If most colleges improved by raising admissions standards and admitting fewer students, this might actually run counter to college match efforts. If, on the other hand, improvements resulted from new institution-level practices and policies, this raises questions about the conditions and incentives that facilitate such improvements. I return to these questions below.

WHAT DO THESE PATTERNS MEAN FOR COLLEGE MATCH?

The analysis above indicates both opportunities and challenges on the supply side of college match. The data really tell two different stories. On the one hand, the enrollment analysis showed that more first-time students were enrolling in top-performing four-year colleges in 2012 than in 2002. Some of this positive trend reflects growth in enrollments at institutions with high graduation rates, but much of it also seems to have resulted from institutions improving their graduation rates over time. These are good signs that the supply side can expand, if necessary.

Still, there are important questions about whether and how policy can encourage good schools to expand and average schools to get better. If high-performing colleges display a willingness to expand their enrollments, then informational interventions that encourage qualified students to apply should pay dividends. If, however, capacity at quality institutions expands more slowly, that might suggest a need for different policy solutions—enticements for good schools to grow. That colleges have shown an ability to improve their graduation rates while more or less maintaining their level of selectivity suggests another route to improvement: policies that give colleges incentive to *become* a better match for students.

Neither of these are easy to do. For most four-year colleges, the incentives point in the opposite direction; the more selective a school gets, and the scarcer the product, the more likely a school is to rise in the college rankings. Increasing in size could hurt that reputation. (See chapter 6 for a more detailed dicussion of ranking and college match.) Likewise, the easiest way to improve graduation rates may be to increase admissions selectivity. Institutional change entails spending time, resources, and political capital on reforms that may or may not pan out. In contrast, raising the SAT requirement is a straightforward change with a more certain outcome. Improving match will require more of the former and less of the latter.

The fact that about half of the four-year institutions in the data set raised their graduation rates over time is a positive sign. Likewise, the expansion in enrollments in four-year colleges with above-average graduation is also encouraging. But these additional seats are a drop in the bucket when it comes to the system as a whole—a system where more than half of first-time students enroll in institutions where fewer than half graduate. No surprise, then, that graduation rates as a whole remain stubbornly stagnant and have actually declined for the most recent cohort. There is clearly more work to be done.

Graduation rates have declined in part because of the parallel story: the significant expansion of enrollment at community colleges with low graduation rates. The recession drove marginal students, many of them adults, into the higher education system, and most of them chose the cheapest and most readily available option. These institutions are inexpensive, have low or nonexistent admissions standards, and are geographically accessible. They also receive about 70 cents from the state for every dollar that is invested in public four-year colleges.[17] The ease of enrolling in community colleges and the lack of student services predispose them to low rates of retention and completion. As seen above, when enrollments boom, these institutions expand dramatically. But expanded enrollment in lower-performing colleges does not raise completion rates, it lowers them.

As the economy improves, this enrollment surge will recede, and the share of enrollments flowing to low-graduation rate schools should decline. But reformers should not lose sight of the fact that students for whom open-access two-year college is the best match—academically, financially, and geographically—deserve better options than they currently have. To an even greater extent than in the four-year context, ensuring that more community college programs are a good match for qualified students will require organizational change, not just shifting enrollments from low-performing schools to high-performing ones. There are simply too few in the latter category.

Research suggests that improvement in this sector is possible but that it can be costly. In chapter 4, Thomas Bailey and colleagues discuss the various ways community colleges could reform their career and academic advising to boost student success. CUNY's ASAP program provides another example of progress, as do the reforms under way at winners of the Aspen Institute's Prize for Community College Excellence.[18] Some of these reforms require upfront investment that pays off in lower costs per completion, as is the case in CUNY's ASAP program. Encouraging community colleges to adopt them in the first place, and to do so with fidelity, also requires policies that reward institutions for student success rather than just enrollment.

Fortunately, reformers at the state and federal level are experimenting with reforms that reward colleges for student success. Thirty-five states are developing and/or implementing some form of outcomes-based funding, where schools are funded based on how many students they graduate rather than how many they enroll.[19] Some even weight disadvantaged students more heavily, ensuring that top colleges have incentives to enroll those who are prone to undermatch. At the federal level, as Robert Kelchen discusses in chapter 9, policy makers are discussing risk sharing, or the notion that colleges should be held financially accountable for their students' ability to repay their loans and should be rewarded for every Pell Grant recipient they graduate. Such a policy would focus institutions on student success both in and after college.[20]

In the end, then, the results above suggest that reforming institutions, rather than just changing the flow of students to them, is key to making significant improvement in student success. As seen, colleges with high graduation rates will expand to accommodate more students, but perhaps more slowly than is optimal. Raising average- or poorly performing institutions up will multiply the number of quality seats available. Future research on the supply side of college match should examine the optimal mix of expansion and improvement.

Enrollment Management and the Low-Income Student

*How Holistic Admissions and Market
Competition Can Impede Equity*

Michael N. Bastedo

Low-income college students are having a moment in higher education, government, and the media.[1] A wide range of actors are taking notice that these students constitute less than 5 percent of the enrollment at our most selective institutions, a percentage that, despite a great deal of effort and policy reform, has remained virtually unchanged for decades.[2] Yet in the past two years, only 11 percent of selective colleges have increased their focus on socioeconomic diversity, and in the past five years, college enrollment among low-income students has fallen by ten percentage points.[3] Meanwhile, students at the upper end of the income spectrum come from families whose wealth has accelerated during that time, leading to greater disparities on campus between the haves and have-nots.

Persistently low enrollment among low-income students is not due to a lack of qualified candidates. If we look at standardized test scores, for instance, there are thousands of low-income graduates each year who earn scores that are typical of highly selective colleges.[4] While estimates of undermatching vary widely depending on how it is measured, all of them find that a disproportionate number of low-income students attend colleges whose academic and admissions standards are significantly lower than others they would be eligible to attend.[5]

This problem is often seen as one of incentives and information. On one side, students are seen as failing to understand the full range of available options, owing to weak college counseling and insufficient funds to apply to a large number of colleges. Low-income students are also more likely to be subject to information asymmetries, leading them to overestimate their college costs.[6] They may not understand that the "net price" of selective colleges, due to these schools' superior financial resources and smaller numbers of low-income students, is often much lower than the price of less selective competitors.[7] Interventions that address such barriers, including application fee waivers and guidance on college options, have been shown to be effective in changing students' application behavior.[8]

Some of these low-income students do gain admission to selective colleges and choose to enroll there. Programs like QuestBridge and the Posse Foundation produce inspirational stories of students whose lives are changed by their college choices. These are more than just heartwarming narratives; the returns to selective colleges among low-income students are undeniable, even in the most conservative models.[9]

We are also seeing some interesting policy shifts. In recent years, Colorado has conducted a fascinating experiment with indexes of disadvantage and overachievement to help assess applications in context.[10] There are also significant initiatives from major institutions—such as the University of Chicago, the University of Michigan, and Washington University—to improve their record of enrolling low-income students.[11]

Commitments from individual institutions are commendable. But what is happening more broadly on the institutional part of this equation—what is often termed "the supply side" of undermatch? As much as the literature deals with this question, we again see a problem definition centered on information and incentives. Because students who do not apply are not visible, admissions officers may believe that they do not exist or use search techniques that disadvantage the recruitment of low-income applicants.[12] Thus, if only we could induce low-income students to apply in greater numbers, they would be admitted on the strength of their academic credentials. If we spent just a bit more on recruitment, application waivers, and information sharing, we would facilitate better matching, and a more equitable, meritocratic system of higher education admissions would emerge.

This may be true at a few institutions, such as Stanford and Princeton, where there are plenty of resources to support low-income students. But these assumptions do not reflect the reality of enrollment management at colleges that are selective but resource-constrained—in other words, the vast majority of highly selective colleges. They do not reflect the pressures that lead higher-income students to maintain a competitive advantage over lower-income students in every aspect of the college choice process. They do not reflect the complete picture of how applicants are admitted via a holistic review process that weighs many factors in addition to test scores. But more importantly, these assumptions do not reflect the pressures on enrollment managers—the people who generally oversee admissions personnel—to generate the tuition revenue needed from each incoming class.

Beyond revenue, there is also substantial pressure on enrollment managers to ensure the continued prestige and reputation of the institution. We have strong evidence that college rankings, such as those published by *U.S. News & World Report*, have a significant influence on college applications. Even more than the real effect, however, is the perceived effect of college rankings on applicants, funders, and other stakeholders. Admitting more low-income students is unlikely to serve the prestige-seeking goals of selective colleges. And sadly, while class-based affirmative action is discussed widely in policy circles, it has not yet been implemented in most colleges, and race-based affirmative action cannot effectively serve multiple purposes.[13]

In this chapter, I draw on the existing literature on college admissions and enrollment management, as well as my own work: fieldwork conducted over a two-year period in two flagship university admissions offices, reading undergraduate applications and conducting sixty interviews with admissions officers and external readers;[14] a number of recent papers I authored on college admissions and stratification; and two experiments I conducted to assess admissions decision making.[15]

Drawing on this work, I review some of the institutional impediments to an equitable system of selective college admissions. I will explore what we know about the crucial factors that shape a student's holistic review beyond the grades and standardized test scores used in most of the existing literature on undermatch. I will also examine what we know about how the drive for revenue and prestige determine decision making and result in intense pressures on enrollment managers to produce results that meet institutional targets. Finally, I will discuss how two important factors—*replacement* and *scale*—are likely to influence any future reduction in undermatching behavior.

HOLISTIC ADMISSIONS

Because of the nature of the available data sets, much of the literature on college undermatch uses simplified models of the admissions process, relying primarily (sometimes exclusively) on standardized test scores and grade point averages.[16] Beyond data set availability, there are some good, research-driven reasons to use simplified models. The existing research shows that standardized test scores are the most significant driver of admissions decision making, playing a particularly strong role for low-socioeconomic status (SES), black, Latino, and female applicants.[17]

However, in their simplicity, these models miss major factors outside of GPA and test scores that are an important part of holistic review. Here I discuss the most important missing pieces: advanced course taking, extracurricular activities, and demonstrated interest.

Advanced Courses

The most important factor missing from simplified models of match is the pattern of advanced course taking in high school. For nearly all highly selective colleges, advanced course taking is a primary criterion for admission. A recent survey of admissions officers conducted by the National Association for College Admissions Counseling (NACAC) revealed that a student's strength of curriculum (defined as AP, IB, dual enrollment, and other advanced/college-level coursework) was rated as "considerably important" by 75 percent of respondents at selective colleges.[18]

Under the philosophy of holistic review, an applicant who achieved high test scores and a 4.0 GPA is unlikely to be admitted to the most selective colleges unless those grades were earned in the most advanced courses offered by the high school. In practice, however, the benefits from advanced coursework are more complicated. In general, my research shows that "maxing out" the high school curriculum—when a student takes the most advanced courses available—is not a strong predictor of admission to selective colleges.[19] In most states, maxing out is only a predictor when considered along with GPA, and does not lead to a significant increase in the probability of admission to the most selective colleges. In states with affirmative action bans, however, maxing out is consistently related to admissions decisions, and leads to a significantly higher probability of admission—likely due to higher fidelity to holistic admissions practices in these states.

These data on maxing out among low-income students should be most concerning to researchers and advocates focused on undermatching. Even among this highly select group, low-income students who apply are significantly less likely to max out their curricula in math and English than students in higher-income quartiles.[20] In mathematics, students from the lowest SES quartile were far less likely to max out their coursework—by nearly half a standard deviation—than those of the most affluent students. This disparity could easily be compounded by intersecting disadvantages, as black, Latino, urban, rural, and female applicants are also less likely to max out their curricula.

Maxing out on advanced courses is impossible for students who lack access to them in the first place. The literature on access to advanced coursework in high schools is complex with respect to race, income, and geography. Researchers have found that the socioeconomic composition of a high school's student body is an independent predictor of advanced course offerings, and that students from low-income families are the least likely to have access.[21] Yet when controlling for SES or high school composition, racial diversity modestly increases the likelihood that a school offers advanced coursework.[22] In Florida, schools serving a higher proportion of black or Latino students are slightly more likely (and schools with a higher percentage of Asian students are much more likely) to offer advanced courses than those serving primarily white students.[23] However, lower-income students have consistently less access.[24]

Extracurricular Activities

At the most selective colleges, participation in extracurricular activities also plays a crucial role in admissions.[25] Applications to top colleges are remarkably self-selecting; for admissions readers, file after file contains near-4.0 GPAs, high test scores, and a slew of AP courses. Among these applicants, extracurricular activities often become a distinguishing factor.[26] Obtaining access to a convincing set of extracurricular activities, and the ability to convey their importance in a holistic review, takes a great deal of social and cultural capital. The effects on admission probabilities can be quite substantial. Athletes, for example, are four times more likely to be admitted to elite private institutions than non-athletes.[27]

Unsurprisingly, athletic and extracurricular activity participation are highly stratified due to differences in high school opportunities, financial limitations, parenting styles, and safety issues, among other factors.[28] This is not a particularly deep area of research, but what has been done shows very consistent results. In North Carolina, for example, the percentage of students eligible for free or reduced-price lunch was negatively associated with the number of activities available, particularly academic honors, service opportunities, and sports activities.[29] It is not uncommon for the low-income families of high-achieving students to be unaware of the importance of extracurricular activities, or even to discourage them as a distraction from academic endeavors.[30] Yet in a holistic review, a file with a high GPA, high test scores, and academic rigor is likely to be deemed "qualified, but not admitted" without substantial evidence of leadership in extracurricular activity participation.

Demonstrated Interest

What is most often overlooked by scholars is the importance of demonstrated interest, or the degree to which applicants connect with the institution and express their likelihood to accept an offer of admission. Currently, 20 percent of admissions offices at selective colleges identify demonstrated interest as considerably important in their admissions process.[31] This is an increase from 7 percent in 2003, the first year the question was asked.

Legacy status can be one aspect of demonstrated interest. In the media, admissions officers often downplay its importance, both in terms of the number of applicants it affects and the amount of consideration it receives in the admissions process. An eye-opening study by Michael Hurwitz demonstrates otherwise. Using data from thirty elite, highly competitive colleges, he finds that legacy applicants were more than three times more likely to be admitted, even conditional on all academic factors. At the most selective colleges in his sample, legacy applicants were over five times more likely to be admitted. A primary legacy at these schools—someone whose father or mother attended the school as an undergraduate—was nearly *fifteen times* more likely to be admitted.[32] Due to the history of elite universities, legacy applicants will most often be whiter and wealthier than their non-legacy counterparts.[33]

The holistic admissions process is undoubtedly complex, and it is often portrayed as a game that is relatively unpredictable. But the patterns are clear. When it comes to holistic review, low-income students are at a disadvantage in nearly every element of the process. Even elements designed to improve the odds for low-income applicants—contextualizing the student's course taking in light of the opportunities available in their high school, for example— in the long run simply do not produce greater socioeconomic diversity.

Holistic review has clear implications for policy and practice as they relate to undermatch. When our research and interventions focus only on standardized test scores or grade point averages, we miss many of the important elements in a holistic review process. Success in academics alone is not enough to get students admitted, so raising application rates alone will not solve the undermatch problem. The admissions office is a gatekeeper that cannot be ignored in this discussion.

MARKET COMPETITION: MAXIMIZING REVENUE AND PRESTIGE

Understanding undermatching behavior requires a description of the rapidly changing market for selective college admissions. The increase in selectivity at elite colleges has been well documented, accompanied by increases in the academic credentials not only of students accepted to elite colleges, but also of average students.[34] For example, low-income students have raised their math course taking by a full year (essentially from Algebra I to Algebra II) since 1982. However, math preparation increased by roughly the same amount across all SES quartiles, ensuring that higher-income students maintained their advantage in the competition for admission.

A similar phenomenon can be seen with respect to AP courses. In *Daniel v. State of California*, a group of Inglewood parents sued the state over inequitable access to AP courses, and the state responded by trying to increase access to such courses. A study by Joshua Klugman shows how the attempt was largely successful, with more low-income students enrolled in AP courses. However, higher-income districts increased their offerings as well, ensuring that stratification of academic coursework remained.[35]

Enrollment managers at selective colleges work in this market. For every low-income applicant with high academic qualifications, there are many more applicants with the same qualifications who are willing and able to pay tuition. Thus, admitting low-income students depends not on institutional self-interest, but on serving the public interest, which unfortunately waxes and wanes with available resources. When resources are strong, enrollment managers have more flexibility to admit additional well-qualified low-income students. When resources become constrained, such as during the Great Recession, selective colleges become less socioeconomically diverse in response.

This phenomenon was demonstrated perhaps most dramatically in the rapid rise in out-of-state enrollment at public universities over the last decade. When state appropriations sharply declined, public universities responded in part by increasing the share of out-of-state students they admitted, students who pay tuition prices comparable to private institutions.[36] The impact on enrollment and equity was significant: a smaller proportion of students admitted were low-income, particularly in states with high poverty rates and at the most highly ranked institutions.[37]

Why did institutions choose to increase out-of-state enrollment as a primary revenue strategy? For many public institutions—particularly highly ranked ones—nonresident students can be added without admitting students who are less well prepared. Indeed, in some states, like North Carolina, Virginia, and Michigan, out-of-state applicants have stronger academic profiles than the in-state applicants who were admitted under quotas set by formal or informal policies. Many flagship universities have also experienced a surge in full-pay, international students (particularly from China) who are eager to obtain an American undergraduate degree. The proportion of nonresident students is also relatively opaque to the campus community, and therefore generates relatively little opposition. The decision often seems warranted when it is driven by declines in state support for incoming students.

These patterns are not simply the outcome of consumer choices. On the contrary, they reflect the work of sophisticated enrollment managers who are able to generate these results with regression-driven models—models that allow them to anticipate how a shift in one input will impact other important variables. In particular, these models allow institutions to understand how shifts in merit aid and tuition discounting will shape enrollment and tuition revenue.[38] Although most studies of merit aid focus on state-level programs (like Georgia HOPE), institutional merit aid programs generally reduce the proportion of low-income students on campus.[39] Even National Merit Scholarships have been associated with lower enrollment among low-income students.[40] In the competitive world of college admissions, merit aid is a key tool for enrollment managers.

Enrollment models help to explain the persistence of early admissions and early action programs despite strong, consistent evidence that these programs have negative effects on disadvantaged applicants.[41] An early admissions application is essentially a form of demonstrated interest, because it signals that the applicant has designated the school as his or her first choice. Early admissions candidates are far more likely to enroll, are generally stronger academically, and need less financial aid than regular admission candidates. A low-income applicant, who will likely want to see multiple financial aid options before making a decision, is less likely to submit an early application. Yet early application is correlated with a 20 to 30 point increase in the probability of admission.[42] Unsurprisingly, despite the negative effects of these programs on low-income applicants, fledgling attempts to eliminate them in the 2000s were generally unsuccessful.

The importance of college rankings also cannot be underestimated for the most highly selective institutions. College rankings significantly affect college admissions indicators, such as applications and yield.[43] Interestingly, most students do not report that rankings are a significant influence on their decision making. However, the *perception* among institutions that the rankings are important to students is quite strong.[44] As a result, there are now many examples of institutions and admissions offices gaming statistics to enhance their *U.S. News* rankings.[45]

Unfortunately, prestige-seeking behaviors rarely benefit low-income students. To increase or maintain their ranking, institutions must focus on the specific indicators that are being used. Many of these require huge investments in resources, particularly increases in faculty resources and reducing class size.[46] Those investments must be funded, which at most institutions means increases in tuition, and low-income students are the most price-sensitive. A focus on admissions indicators has the same result—low-income students are less likely to have high standardized test scores and are less likely to enroll if admitted.

An enrollment management perspective also helps to explain the rapid diffusion of test-optional admissions policies since the 1990s. This trend was driven largely by a concern about the relationship between family income and standardized test scores, and has been particularly embraced by private liberal arts colleges. Andrew Belasco, Kelly Rosinger, and James Hearn recently investigated whether test-optional admissions increased racial and socioeconomic diversity at selective liberal arts colleges. Unfortunately, the researchers did not find any causal relationship between the implementation of a test-optional policy and a more economically or racially diverse student body.[47]

This finding is entirely contrary to the widespread claims made by test-optional advocates and somewhat surprising if only admissions and rankings are considered.[48] A test-optional strategy should allow institutions to produce classes that are more racially and socioeconomically diverse without suffering a decline in reputation or rankings. However, this analysis ignores the problem of revenue: every low-income student who enrolls is quite expensive to the institution, so a test-optional policy without concurrent investments in financial aid is unlikely to produce diverse classes. Instead, these schools are more likely to enroll wealthier students with strong grades and weaker test scores.

From an enrollment management perspective, however, a test-optional strategy is still highly effective. The announcement of a test-free option generates positive publicity for the school, and significantly increases applications. Ironically, reported test scores—to *U.S. News & World Report*, for example—actually increase after a test-optional plan, as students with lower test scores choose not to report them. Thus the strategy is win-win for the college, providing positive publicity, increased applications, and higher reported test scores. Meanwhile, schools that simply stop using test scores entirely, as Hampshire College recently did, are punished by going "unranked" by *U.S. News.*[49]

An enrollment management perspective also helps to explain some of the "innovations" we have seen in college admissions practices over the past few years. The most admirable, by Bard College, allows applicants to submit four academic essays that are graded by college faculty; students who earn a B+ or better on all essays are admitted. Bennington College has implemented "dimensional admissions," which allows students to apply for admission by submitting a portfolio rather than traditional application materials.

The most outlandish scheme comes from Goucher College, which has implemented "transcript-free admissions." Goucher now allows applicants to submit a two-minute video, "an example of your best work," and a single graded writing assignment in lieu of evidence of academic achievement ("There's no need to create anything new!").[50] Its marketing video, which begins with a student ripping up a high school transcript, emphasizes how Goucher cares about each applicant as a "unique person" and assures them that, at Goucher, "you are more than just a number." (The fact that Goucher has been test-optional for over five years goes unmentioned.) Thus the admissions application, which had been relatively standardized, has itself become a form of public relations and marketing.

Goucher and Bennington are thrilled with the results. Although very few applicants have used these options (less than one hundred at each institution), regular applications have hit record highs. Early admissions applications were up 12 percent at Goucher and more than 60 percent at Bennington since implementation.[51] For small liberal arts colleges, we might expect that these sorts of public relations efforts will become more common as schools attempt to build a niche and expand enrollment in a sector that seems to be under serious threat. The recent closing (and subsequent reopening) of Sweet

Briar College will undoubtedly serve as a warning to many institutions that they ignore enrollment management strategies at their peril.

The pressures on enrollment managers to increase applications, yield a class, and generate revenue have become enormous. Chief enrollment officers make or break their careers on measures of marketing and reputation—increased applications, increased test scores, increased rankings—rather than measures of equity or diversity. In recent years, dozens of enrollment managers have been fired for failing to meet expectations, and others are quitting the profession due to stress and anxiety.[52] Enrollment managers are often blamed on campus for pursuing goals that were set by presidents and boards. College presidents can publicly claim that they want more racially and economically diverse incoming classes, while privately demanding that their chief enrollment officer increase tuition revenue and prestige. Enrollment managers become the faceless, pragmatic technocrats of the institution, while everyone else gets to pretend that all enrollment goals can be pursued simultaneously.

IMPLICATIONS FOR COLLEGE UNDERMATCH

To this point, this chapter has made the case that understanding the nuances of holistic admissions, enrollment management, and the competitive higher education market is crucial to addressing undermatching among low-income students. Increasing application rates alone is not a panacea, and a single, low-cost intervention cannot compensate for equitable admissions and enrollment practices.

But there is an important contrary argument to consider. If experiments are shown to increase applications and enrollment, does that not demonstrate that selective colleges are willing and able to admit an increased number of low-income students? There are two problems with this argument. First, there is the *replacement* problem: there are a substantial number of low-income students who have been admitted to highly selective colleges who, when considered by predictive admissions models, have actually been overmatched. That is, colleges admitted these students with weaker academic credentials than are typical for that college. Given the existing set of applications, this admissions practice was necessary to produce even a modest level of socioeconomic diversity in the incoming class. However, if high-achieving, low-income students begin to apply in substantial numbers, these overmatched students can be replaced by higher-achieving students, improving match but failing to increase the overall number of low-income students enrolled on campus. This may help to explain why, for example, QuestBridge cannot be shown to improve socioeconomic diversity in partner colleges.[53]

The second problem is even more important—the question of *scale*. Adding a few additional low-income students is not existentially threatening to highly resourced colleges. However, greater numbers of low-income students are associated with greater costs, and pressures will mount on enrollment managers to produce classes that generate a specific revenue target and meet enrollment targets for legacies, athletes, students of color, special talents, and other priorities. Given that enrollment in highly selective colleges is a zero-sum game—as they have shown no desire to grow enrollment—the solution to these problems is replacing overmatched low-income applicants with higher-achieving, better-matched low-income applicants.

Thus, increasing applications by low-income students is necessary but not sufficient. What should be done to intervene on the institutional side? The simplest answer is money—additional resources to cover the cost of enrolling more low-income students. Institutions would be happy to admit more low-income students if they came with state and federal resources to support their education. Federal policy could be used to incentivize institutions to enroll low-income students by providing specific bonuses, and state policy could include low-income student enrollment and graduation in funding formulas. Thus, for each low-income student who enrolls and graduates, more state appropriations flow to the institution. That provides a specific and targeted incentive for institutions to change their behavior.

Unfortunately, the existing financial incentives often exacerbate undermatching behavior. Lower-status institutions often provide merit scholarships to higher-performing students, and low-income students are the most likely to respond to these incentives. Even state-level policies, like Tennessee Achieves, seem more likely to produce undermatching among low-income students.[54] For all of the possible benefits of providing free community college education, one of the detriments is very likely to be fewer low-income students beginning their education at four-year colleges, and the most selective colleges admit shockingly few community college transfer students.[55] Any move to increase community college enrollment is thus likely to increase stratification and undermatching. If tuition were eliminated at all public colleges and universities—funded by a financial transactions tax, for example— we would most likely reduce stratification and increase graduation rates.[56]

We also need to investigate further the question of *fidelity*—to what degree do admissions offices use the holistic admissions practices they claim? In a recent study, 95 percent of admissions officers at selective colleges said they used holistic review.[57] In theory, the key to holistic admissions is contextualizing student performance within the opportunities available in that student's family and high school. Ideally, this practice should yield improved results for disadvantaged students. However, the move to holistic review in selective college admissions offices has not yielded increases in representation of low-income students, and implementation does not seem to be pervasive.[58]

One intriguing possibility is to design interventions focused on the decision-making process in admissions offices. In my fieldwork at flagship university admissions offices, I identified two cognitive biases that influence decision making: anchoring bias and correspondence bias.[59] *Anchoring bias,* or the undue influence of even arbitrary numbers on the estimation of other quantities, potentially plays a role in the disproportionate influence of standardized test scores on admissions decisions. *Correspondence bias,* or our tendency to attribute decisions to dispositions rather than contexts, potentially plays a role in the discounting of high school and family context, even in holistic review processes.

These biases can be shaped in organizations, however, through the use of *cognitive repairs* that seek to use organizational routines to reduce normal human biases.[60] In my fieldwork, I found that one admissions office was very effective in using cognitive repairs by monitoring the language used by admissions officers in discussing applications, preventing premature closure of decisions before all information was considered, and providing scoring data to readers so that they could identify outliers and self-correct scoring biases. The result was more equitable treatment of the applications from low-income students.[61] Although these repairs varied in their effectiveness—and were often themselves subject to other biases—they give us a sense of what may be possible through future examination of decision-making processes.

Ultimately, the answer to the undermatch problem is not one thing; it is everything. We need interventions that encourage low-income students to examine all of their options, and we need to pave the way through counseling, recruitment, and incentives. Institutional leaders need to intervene in admissions, ensuring that low-income students are treated fairly, considering fully the opportunities they have had to succeed. These interventions should be paired with targeted financial aid interventions at the federal, state, and institutional levels, so that low-income students can afford the education provided by selective institutions and that institutions can afford to admit them.

Most likely, given the degree of overmatching we see in the data, we may well need forms of class-based affirmative action to bring enrollment of low-income students anywhere close to their proportion among high school graduates.[62] Perfect matching is simply inadequate—both in terms of increasing enrollment and in increasing bachelor's degree attainment.[63] However, if selective institutions added more places for low-income students—if they did not treat their enrollments as fixed—we could increase low-income bachelor's degree attainment by about thirty-five hundred students per year without declines in prestige or average academic achievement.[64] There are solutions; if we are serious about these issues, aggressive interventions will be necessary.

These are problems worth addressing. Undermatching is an important issue not only for the students affected, but also for American public policy. By nearly every measure, low-income and students of color benefit disproportionately from enrollment in selective colleges, and their communities benefit disproportionately as well.[65] We are closer now than ever to having significant answers to these challenges, but they will require thoughtful reflection, sustained efforts, and significant financial investments.

7

On Undermatch and College Cost

A Case Study of the Pittsburgh Promise

Lindsay C. Page and Jennifer E. Iriti

P opular press and educational policy efforts have recently paid substantial attention to a seemingly counterintuitive set of facts.[1] High-achieving high school students from low-income families often attend lower-selectivity postsecondary institutions than those for which they are academically qualified. Yet these students would likely benefit both academically and financially by attending the most selective institution to which they could gain admission, precisely because they are qualified for admission to highly selective colleges and universities. These institutions invest more per student in undergraduate education. Further, low-income, high-achieving students who attend highly selective colleges and universities typically pay little to attend them. This is owing to generous need-based financial aid that the schools are able to provide, in contrast to the less selective institutions that students from low-income backgrounds more typically attend.[2]

These facts provide powerful motivation for efforts to improve access to the highest-caliber postsecondary institutions for students from low-income backgrounds. Nevertheless, as noted in chapter 4, these facts may be limited in their generalizability and potential to drive broad improvement in college match, given their focus on a narrow slice of the student population. The standard for being designated as high-achieving—1300 on the SAT or 28 on the ACT—is reached by only 10 percent of test-takers, and nearly 60 percent of high school students never take either college entrance assessment.[3]

A question that naturally follows is whether these same facts apply for low-income students across a wider range of academic preparation. When considering the prices that these students would face—net of grant-based financial aid—to attend college, is it an optimal strategy to attend the most selective institution to which they can gain access? Is the best academic match also the best choice financially? The reality is that for these students, the picture is much less clear. Caroline Hoxby and Sarah Turner illustrate that net price faced by low-income students is inversely related to college selectivity among the top several tiers of institutions.[4] This is not so, however, elsewhere in the distribution. Outside of the most selective institutions, a trade-off exists between net price and college selectivity; net prices are higher at higher-caliber institutions. This is true both for low-income and non-low-income students, although the differential in net price for attending a higher-selectivity institution is larger for higher-income students.[5]

For students outside of the highest levels of academic achievement, attending a less selective institution may seem sensible, at least in managing the immediate challenge of paying for higher education. Yet given that lower-selectivity institutions also have lower rates of student success, the dilemma is clear: if college prices—perceived and actual—drive college choice, they may lead students to choose schools where they are less likely to be successful, especially if cost overshadows other factors like institutional supports or students' qualifications and goals. This potential dilemma motivates our investigation into whether a reduction in the net price of higher education can shift students' choices about whether and where to pursue postsecondary education.

Specifically, we consider the relationship between college financing and college match, drawing on rich quantitative and qualitative data from the Pittsburgh Public Schools (PPS). Pittsburgh provides a useful context, given that in 2007 the city began the Pittsburgh Promise program ("the Promise"), a place-based scholarship program focused on providing every student who graduates from PPS and meets certain benchmarks with financial assistance for college. Today, the Promise provides PPS graduates meeting modest GPA and attendance criteria up to $10,000 per year for up to four years of postsecondary education.[6] We investigate the extent to which the program's advent impacted students' postsecondary trajectories to shed light on the extent to which generous and well-publicized financial aid can influence students' postsecondary match. If postsecondary costs are a driver of students' college choices and institutional match, we should expect to see significantly lower rates of postsecondary undermatch in the years since the Promise was first introduced.

To preview our findings, our analyses indicate that the implementation of the Promise led to higher rates of college-going for PPS graduates. Over time and at the margin of Promise eligibility, PPS students were more likely to attend four-year institutions and persist through the first two years of college.[7] The generosity of the Promise was phased in over time. By the time it reached its full award level, students were not only more likely to continue to college but also more likely to match and less likely to undermatch to their chosen postsecondary institution. At the margin of eligibility, the influence of the Promise on postsecondary undermatch was less clear. We hypothesize that this may have been due to the timing with which Promise awards were finalized and the consequent uncertainty of these "marginal" recipients as to whether they would have access to Promise funds.

Our qualitative evidence underscores that the availability of the Promise increased students' and parents' belief that some form of postsecondary education was financially possible; made "next tier" schools more affordable; and encouraged students to remain in Pennsylvania for postsecondary education. Despite improved perceptions of college affordability, evidence suggests that students still lack information regarding the complexities of financial aid and the true costs they will likely face during the process of college search and application. Therefore, it may be that the size of the Promise scholarship provides a strong enough signal about college affordability rather than serving as motivation for families to look beyond institutional sticker prices. If students are not taking likely costs into consideration at the time of selection and application, they may nevertheless end up with a choice set of institutions that are not financially viable, despite the availability of the Promise.

In the section that follows, we provide background on trends in college pricing nationally and specific to Pennsylvania, introduce the Pittsburgh context, and provide details on the Pittsburgh Promise. We then detail our quantitative and qualitative data collection and analysis. We close with a discussion of learnings from this analysis and implications for research and policy going forward.

COLLEGE PRICING OVER TIME

Over the last several years, annual published tuition and fees (or "sticker prices") have increased dramatically for all sectors and types of postsecondary institutions (see figure 7.1). A primary driver of these increases has been

FIGURE 7.1   Average published sticker price (including room and board) for US colleges and universities by institutional sector and type (1990–1991 to 2014–2015)

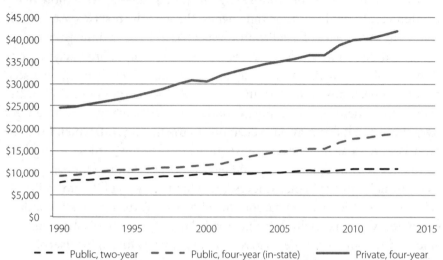

Source: This figure provides a graphical representation of data presented in Sandy Baum, Diane Cardenas Elliott, and Jennifer Ma, *Trends in Student Aid 2014* (New York: College Board, 2014), table 7.

Note: Trends illustrated in 2013 constant dollars.

changes in the relative sources of institutional revenue.[8] While state and local investment in higher education has historically kept tuition increases in check, public investment in public higher education has not kept pace with increasing enrollments.[9] Pennsylvania is a case in point, with state appropriations plunging from two-thirds to one-quarter of institutional revenues for its public colleges and universities between 1984 and 2014.[10] These declines in public investment have contributed to making public higher education costlier in Pennsylvania, compared with most US states.

As greater responsibility for higher education financing has shifted to students and families, financial aid policy has responded to target aid to those who need assistance with managing costs. Today, the majority of college students receive some aid, with billions being invested from all sources, including federal and state governments as well as institutional and private sources. Even so, increases in grant-based financial aid have not kept pace with sticker prices. With the exception of the public, two-year sector, average prices net of grant-based financial aid have increased over the past two

FIGURE 7.2   Average net price (including room and board) for US colleges and universities by institutional sector and type (1990–1991 to 2014–2015)

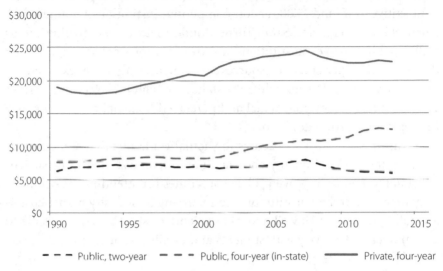

- - - Public, two-year   – – – Public, four-year (in-state)   ———— Private, four-year

Source: This figure provides a graphical representation of data presented in Sandy Baum, Diane Cardenas Elliott, and Jennifer Ma, *Trends in Student Aid 2014* (New York: College Board, 2014), table 7.

Note: Trends illustrated in 2013 constant dollars.

decades (figure 7.2), in turn placing pressure on students to borrow to cover costs. Given its relatively high college sticker prices, it should come as no surprise that Pennsylvania ranks third-highest in terms of average student debt, with the typical graduate of a state-owned or state-related institution amassing $30,000 in educational loans.[11]

The current system of college pricing directs financial risk to students if they take on educational loans and has led to increased variability in what individual students pay out of pocket to attend a given institution. Therefore, more responsibility is placed on students to understand and navigate the increasingly complex landscape of financial aid. Indeed, several aid-related barriers hinder postsecondary access, including a lack of information; discrepancies between actual versus perceived affordability; and the complexity of the application process itself.[12] These barriers are most prevalent for students from the lowest-income backgrounds and likely contribute to their higher rates of institutional undermatch.[13]

Shifts in sources of institutional revenue have brought with them an increase in the variation of per student expenditures across institutions. As

Caroline Hoxby and Sarah Turner have shown, variation in instructional expenditures per student is dramatic, ranging from over $25,000 at the most competitive to around $5,000 at non-competitive institutions.[14] John Bound, Michael Lovenheim, and Sarah Turner found that two-year institutions as well as public four-year institutions outside of the top tier have experienced declines in their per-student resources and, concurrently, declines in rates of degree completion.[15] Thus, while the stakes are high for selecting the right postsecondary institution, actual and perceived financial constraints may hinder students from doing so.

Focus on sticker price obscures the actual trade-offs that students face between institutional quality and cost. Low-income students, in particular, stand to realize improved college outcomes for attending even a modestly higher-selectivity institution and incurring a modestly higher cost as a result.[16] As Jessica Howell and Matea Pender ask, if it were possible to communicate effectively with students and families about actual net price, would this solve the problem?

Financial Aid and the Timing of Undermatch

A key insight from the postsecondary match literature is the attribution of undermatch primarily to actions of students rather than of institutions. Research evidence broadly agrees that undermatch occurs at two stages in the college-going process: when students identify the institutions to which to apply, and when students select an institution from those to which they have been admitted. Undermatch at the exploration phase is somewhat more prevalent among low-income students.[17] These patterns are consistent with the hypothesis that informational barriers (for example, accurate information about college cost and financing) play a key role in postsecondary match. Indeed, even among very high-performing students, those from low-income backgrounds are more likely to undermatch, especially when they are geographically isolated from other high-achieving peers.[18]

Given these facts, what role do *actual* college costs and *perceptions* about college financing play in students' postsecondary search and choice behavior (and, as a result, the rate of undermatch)? From an intervention standpoint, it may be most important to address perceptions about college pricing at the time of application—ensuring that students don't rule out institutions based on assumptions or even ballpark estimates of net price.[19] Actual net prices may weigh more heavily at the college selection stage, when students may be surprised by the generosity of aid they receive or face being "gapped" and negotiating unmet financial need.

The Pittsburgh Promise may impact student decision making at both stages, especially given the current size of the benefit and the place-based nature of its implementation. Clear messaging about the scholarship may motivate qualified students to apply to institutions previously considered unaffordable, and the scholarship itself reduces the out-of-pocket college expenses that students face.

Pittsburgh Public Schools and the Pittsburgh Promise

The Pittsburgh Promise is a place-based scholarship program that supports postsecondary education for students who graduate from PPS and city-based charter high schools.[20] It went into operation with the graduating class of 2008 with significant support from local industry and foundation funders, including $100 million from the University of Pittsburgh Medical Center and contributions of over $10 million each from the Grable Foundation, the Heinz Endowments, and The Pittsburgh Foundation, among many others.[21]

Several ambitious goals guided the establishment of the Promise: to support PPS student success; reform educational systems; help stabilize city and school populations; and act as an engine for an invigorated workforce and volunteer corps. At the time of our writing, the Promise's signature feature was the offer of up to $10,000 per year (for four years) to attend any Pennsylvania postsecondary institution (public or private) that awards a degree, license, or diploma for PPS graduates who meet specific academic, attendance, and residency requirements.[22]

The eligibility criteria and total award amount were phased in over the first five cohorts of students (figure 7.3). The program now includes two award types. "Core scholars" have met all eligibility criteria and are able to use Promise dollars as described. "Extension scholars" have a GPA between 2.0 and 2.49 and are able to use funds to attend the local community college for one year. Upon attaining certain performance goals, extension scholars can attend any other eligible institution.

Promise funds are a *last dollar resource*—students must first complete the Free Application for Federal Student Aid (FAFSA) and apply for federal, state, and institutional aid. Should these sources cover the costs of postsecondary attendance (including tuition, fees, books, and room and board), students may still receive an award of up to $1,000 per year. Students apply for the

FIGURE 7.3   Pittsburgh Promise eligibility criteria by PPS graduating cohort

	Phase I	Phase II	Phase III		Phase IV
Cohort	2007–2008	2008–2009	2009–2010	2010–2011	2011–2012+
Qualifying postsecondary institution	State-funded and private institutions in Allegheny County offering two- or four-year degree programs		All degree-, license-, or diploma-granting public and private institutions in Pennsylvania (300+)		
GPA minimum	2.0	2.25	Core scholars: 2.5 Extension scholars: 2.0 to 2.49		
Attendance minimum	None	85%	90%		
Residence requirement	75% of full scholarship for continuous enrollment since ninth grade, increasing to 100 percent for continuous enrollment since kindergarten				
Award amount	$5,000/year for up to four years				$10,000/year for up to four years

Source: Gabriella C. Gonzalez et al., *Fulfilling the Pittsburgh Promise* (Pittsburgh: RAND Education, 2011), www.rand.org/content/dam/rand/pubs/monographs/2011/RAND_MG1139.pdf.

Promise in the spring of their senior year and are notified of their award the summer after high school graduation. To maintain eligibility, students must maintain a 2.0 college GPA and a full-time course load.

The Pittsburgh Promise has a robust information campaign to promote college-going and educate students and families about the scholarship criteria, awards, and use constraints. This outreach includes direct work with high school counselors, communication with other school staff, and building the capacity of upperclassmen to serve as "Promise Ambassadors" within the high schools.

During the 2014–2015 academic year, the Pennsylvania State Grant program awarded a maximum grant of $4,011, while the maximum federal Pell award was $5,730.[23] In sum, the lowest-income students who meet the current Promise eligibility criteria can access nearly $20,000 annually in grant-based financial support for college.[24] Thus, Promise eligibility has a dramatic impact on the out-of-pocket costs of higher education. Specifically, this combination of benefits implies that low-income Promise-eligible students could attend an in-state, public four-year institution at essentially no cost. While information-related barriers may still hinder students from capitalizing on this benefit, if postsecondary costs are a driver of undermatching in terms of institutional selectivity, we should expect to see significantly lower rates of postsecondary undermatch as a result of the Promise.[25]

DATA AND ANALYSIS

We examined this hypothesis from quantitative and qualitative perspectives. Quantitatively, we compared college-going outcomes and rates of postsecondary undermatch for PPS students from the graduating class of 2007—the year prior to the Promise's implementation—to those from its inception in 2008 to its full implementation by 2012. In addition, we examined students near the margin of Promise eligibility to compare and contrast the college-going outcomes of students who just made and just missed the Promise criteria. We coupled quantitative results with qualitative evidence on the experiences of PPS students and counselors as well as current Promise recipients to describe how the Promise influenced postsecondary exploration and decision-making.

We drew on quantitative data from three sources. First, PPS administrative records provided information on students' enrollment history, demographic characteristics, academic achievement, and school behavior, including indicators utilized to determine Promise eligibility. Second, using data from the National Student Clearinghouse (NSC), we observed students' college-going outcomes. NSC records allowed us to observe whether and where students continued to postsecondary education on a semester-by-semester basis. Our data included students from the PPS graduating classes of 2007 through 2012.[26] Because PPS only obtains NSC records for district graduates, we excluded from our analysis students who failed to graduate from PPS due either to dropout or transfer out of the district. Third, data furnished by the Pittsburgh Promise allowed us to identify those students who actually received Promise funding and the level of that funding on an annual basis.

We additionally gathered qualitative data from PPS counselors and high school seniors as well as from college students currently receiving Promise funding. First, we conducted hour-long interviews with ten school counselors from seven of PPS's nine high schools to investigate support practices related to college exploration, application, and selection. Second, 800 class of 2015 Promise applicants were invited to participate in an online survey; 205 of these students did so. Finally, we invited Promise recipients who had just completed their first year at either the local community college or one of the state-owned institutions to participate in a forty-five-minute phone interview. We completed interviews with thirty students. Both the Promise-recipient interviews and Promise applicant surveys focused on students' experiences exploring, applying to, and selecting a postsecondary institution, and whether and in what ways the availability of the Promise influenced these processes.

Descriptive Statistics

Our quantitative data included 9,665 students across six cohorts of PPS graduates (descriptive statistics are shown in table 7.1). PPS graduating classes have larger shares of females than males (54 percent female, on average). Across the years, 52 percent of graduates are black and 43 percent are white, with far smaller shares of students identifying as Asian, Latino, or multiracial.

TABLE 7.1 Descriptive statistics for Pittsburgh Public School high school graduates, 2007–2012

Variable	Mean
Female	0.54
Black	0.52
White	0.43
Asian	0.02
Hispanic	0.01
Multiracial	0.03
Low SES	0.60
SAT taken	0.57
SAT mathematics score	441 (108)
SAT verbal score	433 (109)
GPA	2.62 (0.73)
Attendance rate	0.93 (0.08)

Source: Pittsburgh Public Schools administrative records for graduating classes of 2007–2012.

Note: N = 9,665. Cells present simple means calculated across the graduating classes. Means only are presented for binary variables. Means and standard deviations in parentheses are presented for continuous variables.

At the high school level, school-meals status is a poor proxy for socioeconomic status. Instead, we linked students to zip code level socioeconomic metrics from the American Community Survey, with which we build a composite measure of neighborhood socioeconomic status.[27] We then dichotomize this measure to identify students living in predominantly low-income versus better-off neighborhoods. While a community-level measure, we use the shorthand "low income" to refer to students residing in low-income neighborhoods. With this strategy, we identify 60 percent of PPS graduates as low-income.[28]

Finally, we report on SAT-taking among PPS graduates. Across cohorts, approximately three of every five graduates take the SAT. Because we use SAT scores to determine postsecondary match (described below), we impute scores for those who did not actually sit for the exam. Therefore, the average SAT scores that we report include both actual and imputed scores.[29]

The average SAT scores of 441 in mathematics and 433 in critical reading place the typical PPS graduate at approximately the twenty-fifth percentile of all SAT test-takers. Thus, the focal population in Pittsburgh is similar, on average, to that considered in chapter 8, in which Joshua Goodman, Michael Hurwitz, and Jonathan Smith examine students near the thresholds of eligibility for attending an institution within the Georgia State University System.[30] It is quite different from the high-achieving, low-income students targeted by the Expanding College Opportunity effort.[31]

Defining College Readiness and Postsecondary Match

Our definition of match is similar to that used by Caroline Hoxby and Christopher Avery and by Jessica Howell and Matea Pender.[32] Specifically, we compared each student's SAT performance (actual or imputed) to the median SAT performance of students attending their postsecondary institution as reported in the Integrated Postsecondary Education Data System (IPEDS). We defined students as "undermatched" if they attended an institution with a median SAT performance more than 15 percentile points below their individual scores. Otherwise, we designated college enrollers as matched. We considered students to be appropriately matched to a two-year institution if their combined math and critical reading SAT score was below 800.[33]

Basic Patterns of Enrollment and Undermatch

The outcomes on which we focused pertained to direct-to-college enrollment in the year after high school graduation. Among PPS students who continued to college, most did so directly. Therefore, expanding the allow-able time frame for first enrollment did not change results qualitatively. Across the cohorts examined, 53 percent of graduates continued directly to postsecondary education (see figure 7.4). Of college-goers, 30 percent continued to two-year institutions (primarily the Community College of Allegheny County), and 70 percent attended four-year institutions. While nearly three hundred colleges and universities are represented in the data, nearly three-quarters of the four-year college-goers matriculated to one of twenty institutions, including the four Pennsylvania state-related institu-tions, six of the fourteen state universities, and other private colleges in and around Pittsburgh. Greater shares of PPS students attended public institu-tions, and the majority stayed within Pennsylvania.

Figure 7.5 presents basic descriptive statistics on postsecondary under-match and match.[34] The top portion considers students eligible for or who attended a two-year institution, and the bottom portion is analogous with respect to four-year institutions. Eight percent of students were well matched at a two-year institution, and another 8 percent were undermatched in this

FIGURE 7.4   College enrollment outcomes for Pittsburgh Public School high school graduates, 2007–2012

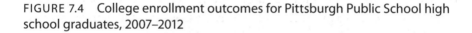

Of all students who continue to postsecondary education

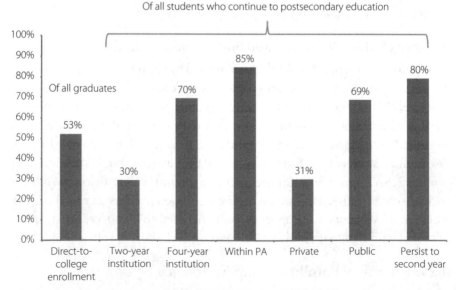

Source: Pittsburgh Public Schools and the National Student Clearinghouse.

sector. Of those who enrolled in four-year institutions, a remarkably small share was undermatched. Rather, among four-year college-goers, many continued to institutions where the typical students exceeded their own SAT-based qualifications. Most notably, the majority of undermatch occurred because students failed to continue to postsecondary education at all. In sum, 40 percent of students matched to postsecondary institutions while the majority (60 percent) undermatched. Of those who undermatched, one in five did so by attending a mismatched institution, and four in five did so by not continuing to college. These findings were consistent with national patterns revealing that undermatch is due primarily to non-enrollment.[35]

To investigate the relationship between college match and cost, we capitalized on the introduction and phase-in of the Pittsburgh Promise, which represented a dramatic and sudden reduction in the out-of-pocket costs that eligible students would face to pursue postsecondary education. Across the years examined, more than half of PPS graduates met the eligibility requirements and over a third received Promise funding in the year following high school graduation.

FIGURE 7.5 College match outcomes for Pittsburgh Public School high school graduates, 2007–2012

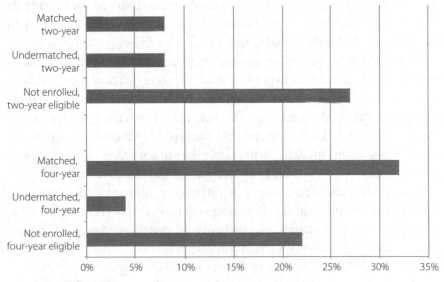

Source: Pittsburgh Public Schools and the National Student Clearinghouse.

Trends over Time

Here, we examine trends in college-going outcomes across the four phases of the Promise. Phases I, II and III correspond to the graduating classes of 2008, 2009, and 2010 and 2011, respectively. Phase IV corresponds to the class of 2012. With each change in phase, stringency of the eligibility requirements increased and, with Phase IV, the maximum grant amount also increased (as seen in figure 7.3). We limited our comparisons to groups of students who graduated from the same high school.[36] In addition, we controlled for student gender, race/ethnicity, and socioeconomic status to limit our comparison to students who are similar, at least with respect to these characteristics.[37] Tables A7.1, A7.2, A7.3, and A7.4 in the appendix to this chapter present our quantitative findings, which we summarize here.

For students overall, we found that compared with the class of 2007, the "typical" PPS graduate in all later classes (and Promise phases) had a greater likelihood of continuing on to postsecondary education. These overall effects were driven primarily by increased enrollment in four-year rather than two-year institutions, particularly when the Promise was increased to $10,000 annually (Phase IV). By Phase IV, impacts on four-year enrollment were larger than impacts on enrollment overall, indicating that students were enrolling at higher rates and shifting from two-year to four-year institutions. Where we observed impacts on overall enrollment, impacts on in-state enrollment are greater. Thus, Promise funding also induced some students to stay in Pennsylvania for postsecondary education, a pattern similar to that observed by Sarah Cohodes and Joshua Goodman in Massachusetts.[38]

Consistent with the shift in student preferences toward four-year institutions, we observed that, over time, students were not only more likely to enroll in college, but also were shifting away from undermatched institutions and toward matched institutions. This was again particularly so in Promise Phase IV. Compared with 2007, by 2012 the typical PPS graduate was nearly 8 percentage points more likely to matriculate to a matched institution and 2.3 percentage points less likely to matriculate but undermatch.

Finally, we examined changes in rates of enrollment and persistence through the second year of college. Improvements were consistent with at least three potential underlying mechanisms: match, academic effort, and affordability. For students attending better-matched institutions, existing research predicts that improved persistence and completion would result.[39] Academically, students needed a minimum college GPA of 2.0 to maintain Promise eligibility. This requirement might have motivated stronger academic effort.[40] Finally, Promise funding might have made college continuation more tenable financially.

Next, we examined these trends separately for low-income and non-low income students. For the class of 2007 graduates, students from low-income backgrounds had a 45 percent chance of continuing to postsecondary education, compared with 57 percent for their non-low-income counterparts. Nevertheless, for both groups, college enrollment rates improved over time by a similar margin of 5 to 6 percentage points. For low-income students, four-year enrollment improved significantly only in the final phase of the Promise, whereas for non-low income students, the shift towards four-year institutions was more immediate. For both groups, implementation of the Promise increased students' preferences toward Pennsylvania institutions and improved rates with which students completed two years of college. Also for both groups, and particularly during the later Promise phases, improvements in the combined outcome of enrollment and match were as large as or larger than the impact on college enrollment overall. Thus, regardless of socioeconomic status, the Promise was not only inducing more students to continue to college but also affording some who would enroll in college regardless of the opportunity to attend a better-matched institution.

Changes in students' approach to college search, application, and selection may have driven improvements in match rates over time. Counselors informed students and families that the Promise would make possible some form of postsecondary education for all recipients, and our qualitative data on student perceptions and experiences indeed revealed that, depending on student characteristics, the Promise's advent put "college on the table" and changed college consideration in three ways. First, it made college an option when it had not previously seemed financially viable. Second, it made attendance at a four-year institution a possibility when previously only the community college was perceived to be financially within reach. Third, it made higher-tier (and more expensive) schools possible. In addition to these "college possibility shifts," there was also a distinct move to considering Pennsylvania options, since the Promise could only be used in-state. In short, the awareness of the funds changed whether and what types of postsecondary institutions students considered.

On the Margin of Eligibility

The trends in college-going for the typical PPS graduate were consistent with the notion that the Promise's implementation would improve enrollment outcomes by improving perceptions of college affordability, reducing out-of-pocket expenses, and motivating improved academic preparation and college-readiness in successive cohorts of PPS graduates. To take a more fine-grained look at the Promise's impact, we also examined changes in college-going outcomes at the margins of Promise eligibility. As noted, over time, eligibility criteria became more rigorous. For example, in 2008, Promise eligibility for funds was contingent on a minimum GPA of 2.0. By 2012, students had to have earned a minimum GPA of 2.5 and a school attendance rate of at least 90 percent. In all years where an attendance criterion was imposed (2009–2012), the vast majority of students met the minimum, while GPA remained a binding constraint for eligibility. For these years, we dropped from our analysis the small number of students who did not meet the attendance criterion. In addition, because students had to have been enrolled in PPS from at least the ninth grade through graduation to be eligible, we did not include those who first entered PPS after ninth grade. We therefore focus on the threshold of Promise eligibility determined by student GPA and use a regression-based strategy to compare college enrollment outcomes for those students who just missed or just achieved the GPA criterion.[41]

Generally, the impacts for students who just meet the eligibility criteria were similar to those that we observe for cohorts overall. For the first two cohorts (years 2008 and 2009), students who were just eligible were 43 percentage points more likely to receive Promise funds than those who just missed the GPA criterion. Marginally eligible students were 7 percentage points more likely to continue to any college, the greatest effect being a positive impact on enrollment in a four-year institution. For students at this margin, impacts on college enrollment were driven primarily by students enrolling and matching to their postsecondary institution.

For the graduating classes of 2010, 2011, and 2012, eligibility for the full Promise required achieving a GPA of 2.5 or above. Students who met the attendance requirement but who earned a GPA between 2.0 and 2.49 were eligible for an extension scholarship to begin postsecondary education at the Community College of Allegheny County. In analyses not included in the appendix tables, we found that just meeting the 2.0 GPA requirement had little impact on any of the postsecondary outcomes examined here. Therefore, we focused on students at the margin of full Promise eligibility. Because students below the 2.5 threshold were eligible for some financial support (which explicitly encouraged community college attendance), we expected patterns of impact to differ before and after the graduating class of 2010.

For the classes of 2010 through 2012, students who just met the 2.5 GPA threshold were 31 percentage points more likely to receive Promise funds, compared with the estimated 37 percent of students just below the 2.5 threshold. Given the opportunities open to students on either side of the threshold, it is not surprising that full Promise eligibility did not impact overall enrollment at this margin but impacted substantially the type of institution to which students matriculated. Those just eligible for the full Promise were 12 percentage points more likely to continue to a four-year institution. Despite this impact on sector shift, with a large share of students moving away from a two-year institution and into a four-year institution as a result of Promise support, the impact on enrolling to a matched institution was more modest. Therefore, although marginal Promise recipients shifted to four-year institutions as a result of Promise support in these years, they were not necessarily shifting to four-year institutions to which they were well matched.

DISCUSSION

Overall, our findings pointed unequivocally to the conclusion that the Pittsburgh Promise improved students' access to postsecondary education. Over time, both low-income and non-low-income students were more likely to continue to four-year institutions and were more likely to persist through a second year of college. The same general conclusions held when we looked narrowly at the margin of Promise eligibility.

The current combination of generosity and flexibility are likely important components of the Promise as it "interacts" with the higher education market. Both public and private higher education are more expensive in Pennsylvania than in most other states.[42] Thus the ability to utilize Promise funds at both public and private institutions in the state may help to open the doors to these institutions for those who would otherwise consider them out of reach.

What, then, is the impact of the Promise on postsecondary match and what does this tell us about the relationship between cost and match? Over time, consecutive cohorts of PPS students were not only more likely to continue on to postsecondary education, but as the Promise matured, they were also more likely to enroll in matched institutions and less likely to enroll but undermatch. These general patterns held (although are less precisely estimated) regardless of socioeconomic status. Within cohorts at the margin of Promise eligibility, however, the impacts on postsecondary match are more ambiguous. Students were enrolling at higher rates and were more likely to enroll in four-year institutions but not necessarily in those that were well matched. This may relate to the fact that at the margin of Promise eligibility, students were not particularly high performing academically. Therefore, the high school academic performance of these students may have rendered them ineligible for postsecondary institutions for which their SAT scores would suggest that they were well matched. A second possibility is that at the time of college search and selection, students on the margin of eligibility were uncertain about whether they would ultimately be eligible for Promise funds, since they would only be told in the summer after high school graduation—only a few months before on-time college matriculation. A high degree of uncertainty may have hindered students at the margin from changing their approach to college search and selection based on potential eligibility.

While our quantitative data prohibit us from understanding the unique impact of the Promise on college application and selection, our qualitative evidence suggests that issues related to college cost had differential impacts at these two stages in the college-going process. At the stage of deciding where to apply, rigorous consideration of college cost and financing appeared largely absent. Counselor interviews suggested that for PPS students, supports for understanding college cost and financing were neither widespread nor systematically available across the PPS high schools at the time of college exploration. Several counselors believed that because colleges lacked transparency about the price that students would ultimately be expected to pay, it was often hard to factor financial issues into decisions about where to apply. While students did report cost to be a consideration during the college search phase, this did not involve a deep understanding of how financial aid operates and what they might realistically pay after grants and other forms of aid were applied. For example, when we interviewed current Promise recipients, two-thirds indicated that during their college application process, they perceived some institutions to be "out of reach" primarily on the basis of cost. These assessments, however, were based on institutional sticker prices and ballpark expectations of Promise funding. Given the level of funding, the expectation of a $10,000 grant has the potential to influence decision making for those comfortably meeting the eligibility thresholds at the time of college search. Thus, the impact of the Promise at the time of college search and application might stem from the clear and simple message that scholarship funds were available to make college financially viable rather than students gaining a comprehensive understanding of all options available for financing higher education inclusive of the Promise. In sum, while the opportunity of the Promise fostered a broad sense that college could be affordable, even in this context, students could fail to apply to institutions that were both academically matched and financially feasible. In stark contrast, once students were deciding from among those schools to which they have been accepted, our evidence pointed to cost as *the* primary factor at play.

This misalignment in the consideration of cost at the various stages of the college-going process may contribute to undermatching. Relating this to Jonathan Smith and colleagues' finding that undermatch occurs at the phases of application and choosing which college to attend, our findings suggest that actual cost is a key driver of undermatch during the latter phase.[43] At the application phase, students may consider a range of schools, but use only sticker price and their sense of Promise eligibility to guide their decisions. If students do not apply to a match school that is ultimately within their price range, they may end up undermatching by default at the decision stage due to a lack of affordable match options.

While our investigation is Pittsburgh-specific, failure to consider net college cost when applying is likely a more widespread phenomenon. Several factors may contribute. First, developmentally, high-school aged students are overly present-focused.[44] They are likely to overemphasize near-term considerations (for example, which colleges do I like or fit me best?) rather than those that seem further in the future (for instance, how am I going to pay for the college that I decide to attend?). In addition, college financing is challenging to understand and ability to pay is uncertain until financial aid packages are actually offered. When faced with such complexity, students may base decisions on constructs that are more transparent and easier to understand or even rules of thumb.[45] Either factor suggests the need for better information and encouragement for students to learn about and consider issues of financing at the time of college application. Encouragingly, policy shifts currently under way to simplify FAFSA and change the timing of filing may help to resolve the decoupling evident in our qualitative data. A Promise-specific policy shift to encourage students to consider college financing at the time of search and application would be to determine eligibility at the beginning rather than the end of senior year. This might be of particular benefit to those students at the margin of eligibility. More broadly, a key question is to what extent a robust effort to educate students and families about higher education financing at the application stage could have impacts outside of the Promise context or could further magnify the Promise impacts that we observe if well paired.

Indeed, even for Promise recipients, there remain financial barriers to higher education that drive students to turn down well-matched postsecondary options, especially given the high-cost context of Pennsylvania. Even with the Promise and other sources of aid, the full cost of attendance is not met for many students. Many students and counselors report that families are extremely debt-averse, and many lack information about educational loans and repayment models. Counselors expressed what they considered to be an ethical dilemma related to student loan debt. "How can I encourage a student from a low-income background, who may or may not ever earn the college degree, to take on debt to go to a match school rather than go to a lower-tier school for free?" one counselor pondered. This dilemma—the likelihood of a student succeeding in college weighed against the value added of going to a school that requires the student to borrow—can drive counselors to encourage even four-year-qualified students to attend the local community college. With this frame, the guidance is not a manifestation of low expectations, but a practical deliberation about the risks and benefits of debt and potential payoff of a college degree. Some counselors believed "a degree is a degree," regardless of from where it is earned, and did not seem to recognize that chances of degree attainment are higher at higher-quality institutions, perhaps for reasons beyond students' own preparedness or motivation. As one counselor described, I had one student who ". . . was accepted to Penn State's main campus. Bright young lady. When it comes down to it, it was about cost. She ended up going elsewhere [a significantly lower academic tier four-year institution with a substantially lower four-year graduation rate] because her family could not bridge that financial gap. We had to tell her, 'Regardless of where you go, your wonderfulness will stand out.'" Unfortunately, mounting evidence suggests that this is not always the case.

Appendix (Chapter 7)

TABLE A7.1   Change in college enrollment outcomes across Promise phases compared to pre-Promise 2007 cohort, all students

	Any college	Two-year college	Four-year college	Penn-sylvania college	Enroll and under-match	Enroll and match	Enroll and persist through year 2
Phase I	0.021	0.011	0.01	0.023	0.008	0.013	0.037*
	(0.016)	(0.012)	(0.015)	(0.017)	(0.011)	(0.016)	(0.015)
Phase II	0.050**	0.013	0.037*	0.057***	0.017	0.033*	0.065***
	(0.017)	(0.013)	(0.016)	(0.017)	(0.012)	(0.017)	(0.016)
Phase III	0.054**	0.01	0.044*	0.059**	−0.003	0.057**	0.061***
	(0.018)	(0.014)	(0.017)	(0.019)	(0.013)	(0.018)	(0.018)
Phase IV	0.055**	−0.019	0.075***	0.080***	−0.023~	0.079***	0.067***
	(0.018)	(0.014)	(0.018)	(0.019)	(0.012)	(0.019)	(0.018)
Class of 2007 rate	0.497	0.156	0.341	0.410	0.126	0.370	0.380
Fixed effects for high school	✓	✓	✓	✓	✓	✓	✓
Covariate controls	✓	✓	✓	✓	✓	✓	✓
N	9,362	9,362	9,362	9,362	9,362	9,362	9,362
R^2	0.124	0.011	0.156	0.049	0.035	0.082	0.159

Source: Pittsburgh Public Schools, Pittsburgh Promise, and the National Student Clearinghouse.

Note: *$p < 0.05$, ** $p < 0.01$, *** $p < 0.001$. Coefficients presented from linear probability models predicting enrollment outcomes from Promise phase corresponding to high school graduating cohort, fixed effects for high school, and baseline covariates including gender, race/ethnicity and socioeconomic status.

TABLE A7.2   Change in college enrollment outcomes across Promise phases compared to pre-Promise 2007 cohort, low-income students

	Any college	Two-year college	Four-year college	Pennsyl-vania college	Enroll and under-match	Enroll and match	Enroll and persist through year 2
Phase I	−0.005	0.008	−0.013	−0.003	−0.003	−0.002	0.018
	(0.021)	(0.016)	(0.020)	(0.021)	(0.013)	(0.021)	(0.020)
Phase II	0.048*	0.019	0.029	0.052*	0.02	0.028	0.062**
	(0.022)	(0.017)	(0.020)	(0.022)	(0.014)	(0.022)	(0.021)
Phase III	0.055*	0.048*	0.007	0.062*	0.004	0.051*	0.060**
	(0.024)	(0.019)	(0.022)	(0.025)	(0.015)	(0.024)	(0.023)
Phase IV	0.051*	−0.01	0.061**	0.076**	−0.014	0.065**	0.077**
	(0.025)	(0.019)	(0.023)	(0.025)	(0.015)	(0.025)	(0.024)
Class of 2007 rate	0.448	0.146	0.302	0.383	0.102	0.346	0.319
Fixed effects for high school	✓	✓	✓	✓	✓	✓	✓
Covariate controls	✓	✓	✓	✓	✓	✓	✓
N	5,542	5,542	5,542	5,542	5,542	5,542	5,542
R^2	0.102	0.013	0.134	0.054	0.034	0.074	0.136

Source: Pittsburgh Public Schools, Pittsburgh Promise, and the National Student Clearinghouse.

Note: $\sim p < 0.10$, $* p < 0.05$, $** p < 0.01$, $*** p < 0.001$. Coefficients presented from linear probability models predicting enrollment outcomes from Promise phase corresponding to high school graduating cohort, fixed effects for high school, and baseline covariates including gender, race/ethnicity, and socioeconomic status.

TABLE A7.3   Change in college enrollment outcomes across Promise phases compared to pre-Promise 2007 cohort, non-low-income students

	Any college	Two-year college	Four-year college	Penn-sylvania college	Enroll and under-match	Enroll and match	Enroll and persist through year 2
Phase I	0.053*	0.012	0.041~	0.054*	0.023	0.03	0.060*
	(0.024)	(0.020)	(0.025)	(0.026)	(0.020)	(0.026)	(0.025)
Phase II	0.045~	0	0.045~	0.059*	0.012	0.033	0.063*
	(0.026)	(0.020)	(0.026)	(0.028)	(0.020)	(0.027)	(0.026)
Phase III	0.048~	-0.044*	0.092**	0.055~	-0.012	0.060*	0.058*
	(0.028)	(0.021)	(0.028)	(0.030)	(0.022)	(0.029)	(0.028)
Phase IV	0.057*	-0.033	0.090***	0.088**	-0.032	0.089**	0.053~
	(0.027)	(0.021)	(0.027)	(0.029)	(0.021)	(0.029)	(0.027)
Class of 2007 rate	0.572	0.171	0.401	0.451	0.161	0.411	0.472
Fixed effects for high school	✓	✓	✓	✓	✓	✓	✓
Covariate controls	✓	✓	✓	✓	✓	✓	✓
N	3,820	3,820	3,820	3,820	3,820	3,820	3,820
R^2	0.132	0.031	0.171	0.042	0.033	0.1	0.155

Source: Pittsburgh Public Schools, Pittsburgh Promise, and the National Student Clearinghouse.

Note: ~ $p < 0.10$,* $p < 0.05$, ** $p < 0.01$, *** $p < 0.001$. Coefficients presented from linear probability models predicting enrollment outcomes from Promise phase corresponding to high school graduating cohort, fixed effects for high school, and baseline covariates including gender, race/ethnicity, and socioeconomic status.

TABLE A7.4 Impacts of Promise eligibility on Promise receipt, level of funding, and college-going outcomes

	Promise receipt	Promise funds, year 1	Any college	Two-year college	Four-year college	Pennsylvania college	Enroll and persist through year 2	Enroll and match	Enroll and undermatch
Classes 2008–2012, pooled									
Promise eligibility	0.379***	1558.012***	0.046	–0.03	0.077***	0.050~	0.061*	0.047~	–0.001
	(0.024)	(106.945)	(0.029)	(0.026)	(0.022)	(0.029)	(0.026)	(0.027)	(0.019)
Rate just below threshold	0.187	604.42	0.436	0.255	0.180	0.409	0.265	0.305	0.131
N	4852	4852	4852	4852	4852	4852	4852	4852	4852
R^2	0.312	0.411	0.249	0.079	0.358	0.168	0.272	0.201	0.124
Phase I and II: Graduating classes of 2008 and 2009									
Promise eligibility	0.425***	1179.528***	0.066~	0.018	0.048~	0.058	0.070*	0.048	0.018
	(0.027)	(106.776)	(0.036)	(0.032)	(0.027)	(0.036)	(0.031)	(0.034)	(0.024)
Rate just below threshold	0.052	161.19	0.327	0.206	0.121	0.293	0.183	0.219	0.107

Phase III and IV: Graduating classes of 2010 through 2012

Promise eligibility	0.313***	2102.770***	0.019	−0.099*	0.118**	0.039	0.049	0.047	−0.028
	(0.044)	(208.803)	(0.046)	(0.042)	(0.038)	(0.047)	(0.044)	(0.044)	(0.032)
Rate just below threshold	0.366	1094.78	0.600	0.336	0.264	0.572	0.388	0.441	0.160
N	4852	4852	4852	4852	4852	4852	4852	4852	4852
R^2	0.312	0.412	0.249	0.08	0.358	0.168	0.272	0.201	0.124

Source: Pittsburgh Public Schools, Pittsburgh Promise, and the National Student Clearinghouse.

Note: ~ $p < 0.10$, * $p < 0.05$, ** $p < 0.01$, *** $p < 0.001$. Coefficients from linear probability models predicting enrollment outcomes as a function of GPA and Promise eligibility as determined by GPA thresholds. Coefficients represent impact of Promise eligibility at the year-relevant eligibility threshold. Data restricted to students who meet year-relevant attendance requirements for eligibility. Models include Table 1 covariates, school-by-year fixed effects and year-specific slopes. Regressions fitted within +/− 1.35 GPA point bandwidth. In 2010–2012, lower threshold extends to −0.50 GPA points due to introduction of the Extension Scholars program. Outcome rates just below the GPA threshold pertain to fitted values for students within 0.20 GPA points below the year-relevant threshold.

The Effect of State Policy on College Choice and Match

Shaping Students' Choices

Joshua S. Goodman, Michael Hurwitz, and Jonathan Smith

S tates play a critical role in the US higher education system, both by funding colleges and students and by regulating various aspects of the college admissions process.[1] This chapter summarizes existing research on a variety of state higher education policies, with a focus on the effect of such policies on students' college enrollment choices, the quality of the colleges they attend, and their degree completion rates. We pay particular attention to the match between a student's academic skills and chosen college, in part because state policies most affect disadvantaged students. Such students undermatch, or choose colleges where their peers have lower academic skills than they do, more frequently than do their more advantaged peers. We emphasize the importance of evaluating state policies not only on the basis of how they affect enrollment rates but also by the extent to which they connect students to colleges that give them the greatest chance of completing their degrees.[2]

This chapter addresses four broad types of state policies that influence students' college enrollment and academic match: in-kind spending—the subsidies that states provide to their public colleges; financial aid, both need- and merit-based, that states provide to their students; state policies that mandate public high school students take college entrance exams, such as the ACT or SAT; and admission criteria imposed by states, including affirmative action regulations, plans such as the Texas Top 10 Percent Rule, and minimum test score thresholds needed for admissibility.

In each of these areas, we provide an overview of the topic, discuss the existing research, and conclude with lessons learned and questions that still remain. Each section clearly demonstrates that state policies, intentionally and unintentionally, can have large impacts on college enrollment, college quality, and college match. We see consistent evidence that improving the quality of college attended improves students' longer-term outcomes such as degree completion. Students appear to benefit, or are at least not harmed, even in instances where attending a higher-quality college results in a poorer academic match, suggesting that match may be less important as a concept than absolute quality.

After discussing these effects, we conclude with a broader discussion of the role of state policy in higher education and how states should consider evaluating such policies that are often geared at enrollment and affordability, not choice and match. The central lesson here is that policy makers should pay more attention to the margins on which students will alter their college choices as a result of policy design. The ultimate impact of any higher education policy depends heavily on the alternative college choices students are forgoing as a result of the policy.

IN-KIND SPENDING

The primary way that states financially support students' pursuit of post-secondary education is through direct subsidies of public colleges. In 2013, states spent a total of around $72 billion on higher education, with local tax appropriations providing an additional $9 billion in support.[3] Of that total of $82 billion, more than three-fourths (or $63 billion) funded "general public operations," meaning direct subsidies to the budgets of public colleges.[4]

The extent to which these public in-kind subsidies have paid for college has varied greatly over time. In 1988, public subsidies amounted to $8,100 per student, or 76 percent of the total cost of higher education. In other words, twenty-five years ago, student tuition accounted for only 24 percent of the cost of a college education. In 2013, public subsidies came to $6,100 per student, or 53 percent of the cost of a college education, with student tuition covering the remaining 47 percent. This substantial decline in per-pupil subsidies for higher education has been particularly noticeable in the last fifteen years or so.

States also vary quite widely in the extent to which students are subsidized to attend public colleges. In 2013, Wyoming and Alaska's per-student spending on higher education were $12,900 and $16,500, respectively. Nine other states spent between $7,000 and $10,000 per student. At the other end of the spectrum, New Hampshire and Vermont spent $1,700 and $2,700, respectively, per student. Sixteen other states spent less than $5,000 per student. We turn now to evidence on the effect of such subsidies.

Evidence on the Effects of State In-Kind Spending

The seminal study on in-kind spending on higher education is by Sam Peltzman, which carefully distinguishes the theoretical effects of in-kind spending from those of an equivalent money subsidy such as a scholarship. Peltzman notes that while direct financial aid unambiguously increases the amount of higher education a student will pursue by lowering its price, an in-kind subsidy's effect is actually ambiguous. In particular, the large amount by which public college tuitions are subsidized can induce some students to enroll in public institutions, where less money in total will be invested in their higher education than if they had enrolled in private colleges. This phenomenon is due in part to the indivisible nature of higher education (such as the inability to take individual classes at multiple campuses).[5]

Peltzman himself estimates that about three-fourths of public spending on higher education simply substitutes for private spending and that at times public spending actually displaces more than its value in private spending. In another study, Philip Ganderton uses student- and college-level data to estimate the impact of public subsidies on college enrollment choices. He argues that such subsidies induce students to choose public colleges of much lower quality than the private colleges they would otherwise have picked.[6] Bridget Terry Long extends this work, arguing that if state appropriations to public colleges could be used at any in-state college, then roughly one-fourth of students would prefer to attend private four-year colleges instead.[7]

In a more recent study, Stephanie Cellini compared two-year college enrollment in communities where college funding bond referenda barely passed to those where it barely failed. She finds that bond passage, which increases funding for public two-year colleges, diverts students from enrolling in private colleges and, by shrinking that sector, leads to closure of some of those private colleges. This suggests that in-kind spending can shift enrollment into the public sector. In this case, it appears such spending did not impact overall enrollment rates and too little time had passed at the study's publication to estimate impacts on degree completion rates.[8]

John Bound and Sarah Turner consider an additional dimension to in-kind spending—the fact that the overall level of state subsidies changes too slowly over time to react to short run fluctuations in the size of the cohorts potentially attending public colleges.[9] This means that students born in an unusually large cohort have access to public colleges where the resources per student are lower than they are for students born in a smaller cohort. The authors find that students in such large cohorts are substantially less likely to have earned a college degree than students in small cohorts. They argue that the most likely explanation for this finding is that such students are less subsidized and thus have fewer resources available to them while on campus. These might include fewer faculty members per student, fewer courses open to enrollment, less academic support outside of the classroom, and perhaps less subsidized housing. This suggests that in-kind spending per pupil affects not only enrollment, as earlier studies showed, but also degree completion.

Finally, states' goals of improving their local economies by financing higher education would be undermined substantially if the additional college graduates produced by such subsidies migrated out of state. John Kennan explores the question of whether in-kind spending ultimately results in a more educated in-state labor force. Consistent with the literature discussed here, he finds that in-kind subsidies do increase college enrollment.[10] More importantly, he argues that improvements to the educational attainment of in-state labor forces are long-lasting because a substantial fraction of students whom in-kind subsidies induced them to earn degrees in-state remain in-state upon entering the labor market.

Lessons and Remaining Questions Around In-Kind Spending

The literature on states' in-kind spending shows that a large fraction of such spending on higher education displaces what the student must bring to the table. Because such subsidies benefit only students who choose public colleges, in-kind spending diverts some students from private colleges, so that college quality and match are likely affected for students on the margin of choosing between public and private institutions. Whether such students benefit from the in-kind spending depends on both the relative tuitions and the relative qualities of colleges in those sectors. Both of these dimensions vary by state, making it difficult to generalize about the effects of in-kind spending on college match and quality.

The key remaining questions about in-kind spending concern which policy option is the appropriate comparison. Much of the existing literature compares levels of in-kind spending and implies that increasing in-kind spending per pupil improves college outcomes. We know much less about how changing policy design—such as a shift from in-kind support to a voucher that students could use anywhere—might affect student choices.

FINANCIAL AID

States also provide subsidies directly to individual students through various forms of financial aid. In the 2012–2013 academic year, states awarded $11 billion in financial aid, about 85 percent of which consisted of grants. Of that grant aid, $7 billion funded need-based grants and over $2 billion funded non-need-based grants, usually in the form of merit aid. States spent the remaining $2 billion of non-grant aid largely in the form of tuition waivers ($900 million) or loans ($400 million). The remaining aid dollars were spent on loan forgiveness, conditional grants, work-study, and other forms of support.[11]

As with in-kind spending, the amount of financial aid being provided to undergraduates and in the form of that financial aid varies widely across states.[12] South Carolina, for example, spends the most of any state on all grant aid, roughly $1,900 annually per undergraduate student. The figure is less than $200 in fourteen states, including New Hampshire and Wyoming, which provide no grant aid. In terms of need-based aid, South Carolina ranks twenty-second among the states with only $300 in aid per student, as over 80 percent of the grants it provides comes in the form of merit-based scholarships. The state of Washington, in contrast, ranks first in the nation in terms of need-based grants, providing $1,300 per undergraduate. This amount represents over 99 percent of the grant aid that the state distributes.

Evidence on the Effects of State-Provided Financial Aid

Some of the earliest rigorous research on the effects of state-provided financial aid explored only the impact of programs on college enrollment, in part because the programs or data were too recent to observe students' degree completion results. Susan Dynarski examined the enrollment impacts of Georgia's HOPE Scholarship, a merit aid program that allowed free attendance at in-state public colleges for graduating Georgia seniors whose high school GPA was at least a B. To identify the impact of the new program, Dynarski compared Georgia's enrollment rates over time with those in nearby states that did not implement such a program. She found that this fairly generous aid program, for which over half of Georgia students were eligible, increased college enrollment rates among eighteen- to nineteen-year-olds by a substantial 7 percentage points, or about 4 percentage points for every $1,000 in aid.[13]

Similar impacts on college enrollment are seen in other early studies on state aid programs. Thomas Kane studied the California's CalGrant program, which had both minimum GPA and financial need requirements. The aid would cover up to $4,000 in tuition and fees at in-state public colleges and up to $9,400 in tuition at in-state private colleges, in part because the state found it cheaper in the short run to subsidize private college enrollment than to expand overcrowded public campuses.[14] Kane compared students just above and below the GPA threshold that determined eligibility, but who were otherwise similar. He found that students eligible for CalGrant were 3 to 4 percentage points more likely to enroll in college at all, and an even larger proportion were induced to switch their enrollment choice from public to private colleges.

Additionally, in another study, Kane focused on a rare example of federal aid that changes the relative price of colleges across states. In 2000, Congress created the DC Tuition Assistance Grant, which allowed Washington, DC, residents to pay in-state tuition rates at public colleges in Maryland and Virginia. The program was designed to expand the options available to DC residents, for whom the only in-district four-year public college, the University of the District of Columbia, was an open admissions campus that functioned much like a community college. Kane found that this dramatic drop in tuition more than doubled the number of DC residents attending public colleges in those two states. Some of this effect appears to be due to the shifting of students among four-year colleges but some also appeared to stem from enrollment of low-income students who would not otherwise have been able to afford college.[15]

With consistent evidence that financial aid generally, and state aid in particular, has relatively strong impacts on college choices and overall enrollment rates, subsequent research has turned toward the question of whether such aid translates into increased degree completion rates. Enrollment and completion effects might be quite different if, for example, the marginal student induced to enroll due to increased financial aid faces further constraints (financial, academic, or other) that prevent graduation. With this in mind, Susan Dynarski conducted a follow-up study of the Georgia HOPE program, as well as of a similarly generous scholarship program run by Arkansas. She found that exposure to these programs increased the fraction of young people enrolling in college by 1.6 percentage points and the fraction completing a college degree by 3 percentage points. This means that at least half of the increased degree completion came from inframarginal students—those who would have enrolled even in the absence of the program, but now faced lower costs than they otherwise would have.[16]

Recent work by Ben Castleman and Bridget Terry Long explored the impact of Florida's Student Access Grant, a need-based grant that gave students from low-income families an additional $1,300 annually in addition to any Pell Grant funding. This amount was sufficient to cover over half the average cost of tuition and fees at in-state four-year public institutions. The authors identified the impact of the grant by comparing students whose estimated family contributions placed them just above or just below the threshold for grant eligibility. They found that eligibility for this aid increased both enrollment in four-year public colleges (by 3.2 percentage points) and also the probability of earning a bachelor's degree within six years (by 4.6 percentage points). The estimated impacts were greatest for the academically strongest students—those with relatively high GPAs in high school.[17]

Evidence from Georgia, Arkansas, and Florida thus suggests that state aid can increase not only enrollment in college but also degree completion. Recent evidence from Texas and Massachusetts suggests, however, that not all aid programs improve degree completion rates. Jeffrey Denning studied students in Texas whose school districts were annexed into a local community college's taxing district and thus became eligible for a substantial tuition discount at that college. He found that a $1,000 drop in the sticker price increased community college enrollment rates by about three percentage points. Most of the marginal students would not have attended any college otherwise and very few if any gave up four-year college options as a result of this price change, suggesting small effects on match. Importantly, Denning found little clear evidence of any increase in degree completion rates, perhaps because the community college students affected by this aid had very low completion rates to begin with.[18]

In Massachusetts, Sarah Cohodes and Joshua Goodman studied the Adams Scholarship merit aid program that subsidizes tuition at in-state public colleges for students in the top quartile of each graduating high school class. The authors found little evidence of increased enrollment rates, largely because the marginal student is already very likely to enroll in a four-year college. They did, however, find that the scholarship induced a substantial number of students to switch from private four-year to public four-year colleges and, more importantly, that receipt of the scholarship actually reduced degree completion rates. Cohodes and Goodman argue that this negative impact of aid on completion can be explained by the fact that recipients would forgo private colleges that are academic matches with relatively high graduation rates in order to enroll in public college with relatively low graduation rates, and that the lower quality of the institution negatively affected the individual students.[19]

This evidence on the relationship between financial aid, college quality, and degree completion is consistent with evidence from the Georgia HOPE Scholarship. Rajashri Chakrabarti and Joydeep Roy document that Georgia's aid program caused students to enroll in more selective colleges because the state's public four-year colleges were more selective than the private and out-of-state colleges that students would have attended in the absence of the scholarship.[20] Coupled with Dynarksi's evidence that the HOPE Scholarship increased graduation rates and contrasted with Cohodes and Goodman's evidence from Massachusetts, Chakrabarti and Roy's study suggests that financial aid may improve degree completion rates as long as the given program is not designed in such a way as to induce students to sacrifice college quality.

Lessons and Remaining Questions on Financial Aid

Research on state-provided financial aid provides a few clear lessons. First, such aid can have substantial effects on the probability that a given student will enroll in college at all. Second, it can also have a substantial effect on the type of college students choose—public or private or in-state or out-of-state. Much of the research demonstrates a jump in four-year college enrollment, instead of two-year enrollment, which is one of the largest undermatch margins.[21] Third, aid can improve completion rates, particularly if the aid program's design raises, or at least does not lower, the average quality of the college students choose to attend.

These lessons suggest some critical questions that those designing or evaluating state-provided financial aid programs should consider. First, how does the program's design determine the marginal student whose college enrollment decision is changed by the aid? The marginal student's income and academic skill will relate strongly to the set of his or her college options in terms of four-year, two-year, or none; public or private; in-state or out-of-state; and higher or lower quality.

Second, how does the program's design determine what fraction of aid recipients would have enrolled in college absent such aid, and how many aid recipients choose to enroll because of the aid? Third and related, does the program's design create price wedges between different colleges that may distort college choices in potentially perverse ways? All state aid programs lower the relative price of in-state colleges, but only some alter the relative price of private and public colleges. In different state contexts, these changes in relative prices can differ dramatically in their effect on the quality of college students choose, which in turn affects the long-term impact of these programs on degree completion, among other outcomes. To what extent do these price distortions help or harm students?

EXAM-TAKING POLICIES

In 2001, No Child Left Behind required states' publicly funded K–12 school systems to administer standardized tests for accountability purposes. Since then, at varying times, a handful of states have chosen to use a college entrance exam such as the ACT or SAT to satisfy that requirement for high school testing.[22] In such states, nearly all public school students must take a nationally recognized college entrance exam, typically as juniors. Many of these students would not have taken the exam in the absence of the state policy. In Maine, for example, the number of SAT takers increased by 43 percent in the year the SAT was mandated.[23] In Colorado and Illinois, between one-third and one-half of high school students take the ACT as a result of the state requirement.[24] Policy makers in those states may have been motivated in part by the belief that taking college entrance exams might improve college enrollment rates. But do such mandated exam-taking policies affect college enrollment? There are three reasons why exam-taking requirements might affect decisions to enroll. First, such entrance exams are required by many colleges' admissions processes, so that failure to take such an exam is automatically disqualifying. George Bulman, for example, showed that the opportunity to take the SAT at a student's own high school, rather than traveling to a different testing center, resulted in an 8 percentage point increase in test-taking rates and that nearly half of those new test-takers ultimately enrolled in four-year colleges.[25] State policies requiring college entrance exams may counteract some students' tendencies to let small, short-term costs affect decisions with large long-term implications.

Second, taking such exams may improve students' information about the college application process, specific potential colleges, and their own academic skills. Exam takers have the option to receive information from specific colleges. This is important because ample research suggests that some students, particularly low-income students, lack valuable information when choosing colleges. For example, Christopher Avery and Thomas Kane show that students from low-income households have college aspirations similar to neighboring high-income students, but their unfamiliarity with the college application process prevents similar college-going patterns.[26] The lack of information and support among poor and rural students, often leading to undesirable college application and enrollment decisions, is well documented.[27] Caroline Hoxby and Sarah Turner show that low-income, high-achieving students who receive information about colleges and application procedures have a greater chance of enrolling in a relatively selective college over a less-selective one and thus improving their academic match.[28] Students may also learn from exam-taking that they had previously underestimated their own academic skills, so that exam-taking induces them to choose higher-quality college options than they would otherwise have chosen. Conversely, some students may have previously overestimated their skills, in which case mandatory exam-taking may cause them to shift down the college-quality distribution. The net effect of this last point depends on whether the lower-quality or improved match has a dominant effect.

A third reason such policies may affect enrollment is that schoolwide college entrance exam administration may create a college-going culture in high schools. Studies by both Michael Hurwitz and coauthors and the Strategic Data Project show that observably similar high schools can have vastly different college-going and undermatch rates.[29] If students learn from one another, perhaps about new colleges or about the benefits and costs of selective colleges, then there may be positive spillovers from students to each other. These externalities may mean that schoolwide administration of college entrance exams has larger college enrollment impacts than would interventions to induce individual students to take such exams.

Evidence on the Effects of State Exam-Taking Policies

Recent research has estimated the impact of states' mandatory college entrance exam-taking policies on students' college choices. The three main questions addressed by this literature include whether such policies increase enrollment rates in four-year colleges, whether they change the type and quality of the colleges students choose, and which kind of students are most affected by such policies.

Four-year college enrollment rates clearly respond to mandatory exam-taking policies. Michael Hurwitz, Jonathan Smith, Sunny Niu, and Jessica Howell found that Maine students induced to take the SAT were 10 percentage points more likely to enroll in a four-year institution, which translates into a roughly 5 percent increase in Maine's overall four-year enrollment rates.[30] Daniel Klasik found that Illinois's four-year colleges saw enrollment increases of 12 percent and that Colorado's private four-year colleges saw a 10 percent increase in enrollment.[31] Sarena Goodman estimated that four-year enrollment in Colorado and Illinois actually increased by about 14 percent.[32] A study by Joshua Hyman found that enrollment at Michigan's four-year colleges increased by 0.6 percentage points, or 2 percent.[33] All of these studies suggest that, for some subset of students, the state's requirement that they take a college entrance exam does induce them to enroll in four-year colleges.

Do such policies affect the type and quality of college that students choose? It appears that some of the marginal students induced to enroll in a four-year college would otherwise have attended a two-year college. Klasik found, for example, a sharp decrease in two-year public college enrollment in Illinois and Maine after the new exam-taking policy was enacted, implying that more students were induced to forgo two-year colleges in favor of four-year colleges than were induced to choose two-year colleges instead of no college.[34] This is not true in all states: Klasik found a marginal increase in two-year public college enrollment in Colorado, and Hyman observed no significant change in two-year enrollment in Michigan, though his point estimate was negative.[35] Mandatory exam-taking also appears in some contexts to increase the selectivity of colleges students choose. Goodman estimated that the new policy made students 20 percent more likely to enroll in selective colleges as opposed to less selective four-year and two-year colleges.[36] Klasik observed a similar result in Colorado, though not in Maine or Illinois.[37] These mixed findings suggest some evidence of increases in college quality, though that result is not consistent across all contexts.

Finally, the type of student most affected by mandatory exam-taking policies appears to be consistent with previous research that suggests isolated and low-income students have a difficult time obtaining information on colleges.[38] Hurwitz et al.'s results, for example, were driven by students from Maine's rural high schools.[39] Similarly, Hyman's study revealed that the modest improvements in four-year enrollment resulted from sizeable improvements among low-income students and students in high-poverty high schools.[40] He also showed that these effects were driven more strongly by high-scoring, low-income students, a result consistent with the finding in Goodman that many high scorers would not have taken the exam in the absence of the mandate and therefore would have undermatched.[41] These two studies show that it is not only those students who are on the margin of college readiness who may benefit from such a mandate.

Lessons and Remaining Questions on Exam-Taking Policies

A few clear lessons emerge from research on exam-taking policies. First, such policies have the potential to change four-year college enrollment rates. Second, they can also improve the quality of the college that students attend and thus affect match. Third, the marginal students whose college choice is most affected by such policies tend to be geographically isolated or from a low-income family or school. Fourth, not all such marginal students have low academic skills. Some are highly skilled students for whom attending a matched selective four-year college may have long-term benefits.

Three major questions remain. First, which of the underlying mechanisms discussed earlier is responsible for the observed enrollment effects? Second, what fraction of the marginal students whose college choice is altered by exam policies successfully complete their college degrees? These policies are too recent to estimate six-year graduation rates, but Hyman observed relatively high persistence among Michigan students, suggesting future studies may find positive graduation impacts.[42] Third, and most broadly, how do these mandates compare in terms of cost effectiveness to other state policy options for improving enrollment and completion?

PUBLIC COLLEGES' ADMISSIONS CRITERIA POLICIES

Affirmative Action

While much college match research focuses on undermatch, overmatch also attracts attention, particularly as it relates to affirmative action. Some critics of race-based affirmative action argue that it does a disservice to those students who would not have been admitted otherwise on the basis of their academic record. Such students, those critics argue, find themselves among the least academically prepared students on their college campus and may suffer as a result. The skill gaps between racial groups on a given campus have been documented by William Bowen and Derek Bok, who found that black students entering their sampled college between 1976 and 1989 had SAT scores between 150 and 200 points lower than white students on a 1600-point scale.[43] At Duke, Arcidiacono et al. document a recent black-white SAT gap of about 140 SAT points. These point gaps point to academic overmatch.[44]

Several recent studies have attempted to estimate whether affirmative action may actually harm the students that it is intended to help. Richard Sander argued that overmatched black law students failed the law bar at a higher rate as a result of an admissions process that inappropriately matched those students to overly selective law schools.[45] In response, Daniel Ho noted a number of flaws in that analysis, including the use of correlational analyses to make causal claims.[46] Jesse Rothstein and Albert Yoon made different statistical choices and concluded that, except for the weakest law school students, academic "mismatch" did not disadvantage black students' law school graduation rates, bar passage rates, or employment prospects.[47] Arcidiacono and Lovenheim, in an extensive review of this literature, conclude the question of mismatch "merits further attention, where more definitive answers could be answered with better data."[48]

One reason that research has not clearly answered the question of the long-term impacts of affirmative action on underrepresented students is that the counterfactual is hard to identify. Recent state-level policy changes have, however, generated clearer evidence about the short run college enrollment effects of affirmative action. California, Texas, Florida, Michigan, and Washington now forbid race from factoring into the admissions processes at public colleges.[49] Several researchers have documented how such affirmative action bans have impacted the college match process for underrepresented students.

Marta Tienda et al., for example, showed that both of Texas's most selective public postsecondary institutions (University of Texas at Austin and Texas A&M) experienced declines in the fraction of enrollees identifying as black or Latino after the ban on affirmative action imposed by *Hopwood v. University of Texas*.[50] Subsequent studies have echoed this findings that underrepresented minorities are shut out of some, particularly very selective, postsecondary institutions as a result of affirmative action bans. Peter Hinrichs, for example, demonstrated that a similar ban imposed in California in 1998 generated a cascading effect in which underrepresented minorities shifted from the more selective University of California institutions (UC Berkeley, UCLA, UC San Diego, and UC Davis) toward the least selective institutions (UC Irvine, UC Riverside, UC Santa Barbara, and UC Santa Cruz). Underrepresented minority students' enrollment at the more selective institutions dropped by 4 percentage points, a decline partially offset by a 2 percentage point increase in enrollment at the less selective institutions.[51] This is some of the clearest evidence that affirmative action does substantially improve the average quality of college attended by underrepresented minority students.

The Texas Top 10 Percent Rule

Just one year after affirmative action was banned by the *Hopwood* decision, the Texas state legislature passed a bill now known as the "Top 10 Percent Rule." Anticipating that the affirmative action ban would reduce the number of underrepresented minorities at Texas's most selective colleges, the Top 10 Percent Rule mandated that any Texas high school senior in the top 10 percent of her class would be admitted automatically to the Texas public college of her choice.[52] Given the extent of racial segregation in Texas's public high schools, the Top 10 Percent Rule allowed for the admission of underrepresented students who might have been shut out of the most selective institutions were they to be compared with the statewide distribution of applicants. The new rule essentially allowed for the continuation of academic overmatch for some students without explicitly using race to justify this overmatch.

How much did the Texas Top 10 Percent Rule allow for the preservation of diversity in a legal environment where the consideration of race in the admissions process was forbidden? Mark Long and Marta Tienda examined data from the three most selective Texas universities (University of Texas at Austin, Texas A&M, and Texas Tech) for the entering classes of 1990 through 2003, a period that encompassed three distinct admissions policy regimes. The authors found that at UT-Austin, the most selective of the three institutions, black and Latino applicants enjoyed a thirteen-percentage-point admissions advantage relative to academically similar white applicants between 1990 and 1996, when race could be considered in admissions. In 1997, when consideration of race was banned, that admissions advantage disappeared. Upon implementation of the Top 10 Percent Rule in 1998, black and Latino applicants regained some, but not all, of that pre-*Hopwood* admissions rate. At the somewhat less selective Texas A&M, the admissions advantage did not return with the Top 10 Percent Rule. At the least selective of the three colleges, Texas Tech, there was little evidence in the earliest period of an advantage for black and Latino students, and after implementation of the Top 10 Percent Rule, such applicants had lower probabilities of admission than academically similar white students.[53]

Long and Tienda's analyses, while descriptive in nature, strongly suggest that the affirmative action bans and subsequent Top 10 Percent Rule markedly reshaped admissions policies, at least at Texas's two flagship institutions. In a subsequent study, Niu and Tienda compared students on either side of the GPA threshold defining the top 10 percent to identify the impact of automatic admission on college enrollment decisions. They found large but imprecisely estimated differences in the probability of enrollment at a flagship institution as a result of automatic admission, with Latino students showing a particularly large and statistically significant difference.[54] Eric Furstenberg's study also showed a substantial increase in the quality of college attended as a result of eligibility for automatic admission, and a decrease in graduation probability.[55] This last finding, however, should be treated with caution, as Furstenberg was not able to observe college enrollment and graduation outside of the Texas public sector, thus missing students who attended private or out-of-state colleges.

Daugherty et al.'s study of a single, large school district uncovered clear evidence that eligibility for automatic admission substantially increases enrollment at the flagship universities.[56] This enrollment entirely displaced enrollment in private universities of similar quality, so that overall enrollment and average college quality were unchanged. Such enrollment changes were driven by students at schools with relatively high college enrollment rates, so that students from the most disadvantaged schools appear not to have benefited from the policy. Taken as a whole, the evidence suggests that the Top 10 Percent Rule does increase access to Texas's flagship public colleges for minority students, though the longer-term effects on degree completion and labor market outcomes are still unclear.

Minimum Admissions Criteria

A recent survey by the National Association for College Admissions Counseling found that one in five colleges used specific test scores as minimum thresholds for admission, often in combination with minimum GPAs. These statewide policies help public colleges process large applicant pools with limited resources and serve to screen out applicants who may be academically unsuitable for those institutions. States that use such criteria across their entire public higher education systems include California, Texas, Florida, and Georgia. For example, the Georgia Board of Regents requires that students score at least a 430 on the critical reading section and a 400 on the math section of the SAT in order to gain entry into one of the state's four-year public colleges.[57] The survey found that such admissions criteria created a dichotomy: students who just met the criteria had access to public four-year colleges and were more likely to attend and, consequently, overmatch. Students who just missed the criteria are more likely to attend two-year public colleges and consequently undermatch.[58]

Goodman et al. compared the college enrollment choices of Georgia students just above and below those thresholds, students who are otherwise identical except for differences in eligibility for admission. They found that access to four-year public *sector* institutions increased the probability of enrollment in that sector by as much as 10 percentage points. If not for access to the four-year public colleges, as much as three-quarters of such marginal students would have instead attended two-year community colleges. The remaining students would largely have attended other four-year institutions.[59]

Seth Zimmerman performed a similar study of Florida International University (FIU). FIU is the state's least selective public four-year college, with minimum GPA requirements for admission. Zimmerman showed that GPA-based eligibility increased the likelihood of enrolling at FIU by about 10 percentage points and, as in Georgia, that many of the marginal students would have attended community colleges if they had not been eligible for admission to this four-year college.[60]

Both studies thus indicate that strict minimum admissions criteria in public college systems can substantially change the type and quality of college that a student attends. This implies that the set of choices students face is not a continuum. In part because of the in-kind subsidies states provide by funding public colleges directly, it is hard to find colleges of similar price and quality to the four-year public colleges to which some students want access. Private colleges of similar quality are often substantially more expensive.

Given the clear enrollment and match effects, it is unclear whether states consider the effects of the policies on marginal students' longer-term outcomes. Interestingly, both studies clearly show that the benefits of being at a more selective college, or a four-year college instead of a two-year college, far outweigh any disadvantages of such overmatch. In Georgia, marginal students who enroll in a four-year public college roughly double their chances of earning a college degree. In Florida, enrollment at FIU yields substantial gains in labor market earnings about a decade later. Both studies find that the degree completion gains and earnings gains are concentrated among students from low-income backgrounds.[61]

Lessons and Remaining Questions on Affirmative Action and Admission Criteria

The literature on affirmative action bans makes clear that affirmative action has a substantial impact on the quality of colleges that underrepresented minority students attend, often resulting in overmatch. The Texas Top 10 Percent Rule appears to mitigate some of the effects of affirmative action bans, though perhaps not for students from the most disadvantaged schools. Much less clear is whether access to more selective colleges as a result of affirmative action or automatic admission has a positive impact on students' longer-term outcomes. Also unmeasured in this research is the impact on those applicants displaced to other colleges by students admitted because of affirmative action.

Research on minimum admissions criteria at public colleges makes clear such criteria can substantially change the type and quality of college students choose. The two studies reviewed suggest, however, that attending a higher-quality college is beneficial to disadvantaged students even if they are academically overmatched. In other words, absolute measures of college quality appear to matter more than the match between students' skills and the college they attend. That the relatively low-skilled students in these studies benefited from attending a public four-year college suggests that such admissions criteria may be screening out some potentially successful students. No research yet has explored the effect of relaxing such criteria on either students at the margin or public higher education systems as a whole. Doing so might increase access for some potentially successful students but might also involve admitting a higher number of incorrectly matched students, while increasing the costs of the admissions process itself. The net result of such a change is ex ante difficult to predict.

CONCLUSION

The evidence reviewed here shows that state higher education policy clearly impacts students' college choices. In-kind subsidies, financial aid, mandatory college entrance exams, and admissions regulations all affect college enrollment rates, college quality, and academic match. Policy makers often mistakenly focus on increasing overall enrollment rates while neglecting the potential for policies to affect students' choice of different types of colleges. The evidence suggests that match quality itself matters relatively little for longer-term outcomes but that absolute college quality does matter. To the extent that students have viable choices between colleges, choosing the highest-quality college appears to improve degree completion rates more than choosing the closest academic match.

As a result, to increase degree completion rates requires designing policies that on balance shift students to higher-quality college options than they otherwise would have selected, where quality is measured by an institution's track record of graduating students. This can mean shifting students from no college to the community college sector or from the community college sector to the four-year sector. It can also mean shifting students within the four-year sector to colleges with higher institutional graduation rates. Policies that, often unintentionally, distort student decisions toward lower-quality colleges are almost certainly poor uses of public funds. One plausible hypothesis is that the best use of a public dollar in this context is the policy that most improves the graduation rate of the institution a student chooses to attend.

At least two fundamental questions remain largely unanswered by the existing research. First, nearly all of these analyses abstract from general equilibrium effects. Do students displace one another or are there a flexible number of seats at colleges? Michael Bastedo discusses this potential issue at length.[62] Second, what are the effects of these policies away from the margins, if any? Are students whose college choices remain unchanged nonetheless indirectly affected by the changing composition of their peer groups? We hope future work will address these bigger picture questions.

Finally, though states can affect students' college choices in meaningful ways, such policies are not the only options available for improving longer-term outcomes. In addition to encouraging students to choose institutions with better historical completion rates, states could, for example, focus on improving colleges' degree completion rates. The best state policies could both improve the college choices students make and the quality of the choices students have.

9

Federal Mechanisms for Improving College Match

Information, Aid, and Accountability

Robert Kelchen

A small body of research has examined strategies to increase college enrollment rates, which would improve the percentage of students who match with any institution of higher education. These strategies include allowing students to submit standardized test scores to an additional college free of charge, assistance completing the Free Application for Federal Student Aid (FAFSA), text message reminders of important deadlines, near-peer counseling, and supplemental guidance counseling.[1] All of these strategies are relatively inexpensive and easy to implement, making them excellent potential private-sector or institutional-level approaches to mitigating undermatch.

Due in large part to these promising efforts, the topic of college match has become a key higher education policy goal of the Obama administration as it seeks to meet its ambitious goal of having America lead the world in the proportion of citizens with postsecondary degrees by 2020.[2] The White House hosted two summits related to undermatching in 2014, bringing together hundreds of colleges that made new commitments to help students from low-income families succeed in higher education.[3] The impending reauthorization of the Higher Education Act, legislation affecting nearly all portions of federal higher education policy, provides an opportunity for Congress and the White House to work together on common goals of increasing college access and completion—and strategies to improve college matching could be incorporated into the legislation.

There are three primary mechanisms through which the federal government can strive to improve students' college choices and hence the quality of a student's match with his or her college of attendance. The first is by making better information about the postsecondary education landscape, the prices of various colleges, and post-college outcomes available to students and their families. The federal government can directly reach prospective students in some situations, such as when students fill out the FAFSA, but needs to work with partners such as college access organizations and high school guidance counselors to make sure other information reaches students in user-friendly ways.

Yet information alone is unlikely to lead all students receiving it to reconsider a potentially suboptimal choice of colleges. The second mechanism is the approximately $125 billion in federal grants, loans, and tax credits given annually to undergraduate students and their families to help them afford college.[4] However, these funds have traditionally followed students to nearly any accredited college they choose to attend. This tells students very little about whether they are likely to be matched suitably with their college of choice. In theory, additional federal financial aid dollars could be given for students who attend colleges considered to be high-quality, in order to induce students to attend particular colleges.

The third mechanism that the federal government can use to influence college match is through accountability policies. The converse of potential reforms that would give extra money to students attending certain colleges, the goal of federal accountability policies has typically been to cut off financial aid dollars at the very worst institutions. This alone is likely to do little to improve college match for most students, but heightened accountability policies could help reduce the number of truly awful matches. Another possibility to consider is risk-sharing policies that require colleges to put up matching funds if student outcomes are substandard, as this has the potential to influence how colleges recruit academically capable students from lower-income families.

In this chapter, I discuss each of these three mechanisms, focusing on current policies and practices as well as what else could be done to potentially influence college match. I then address some of the concerns and limitations of possible federal policies before concluding with recommendations for policy makers.

CONSUMER INFORMATION

The most straightforward way the federal government could help improve students' matches with colleges is through the provision and dissemination of information, as colleges are already required to submit a large quantity of data to the US Department of Education for informational and compliance purposes. Yet these data sources are flawed in important ways that often limit their utility. In this section, I detail the types of information the federal government directly or indirectly makes available to students and their families and discuss some potential improvements that might affect college match.

Existing Federal Policies

Since the 1992 reauthorization of the Higher Education Act, the federal government has required colleges receiving federal student financial aid dollars to submit data on student financial aid, enrollment, human resources, graduation rates, and other components to the Department of Education's Integrated Postsecondary Education Data System (IPEDS). This data set does not come without a burden to colleges. In the 2015–2016 academic year, the federal government has estimated the burden of completing all required IPEDS surveys at just over one million hours across the entire higher education system and at an approximated cost of over $40 million.[5]

This information is presented to the public in three main ways. The Department of Education has created a consumer-oriented website, College Navigator, that seeks to display key IPEDS data in a student-friendly manner and allow for comparisons across colleges.[6] Postsecondary institutions with the highest and lowest tuition prices, net prices of attendance, and largest percentage increase in prices by sector are available through the College Affordability and Transparency Center.[7] Colleges in the top 5 percent of tuition, net price, or price increases by sector are required to submit explanations for their increases.[8] Finally, the College Scorecard, which was first released to the public in 2013 and relaunched in 2015, has data measures such as the average net price of attendance, the graduation rate for first-time, full-time students within three years at a two-year college and six years at a four-year college, student loan default rates and repayment rates, median borrowing amounts, and median earnings of former students ten years after entering college.[9]

In addition to the data that colleges must submit to the federal government to post on a centralized website, colleges are also required under the Higher Education Act to disclose additional crucial information to students and their families, including employment and job placement rates, transfer-out rates, graduation rates for Pell Grant recipients, and net price calculators.[10] Colleges can comply with the requirements by posting the information on their websites, or in some cases by providing the data to interested individuals upon request. Yet these outcomes are often presented for either all students or for large subgroups, meaning that students are typically unable to see how those similar to them perform in college. For example, colleges are required to report graduation rates by race and ethnicity, but not for other important measures such as academic preparation, family income, and parental education.

Although a large amount of information on colleges' outcomes is available to the public, it often fails to reach prospective students and their families. One reason is that many colleges do not make federally required information (such as Pell Grant recipient graduation rates) publicly available.[11] Students are less likely to use government websites than many other sources in their college search processes.[12] There is some evidence that the federally required net price calculators on institutional websites are underutilized and that tuition watch lists are relevant only to students in certain states considering particular fields of study.[13] Finally, a survey of adult students considering a return to college found that they do not consider performance metrics to be important in the college decision process and thus did not use those sources.[14] These factors likely contribute to lower-income students and their families consistently overestimating the price of college.[15]

Although a substantial amount of data is available, its value is often limited because measures are not easily comparable across institutions. Net price calculators are a case in point. Although all colleges are required to post these calculators, they can take different forms across different institutions. Some forms ask for the most basic information (family income, household size, and number in college), while others ask for standardized test scores and information about parental assets. Recent aggregation services such as College Abacus allow students to compare net prices across multiple colleges while only entering information once, but some colleges have chosen to block access to the website over alleged accuracy concerns.[16]

Finally, while surveys show that a majority of students considered career training, employment outcomes, and graduate school preparation as crucial factors in the college choice process, they are unable to get comprehensive information from the Department of Education or the vast majority of colleges about longer-term program-level outcomes such as employment, loan repayment, or midcareer earnings.[17] Although the College Scorecard was a large step forward, the federal government trails well behind both many states and the private sector in obtaining data on completion rates, employment, and earnings to students and their families. This is because federal efforts to collect such data were severely hamstrung in the 2008 Higher Education Act reauthorization that banned the creation of a federal student unit record system. This system would have allowed labor market data to be tied to individual students' college records, but was outlawed due to concerns of student privacy and a strong lobbying effort from the National Association of Independent Colleges and Universities, an association representing private nonprofit colleges.[18]

Some states with student unit record data sets that track students from K–12 education through college and into the workforce have made their data available to the public through consumer-friendly dashboards. Two good examples are College Measures, a Lumina Foundation–funded collaboration of six states with longitudinal data systems, and the data portal of the State Council of Higher Education for Virginia, which contains over a decade of information on many measures.[19] Private-sector data sources such as LinkedIn and PayScale have provided information on self-reported earnings and employment to the public, and both have been used to create college rankings.[20] But these systems are necessarily incomplete and, in the case of self-reported data, unreliable.

Potential Reforms to Consumer Information

In addition to the federal government's current policies and practices that have the potential to influence college match, policy makers have the ability to take additional steps if desired. I suggest three overarching principles that should guide federal policy development, as well as some potential policies that satisfy these principles.

Principle 1: The federal government needs to make data available to the public, with a focus on outreach to nonprofit partners.

As discussed earlier, research suggests that students and their families do not first turn to government resources in the college search and choice processes, but rather to family members, guidance counselors, and external sources such as college rankings.[21] The federal government can still play an important role by making data available. But it should also actively reach out to state education agencies, high schools, and community service providers to make sure those organizations are aware of the information and know how to interpret it. A body of research has shown the influence of high schools on improving the college match process, and improved federal outreach to these intermediaries has the potential to help reduce the disparities in college matching across high schools.[22]

While the focus for federal outreach should be toward nonprofit organizations, it is important to recognize that the impact of any additional data will be magnified by for-profit organizations such as college rankings providers. These college rankings are most heavily utilized by students from higher-income families, but higher-achieving low-income students also commonly use rankings.[23] As college rankings rely heavily on data collected by the federal government, additional data releases are likely to be included in both existing and new rankings measures.

There are two main actions that policy makers should consider taking in order to improve the utility of data. The first action is to enforce and strengthen the current provisions under the Higher Education Act that require colleges to make data readily available on their websites—something they have been very slow to do; as former US Department of Education official Ben Miller wrote, "The results [of the disclosure requirement] have gone over about as well as a voluntary broccoli eating contest with toddlers."[24] If colleges do not have required information available on their websites from a link on the home page, they should face sanctions. The second action to consider is to repeal the ban on a federal student unit record data set to allow for more complete data on employment and earnings for all students as well as for outcomes for subgroups of students. Senators Ron Wyden (D-OR) and Marco Rubio (R-FL) have introduced the Student Right to Know Before You Go Act in three consecutive Congresses, but the bill has yet to pass the Senate.[25] In order for the unit record system to be useful, a public-facing dashboard must be created that is user-friendly and targeted toward students, their families, and guidance counselors.

Principle 2: The federal government should help students avoid matching with very bad colleges through the provision of information.

Although it is difficult to define exactly what a "bad" college looks like, one potential indicator is if outcomes are poor for all students. Student loan default rates, for example, exceed graduation rates at several hundred colleges.[26] Additionally, over one hundred programs within for-profit colleges have more students who defaulted on their loans in one cohort than completed in two cohorts.[27] The traditional gatekeeping process of accreditation, a requirement for colleges to receive student financial aid dollars, does little to keep out colleges with the lowest graduation rates or highest student loan default rates.[28] It is also important to consider whether a college does a particularly poor job serving certain groups of students, as the completion rates for students attending the same college can vary drastically by racial/ethnic group. Some colleges that do a respectable job of graduating white students are equally adept at graduating minority students, while others graduate minority students at abysmal rates.[29]

The federal government could provide information in several ways that might reduce the number of students matching with bad colleges. The most straightforward policy change would be to require a college to disclose prominently on its website, advertising, and/or application materials that it has poor outcomes for all students, similar to the Surgeon General's warning that must be displayed on all tobacco-related materials. Students who file the FAFSA could also be targets of this information; if a student checks a box to send the FAFSA to a college with poor outcomes, a warning label would appear encouraging students to reconsider that decision. This could also be done for colleges that serve some groups of students well, but not others. Although students might not consider outcome information such as graduation rates in their college choice process, a stern warning label might give this information more weight in their decision making.

A more nuanced approach to discouraging students from attending the worst colleges would be to include outcome information on the College Scorecard and other federal material oriented toward high school guidance counselors. This approach would be most effective if it was targeted and customized to colleges within a student's region, as was the case in Caroline Hoxby and Sarah Turner's intervention for high-achieving, low-income students, which helped spark the public focus on improving college match.[30] For example, materials could be tailored to particular K–12 schools or districts based on their demographics and colleges where local high school graduates have successfully completed college degrees. Federal databases could allow students to customize results based on their family income, academic background, or race.

Principle 3: The federal government should encourage students to match with a college where they are likely to succeed.

Even among colleges of similar selectivity, students with similar levels of academic preparation can have substantially different completion rates. A 2006 study using data from graduates of Chicago Public Schools shows the magnitude of the variations. While fewer than 20 percent of students with a 3.5 high school GPA graduated from Northeastern Illinois University, students attending Illinois State University graduated at a rate of 57 percent.[31] Additionally, research suggests that parents' perceptions of otherwise similar colleges can be significantly changed if their graduation rates are quite different.[32]

The federal government could take two steps to get information into the hands of the public that might help more students match with high-quality colleges. First, students should be able to readily access information on the outcomes of students similar to themselves. Some of this can be done through existing federal data, but much of this information (particularly that on academic preparation and socioeconomic status) requires a federal unit record data set. A more immediate step could be to issue some "seal of approval" or endorsement of colleges with unusually high success rates for all groups of students, given the types of students admitted. If properly designed, such a system would reward colleges across the selectivity spectrum that do a good job educating the types of students they already have— not the ones they would like to enroll.

STUDENT FINANCIAL AID

Current federal financial aid policies send very few messages to students about whether they are matched with an appropriate college. This is due to the historic aims of federal financial aid based on making college affordable for a broad swath of the population instead of centering on the success of a small subset of students.[33] The vast majority of federal aid functions as a voucher, and students can take this aid to any accredited college that meets basic quality criteria.[34] Although this makes considering a comprehensive set of federal financial aid policies to improve college match difficult to imagine, there are still some steps that could be taken to potentially improve match.

Existing Federal Policies

A limited portion of federal financial aid dollars are allocated directly to colleges instead of to students, which presents an opportunity to improve college match. The Supplemental Educational Opportunity Grant and Federal Work-Study programs together accounted for approximately $1.6 billion in federal aid in the 2013–2014 academic year, or approximately 5 percent of the $31.4 billion in Pell Grant expenditures.[35] Colleges are typically expected to cover one-fourth of the total cost of the programs, which are limited to students with at least some financial need. These funds are disproportionately available to students attending selective, expensive, private nonprofit colleges—a result of historical allocation formulas that have been changed very little since the 1980s.[36] In a sense, these funds are more available to high-achieving students attending colleges where they may be better matched, but this is the result of historical accident rather than an active policy decision.

Another way in which current federal financial aid policies send a muted signal about college match is through Satisfactory Academic Progress (SAP) requirements. Although the exact definitions of SAP vary somewhat across colleges, students are typically required to maintain a 2.0 GPA and complete at least two-thirds of attempted credits by the end of their third semester. Research has found that as many as 40 percent of Pell recipients are at risk of failing to make SAP, resulting in lower college persistence rates for these students.[37] If students are matched well with colleges, they might be at a lower risk of failing to meet SAP, but that question has never been empirically tested.

Potential Federal Policies Regarding College Match and Student Financial Aid

While some of the potential federal policies to improve college matching through increased information are relatively noncontroversial, changing federal financial aid programs to improve college match is likely to be much more difficult. I discuss three key principles in this section that could help policy makers send signals to students about their match by first committing to provide support to students before they enter college and then making them eligible for additional financial aid if they attend a high-quality college or one in line with their academic ability.

Principle 1: Promising students from low-income families should receive additional support before even reaching college.

The gaps in college enrollment between the top and bottom of the family income distribution are staggering; while 80 percent of students from the top income quartile enroll in college, just 30 percent from the bottom quartile do so.[38] Under the current financial aid system, students did not receive information about their financial aid eligibility until completing the FAFSA—no earlier than January 1 of the year in which they wish to enroll in college. The lateness of this information likely contributes to the enrollment gap. Beginning in fall 2016, students will be able to file the FAFSA on October 1, allowing students and their families to use income and asset data from the previous tax year, which gives students more time to compare financial aid packages and make informed choices.[39]

While advancing the aid notification timeline might help some students, earlier financial aid interventions are likely to be more effective in helping low-income students academically prepare for college and then make the decision to enroll in a quality institution. Local-level and state-level college promise programs commit to offering middle and high school students additional grant aid in exchange for meeting residency, academic performance, and/or community service requirements. A small body of research has found that these college promise programs have increased college enrollment and completion rates across the income distribution.[40]

Promise programs have influenced the development of state and federal tuition-free community college proposals; for example, the wildly popular Tennessee Promise program increased year-over-year FAFSA filing rates by 12 percentage points in its first year of operation.[41] Letting low-income students know that they will qualify for Pell Grants in middle school rather than in twelfth grade might have similar positive effects.[42] Another potential model is that used by the federal TRIO, GEAR UP, and Upward Bound programs, which help prepare low-income middle and high school students for college by offering services such as tutoring, financial aid, and additional information about college match. The best available evaluation of any of these college access programs found a significant increase in college enrollment and completion rates for Upward Bound students.[43]

Principle 2: Reallocate campus-based financial aid dollars to colleges that do a good job serving low-income students.

Federal work-study and Supplemental Educational Opportunity Grant dollars should be awarded in a way that rewards colleges that do a good job of enrolling and graduating students with financial need instead of continuing the allocation formula that was set before most of today's students were even born. Although funds are disproportionately allocated to selective colleges at this time, the success rates of Pell recipients may be lower at some of these institutions than at less selective colleges with strong pre-college outreach and support programs. Encouraging colleges to better recruit and serve academically capable students from lower-income families could be accomplished by directing campus-based aid toward these institutions that effectively serve Pell recipients.

Principle 3: Provide additional grant aid to academically prepared students with financial need.

Although students currently need to maintain only a 2.0 GPA to meet satisfactory academic progress requirements, two earlier federal programs, the Academic Competitiveness Grant (ACG) and SMART Grant, targeted relatively high-achieving, low-income students. The ACG was available to first- and second-year students who completed a rigorous high school curriculum and maintained a 3.0 GPA in the first year of college, while the SMART Grant was available to upper-level students in selected majors who also kept a 3.0 GPA.[44] These two programs received less than $4 billion in federal funding between fiscal years 2006 and 2011, when they were phased out.[45]

To improve college match, it might be worth considering reviving a merit-based program for financially needy students similar to the ACG or SMART. The GPA requirement should be set at 2.5, as a 3.0 GPA is higher than what many students can maintain while taking a full course load. The additional grant program could also be limited to students attending colleges that meet certain quality thresholds so that students can better match with colleges whose admissions standards are similar to their own academic qualifications. It is also important that students attending part-time be eligible for any grants with additional merit-based criteria, as was the case for the ACG and SMART grants.

ACCOUNTABILITY

In addition to policies designed to improve information available to consumers and financial aid policies designed to encourage students to attend high-quality colleges, the federal government has a third policy lever that could improve student matching. Existing federal accountability policies in higher education are designed to restrict the access of the lowest-performing colleges to federal financial aid dollars. But accountability policies could also be used to give all colleges "skin in the game" regarding the enrollment and success of academically prepared students from low-income families.

Existing Federal Policies

The federal government has several policies that can restrict or eliminate colleges' access to federal financial aid dollars and therefore limit the risk of students matching to the lowest-quality colleges.[46] The first operates through *cohort default rates*—the percentage of students who defaulted on their federal loans within three years of leaving college. Colleges with a cohort default rate of over 40 percent in any given year are subject to the loss of federal student loan eligibility, while colleges with default rates over 30 percent for three consecutive years are subject to the loss of all federal financial aid dollars.[47] Only eleven colleges have actually lost access to all federal aid in the last fifteen years, as colleges have either opted out of loan programs or successfully appealed the initial judgment.[48] Community colleges serving approximately one million students completely opt out of offering federal student loans, and these colleges are more likely to have higher percentages of minority students—potentially limiting these students' access to higher education.[49]

The second accountability policy is *heightened cash monitoring*, which essentially delays federal student aid payments to colleges if they fail to meet certain conditions regarding financial statements, their financial responsibility score—a proxy for fiscal health—their leadership structure, or other oversight issues.[50] For example, Corinthian Colleges, formerly one of the largest for-profit college chains, was placed on heightened cash monitoring on account of fraudulent job placement rates.[51] The resulting three-week delay in federal student aid reimbursement under heightened cash monitoring is blamed for Corinthian's collapse. The list of colleges under heightened cash monitoring was first made public in early 2015, giving students additional information about colleges that might not be of sufficient quality.[52]

The third accountability policy to highlight is *accreditation*. The Department of Education requires colleges to be accredited by a federally approved agency in order for students to receive federal financial aid.[53] There are different types of accreditation, with regional accreditation—which most nonprofit colleges have—viewed much more favorably than national accreditation, which is dominated by for-profit and small religious colleges.[54] Accreditation in theory is supposed to reflect that a college meets minimal academic quality standards, but some question whether the standards are set high enough. For example, eleven four-year colleges with graduation rates below 10 percent had regional accreditation in 2013.[55] Additionally, a recent report from the Government Accountability Office showed that both regional and national accrediting bodies were more likely to sanction colleges over financial concerns than academic concerns, and that only 1 percent of colleges lost accreditation during a recent five-year period.[56]

The federal government is implementing a new accountability system that has the potential to provide more useful information to students about the quality of the colleges they are considering. A select number of vocational programs, primarily at for-profit institutions and community colleges, are newly subject to *gainful employment* regulations designed to ensure graduates are able to repay their federal loans. If a program fails to meet the threshold in a number of consecutive years, it will be subject to the loss of federal financial aid eligibility. The rules took effect in July 2015 after a legal challenge from the for-profit sector was unsuccessful.[57]

Potential Federal Policies Regarding College Match and Accountability

The federal government has the ability to create accountability policies that could incentivize colleges to recruit, accept, and support academically capable students from low- to middle-income families while cutting off access to federal financial aid for low-performing colleges. Some of the strategies for federal accountability policies are similar to those previously described regarding consumer information, but it may be easier to obtain desired changes by leveraging federal financial aid dollars to get a smaller number of colleges to change than try to affect the individual actions of millions of students through information alone.

Principle 1: Consider allocating bonus funds to colleges with high graduation rates for Pell Grant recipients.

Allocating bonus funds to colleges with high graduation rates could be done in two different ways. The first way is by providing colleges with a carrot, giving institutions extra funds that successfully graduate high numbers of Pell recipients and encouraging them to better serve students with financial need. President Obama has proposed a similar Pell graduation bonus in his past few budgets, but the proposals have yet to see any congressional action.[58] The now-abandoned federal college ratings proposal also aimed to tie federal funds to performance on some of the same metrics by 2018.[59]

Principle 2: Require colleges to share risk for their performance on enrolling low-income students and helping them succeed.

Requiring colleges to have some skin in the game would work by having them put a percentage of low-income students' financial aid awards at stake if outcomes (e.g., Pell enrollment, Pell graduation rates, or post-college outcomes such as student loan default rates) are lower than a predefined threshold. The general idea of risk-sharing has bipartisan support in Congress, although Democrats and Republicans disagree on many of the details. However, care must be taken to design a system that encourages colleges to enroll low-income students—thereby improving college match—instead of only enrolling students with a high probability of completion.[60] This could be done by incentivizing both enrollment and completion instead of just completion rates.

POTENTIAL LIMITATIONS OF FEDERAL COLLEGE-MATCHING POLICIES

Although the federal government is in a unique position to make data available to students and the general public, change financial aid awards in a way that might improve college match, and impose accountability policies that might make colleges more amenable to enrolling academically qualified students from the bottom half of the income distribution, any potential federal policies face a number of substantial limitations that may reduce their effectiveness. Many of these limitations have been described in earlier chapters in this volume, but they bear summarizing here in the context of the federal government's potential to address them.

Encouraging students to attend a college that is more closely in line with their academic qualifications may not make sense for non-academic reasons. For example, although 31 percent of freshmen reported that a college's graduation rate was a "very important" factor in their college choice process, about 45 percent said that price was a major concern and 21 percent of students responded that living close to home was very important.[61] Both price and location are reasons why students choose to attend community college, although research has found that students who begin at four-year colleges complete bachelor's degrees at higher rates than students with similar academic profiles who began at community colleges.[62] Other reasons why students choose a particular college, such as size, religious affiliation, and campus climate, are factors that the federal government is unable to influence through a college-matching policy and thus limit the effectiveness of any federal policies. Third-party organizations like college rankings can provide these types of information to students, while the federal government focuses on providing data on key outcome metrics.

While addressing concerns about price are difficult, it is far from a guarantee that asking students to move farther from home for college is a good idea. Students from low-income families often bear a number of responsibilities for their family and community—financial and otherwise—and leaving home to attend college is difficult if not impossible for them.[63] Unfortunately, in many parts of the country, there are few colleges within a reasonable commute; Nick Hillman at the University of Wisconsin-Madison has called these regions "education deserts."[64] Better serving these areas, which tend to be sparsely populated, may require online or hybrid education models given the diseconomies of scale in these regions.

There is also no guarantee that federal efforts to improve academic match would actually reach or affect the choices of many students. The existing efforts to reach out to low-income, high-achieving students have focused on a fairly small group. The most comprehensive effort to date has been a push by the College Board—which administers the SAT—to give students with SAT scores in the top 15 percent and family incomes in the bottom quartile of the income distribution fee waivers to send their scores to up to six colleges. This is estimated to reach twenty-eight thousand students, a small fraction of the potential college-going population.[65] There is no guarantee that other students with lower test scores who still meet admissions criteria to four-year colleges would respond in the same way as high-achieving students, and there is no comprehensive way to reach out to students who decide not to take the ACT or SAT.

Even if academic match was improved, the potential gains to college completion rates might be fairly small. This is true even though a body of research has concluded that students who attend more selective colleges are more likely to graduate, especially students from lower-income families and those with lower likelihoods of completing college based on their academic preparation.[66] Additionally, while a body of research has found economic returns to attending more selective colleges, the largest effects appear to be for attending elite public and private universities.[67] The effects of going from a less selective four-year college to a moderately selective four-year college may very well be modest, and these institutions represent a far larger portion of the higher education system than the small number of highly selective colleges.[68]

Another factor potentially limiting the effectiveness of federal policies designed to improve college match is that the number of available seats at selective four-year colleges has grown more slowly than the number of available seats at less selective colleges.[69] While low-income students have substantially improved their academic preparation over the last several decades, higher-income students have made even larger gains.[70] As a result, lower-income students have been able to make relatively little headway into elite colleges. But even if that could be resolved, improving college match for some students is likely to displace other students and hurt their likelihood of graduation. Matthew Chingos conducted a simulation of improving college matches, reallocating students already attending four-year colleges to other colleges based on their academic preparation. While this simulation showed a modest decline in socioeconomic gaps in bachelor's degree attainment rates, overall completion rates rose by just 0.2 percentage points.[71]

The federal government could potentially work to help create more seats at high-quality four-year institutions—both at the most selective institutions and at moderately selective institutions that have shown a commitment to increasing access while also increasing completion rates. Some of these latter institutions, such as Arizona State and Georgia State universities, have substantially increased enrollment while decreasing per-student expenditures and increasing graduation rates.[72] These additional seats could be offered to students attending lower-quality four-year colleges (regardless of selectivity), students attending community colleges or for-profit institutions, or academically qualified students not attending college at all.

However, this policy may have limitations as well. Encouraging higher-achieving students to attend more selective colleges could have significant impacts on equity and the students who can only gain admission to open-access institutions. A small body of research has found that the quality of their peers affects students' academic performance in college after controlling for other factors, suggesting that taking higher-performing students out of less selective colleges may have negative implications for the students who remain.[73] This could also reduce enrollment and completion rates at less selective colleges to the point where they face sanctions from accreditors or the federal government, potentially taking away the only local educational option for some students.

Finally, a push to have more students attend more selective colleges could increase the cost of higher education for taxpayers in addition to the price paid by students. In 2011, the average master's-level public university (primarily less selective comprehensive institutions) spent $6,681 per full-time equivalent student in education and related expenditures, while the average public research university spent $9,194.[74] Even if public research universities were willing to expand to accommodate additional students, additional public support is likely needed to allow for the expansion unless the entire price is passed along to students and their families. This also contradicts state and federal efforts to encourage enrollment in community colleges as a cost-effective option, as evidenced by statewide tuition-free community college efforts and President Obama's proposal for a national tuition-free community college program.

CONCLUSION

Recent interest by policy makers in the idea of improving students' academic matches with colleges, coupled with the upcoming reauthorization of the Higher Education Act, make the next few years a rare opportunity to take potentially meaningful action to improve match. The federal government has a number of powerful tools at its disposal, including required data disclosures from colleges, the approximately $150 billion in student financial aid dollars distributed annually, and potentially even issuing an opinion on some metrics of quality should federal college ratings and gainful employment regulations take effect in the future.

The federal government can make its greatest contribution to improving college match through making information available to students, their families, and the general public. Although the US Department of Education has made repeated, good-faith efforts to make data available in a student-friendly format on its website, the information is often not reaching students and their families as they choose colleges. While the data should still be available on official government websites, the main goal of the federal government should be to require colleges to disclose information on relevant outcomes for different subgroups of students working with partners such as guidance counselors in order to get that information to students. Additionally, once data are made public, third-party organizations such as college access organizations and rankings providers can put the information into different formats that students may find useful.

While changes to how student financial aid dollars are distributed to students and colleges may both affect where some students enroll and how many students complete college, it is extremely difficult to imagine a situation in which a meaningful amount of money is reallocated toward colleges determined to be higher-achieving. Higher education funding is likely to be a zero-sum game for the foreseeable future, meaning that any additional money given to colleges successfully serving academically qualified students will likely have to come from other colleges. Given the power of higher education lobbying groups and that the median congressional district has eleven colleges, improving college match through the financial aid system appears to be a long shot at best.[75]

However, the federal government should also work to recognize colleges that are successfully enrolling, educating, and graduating academically qualified students from across the family income distribution. Although this is unlikely to happen through systemic financial aid reforms, the federal government may want to consider rewarding these colleges when one-time funds—such as improvement grants—become available. Labeling certain colleges as "exemplars" may also be worthwhile, although labeling colleges as "needing improvement" is likely to result in a major political fight.

In the long run, the percentage of students able to attend a college for which they are academically qualified will only increase if the number of seats in somewhat selective colleges increases. This can happen through expanding current colleges, building new colleges, or imposing admissions standards at currently open-access institutions. But efforts to make colleges more selective should be carefully weighed against the potential of shutting out students from less rigorous high schools, for whom open access institutions are their only immediate way to access higher education. In any case, improving the quality of higher education is likely to carry a substantial price tag—one that will probably pay off in the long run but create shorter-run fiscal concerns.

Conclusion

Andrew P. Kelly, Jessica S. Howell, Carolyn Sattin-Bajaj

The concept of college match has come a long way in less than a decade. What started as an exploration of Chicago high school students' college-going behavior has evolved into a national research and policy effort designed to help students capitalize on the postsecondary opportunities they have earned. Quite a lot has changed in that time. The term *undermatching* now conjures images of high-achieving students from low-income backgrounds who fail to secure spots in top universities that desperately want to find them, enroll them, foot the bill, and catapult them to the upper echelons of the labor market and civil society. While this definition of college match has attracted significant media and political attention to an important issue of equity, it is inherently limited, obscuring the vast and diverse population of students that is engaging in an increasingly complicated and risky college choice process.

The chapters in this volume chisel away at the narrow image of undermatch that has dominated scholarly and media coverage of the topic, broadening the lens to include more students, more institutions, and more definitions of *match*. In doing so, they push our understanding of the nature and extent of the problems and how those problems are often very different across groups of students and institution types. The volume also identifies new opportunities to address ongoing disparities in access to college and highlights significant challenges in improving college completion rates overall.

The contributors set out to move the conversation about match forward in four key ways. First, we argue that current definitions used by researchers and embraced by policy makers and the media that focus exclusively on the *academic* match between students and colleges are missing essential aspects of student-institution dynamics. We show empirically the power of incorporating other measures of match to estimate the scope and conse- quences of the phenomenon. Second, we push to expand the undermatch discussion beyond the particular and unique plight of high-achieving, low- income students. Third, we highlight the near-total lack of discussion of the constraints and incentives on the supply side of the higher education mar- ket that limit the opportunities available to students. And last, we explicitly focus on the policy implications of college match, introducing evidence of how institutional, local, state, and federal policies affect student choices and capacity constraints. What did we learn? And what new questions emerged over the course of the volume?

LESSONS LEARNED

Below we highlight some of the cross-cutting themes and points of tension that arise from reading the chapters as a whole. Both the areas of concor- dance and conflict serve to identify opportunities for research in this rap- idly changing and influential field.

The Need to Broaden from Academic Match to Overall Fit

Anyone who has engaged in the college choice process in recent years or has discussed it with a student, parent, or college counselor will recognize that the choice of college is based on a wide range of factors that extend beyond academics and admissions selectivity. Students also weigh financial, geo- graphic, and cultural fit considerations. In chapter 2, a team of College Board researchers (including one of the volume's editors) demonstrated empirically that some of the additional dimensions they were able to measure—what they label "fit"—help to explain observable differences in college comple- tion above and beyond what is explained by academic match alone. That these same broader concepts of fit are also important to the "holistic admis- sions" process described by Michael Bastedo in chapter 6 is no coincidence.

Future contributions in this area should broaden the definition of match to incorporate fit and more clearly delineate the core components of this con- cept. They should also improve upon the data available to accurately assess fit in a way that is consistent with use by college admissions professionals. The strongest future contributions to data and measurement will have to overcome substantial challenges—we do not merely need more and better data on student preferences for college attributes, but also better ways to help high school students assess whether they will fit in and feel comfortable on particular campuses. In addition, we need a clearer understanding of how postsecondary institutions attempt to appeal to potential students on the basis of fit, as well as how admissions professionals look for signs of a good fit in students' application portfolios. These questions will be particularly important in light of recent calls to revise the college application to resemble something closer to a portfolio of student work.[1]

Another important facet of broadening the match definition is recognizing the salience of choice of major in students' postsecondary experiences and outcomes. In chapter 4, Thomas Bailey and colleagues at the Community College Research Center introduce the idea of redirecting the match discussion toward "program match," in which a student finds a program of postsecondary study that corresponds to his or her interests, goals, and aptitude. The ideas laid out in chapter 4 put forth a much more dynamic concept of match—although still primarily academic—where students continually update their preferences through exposure to different courses, experiences in various careers, and information about earnings during both high school and college. Because reimagining match as a program-level concept is a dramatic departure from its current definition and we know very little about how to effectively guide students through the process of choosing a college major, we are optimistic that this area of inquiry will attract the attention of more researchers and practitioners moving forward. Chapter 4 also calls on institutions to examine variation in student success across majors, use and share these data for programmatic improvements, and encourage informed decision making on the part of school counselors and students.

The Need to Include Students Outside of the Top of the Class

The recent focus on high-achieving, low-income students has moved the match discussion too far from the vast majority of students and institutions in the United States. We now have good data that show the extent to which undermatch is a phenomenon that affects students at a wide range of academic ability levels. For instance, in a separate study, Jonathan Smith, Matea Pender, and Jessica Howell estimate an undermatch rate between roughly 35 and 50 percent among students with the modest academic credentials that are good enough to get them into all but the top colleges.[2] Awilda Rodriguez and Christian Martell drive home this point in chapter 3; there are an estimated 1.1 million "average-performing" students who are college bound, more than thirty times the number of high-achieving, low-income students estimated by Caroline Hoxby and Christopher Avery.[3] High-achieving, low-income students were an attractive subject for researchers and the media. This stems in part from the fact that they are strong enough academically to gain admission to elite colleges if they would apply yet poor enough to qualify for a full ride at many institutions with the ability to sharply discount their astronomical tuition.

However, now that we know more about improving match for the highest-achieving students, it is time to turn our attention to the large swell of students in the middle of the achievement distribution. Modest achievers are in many ways a more challenging group to address, since the institutions considered an academic match for them tend to have lower completion rates and fewer resources to support tuition discounting. Furthermore, questions about the supply of matched institutions at lower levels of selectivity and in particular geographies (such as those raised in chapters 1, 3, and 7) suggest how complicated it may be to improve match for students in the middle. Expanding the field to include these middle-achieving students will likely bring issues of financial fit to the fore. It will raise potentially charged questions about the relative importance of solving the undermatch problem for modest achievers or for high achievers.

Future contributions in this area will necessarily expand the evidence and discussion to better incorporate community colleges and broad access four-year institutions, which, as Thomas Bailey and colleagues argue in chapter 4, collectively serve a substantial proportion of students with more modest backgrounds. While this volume touches only briefly on match as it relates to non-traditional students, we believe that future attempts to broaden the discussion to community colleges will need to focus on this demographic as well. They are harder to reach and often far removed from any counseling and advising services available to traditional-age students. In light of the various proposals for free community college and the potential effects of such policies on undermatch, future work in this area would be both timely and policy-relevant.

The expansion of the match discussion to a broader swath of students raises questions about how to successfully deliver college counseling and advising services to a much larger population, including parents. Likewise, reimagining match as a program-level construct may involve additional expectations of high school and college counselors in advising students about different majors and career paths. There are currently a variety of different "virtual advising" models being tested, and evidence on the effectiveness of those models—particularly with regard to undermatch—will be extremely informative for those who move the work forward in this direction. The Expanding College Opportunities intervention by Caroline Hoxby and Sarah Turner showed us how college information and advice could be customized and delivered to high-achieving, low-income students without utilizing a counselor. However, we know almost nothing about how low-cost, light-touch alternatives might work for prospective students with average academic credentials, different goals, and very different postsecondary options. Chapter 1 demonstrates that there are currently mixed findings regarding the degree to which more modest achievers would benefit from improved match, so this is also an area ripe for further investigation.

The Supply Side Is Critical

The descriptive portrait of the supply side of the higher education market painted in chapter 5 reveals that the highest-performing institutions—those that graduate their students at the highest rates—are also the smallest segment of the higher education market and grow only modestly over time. In contrast, the colleges that would be academic matches for students with more modest academic credentials are precisely the types of institutions that serve the majority of students and have expanded their supply the most.[4] This is partly why widening the undermatch umbrella to encompass modest achievers is so important; it successfully pulls into the conversation the set of colleges and universities that educate the bulk of American students. These institutions have the greatest potential to respond to increasing demand since they usually do not have the same fixed capacity constraints of the most elite colleges and universities.

At the same time, however, once outside of the ranks of the top two hundred or so colleges, there is tremendous variation in college quality—particularly as measured by graduation rates and credentials per student. In fact, as the examples from Chicago in chapter 1 illustrated, there can be wider variation institutional graduation rates within selectivity categories than across them. Although it is outside of the scope of this volume to address the very real challenge of how to improve student outcomes at postsecondary institutions with lackluster records of student success, the way in which we might effectively improve the quality of the colleges where most students enroll remains a critical piece of the supply-side discussion that is currently missing.

The issues of quality and supply are central to any large-scale response to undermatch, but they are also some of the thorniest. In chapter 6, Michael Bastedo helps explain how the reward structure that colleges face makes it complicated for admissions offices to prioritize decisions that would likely improve the rate at which students match to quality colleges. Until now, what scant attention researchers have paid to supply-side questions in the context of undermatch has been restricted to the unwillingness of elite institutions to expand. Consequently, match has been reduced to a zero sum game where improving outcomes for some students necessarily comes at the expense of others. Bastedo clarifies the "replacement" concerns around undermatch, yet many questions remain about how college admissions professionals balance competing priorities as they assemble their class.

There is no question that elite institutions will never sufficiently expand to serve all of the academically qualified students who desire admission. Yet, there exists evidence of growth over time in this sector and perhaps potential for that trend to continue.[5] For example, undergraduate enrollment has steadily grown over the last decade at Princeton University, and the administration recently announced its intention to grow further without sacrificing academic quality.[6] In fact, many more elite institutions have pledged to engage in a variety of efforts to better support academically prepared students from disadvantaged backgrounds and the calls for these institutions to do more are increasing.[7] Future contributions to the supply-side literature might track the implementation and success of these institutional pledges and activities. Such studies could build the knowledge base about which institutions achieve success in serving students who would have otherwise undermatched, what they are doing, and how their methods might be scaled.

This volume provides a fuller and clearer picture of the way institutional objectives play into the undermatch discussion—particularly with regard to the enrollment managers tasked with crafting incoming classes. Bastedo's ongoing experiments on fixing admission officers' cognitive biases demonstrate that institution-level policies—in this case, presenting applicants' information in a slightly different context—have the potential to generate more equitable admissions outcomes for certain subgroups of applicants. Better and more nuanced understandings of what happens inside the admissions office and why will allow us to identify opportunities to improve match and collegiate outcomes for low-income students on particular campuses. Chapter 6 naturally raises questions about the role of policy in changing the incentives facing colleges and their admissions officers.

Future contributions in this area will build on the institution-level evidence with a careful eye to the places where institutional policies intersect with local, state, and federal ones.

Policies Affect College Match—and Often Not in a Positive Way

A wide variety of policies at the institutional, local, state, and federal levels influence students' propensity to attend a college or pick a major that is a good match, yet studies of undermatching have largely neglected public policy as an important variable. The final three chapters provide evidence of the importance of policies in shaping student choices, and the effects are by no means universally positive.

Local government is often ignored in higher education, as most of the spending and regulation is done at the state and federal levels. But local communities, like local schools, likely have an important impact on college-going behavior. In chapter 7, Lindsay Page and Jennifer Iriti describe how one local effort—the Pittsburgh Promise scholarship—improved college-going, the probability of choosing a four-year institution, and persistence. The authors argue that it did so through a combination of alleviating financial barriers to college and informational barriers about financial aid. The quantitative results for college match in Pittsburgh are suggestive. At full program generosity, the Promise also reduced undermatch in a location with a very high rate of undermatch. Page and Iriti's qualitative findings indicate that the Pittsburgh Promise helped to remove uncertainty about how to finance a college education much earlier in a student's life and provided support through the financial aid process.

Early results from promise programs suggest that notifying families about financial aid eligibility can have a dramatic effect on student behavior, though the effect on matching is still unclear. These results have implications for federal and state policy. For instance, a recent policy change will now allow families to use income from two years prior on the Free Application for Federal Student Aid (FAFSA) form. Like the Pittsburgh Promise, this change will send an earlier message to eligible students, helping to alleviate some uncertainty by allowing students to learn about their financial aid eligibility much earlier in the college choice process.[8] As Robert Kelchen highlights in chapter 9, earlier notifications about available financial aid can support more thoughtful college choice based on more complete information. Information provision is just one way that the federal government can support improvements in college match, a topic we return to in a moment.

Promise programs are just one example of a local education policy that may bear on college match, albeit one that is also well aligned to both K–12 and postsecondary institutions. Chapter 4 highlights another area that receives less attention but is worthy of future research: the relationship between policy, employers, and programs of study. We know very little about how, if at all, employers, economic development agencies, or institutions themselves signal to prospective students (or their high schools) which skills and credentials are in demand. How responsive are institutions to labor market information in their advising? How much do high school counselors know about the relationship between college major and labor market prospects and to what extent do they include such information in their work with students? A starting point for empirical investigation on this topic might be an analysis of the existing policies that might encourage or discourage this kind of behavior.

Moving from the local to the state level, chapter 8 serves to remind us that state policies have a massive impact on college enrollment and choice, and often with mixed results from the perspective of college match. State subsidies for public institutions, state-sponsored financial aid programs, and several other state policies induce college enrollment among students who would not have otherwise gone to college; these policy levers have been shown to improve completion outcomes in several states.[9] Such changes in student behavior may benefit states through an increased probability that those college-educated students remain in the state labor market after college. Yet, some of the evidence highlighted in chapter 8 also reveals that, by changing students' choice of college, some state programs actually result in worse degree completion outcomes. The evidence is particularly damning where state policies are shown to divert students into community colleges and broad-access four-year institutions; new evidence suggests that nontrivial proportions of students who attend these institutions default on their student loans, often on small amounts of debt.[10]

Future contributions in this area will better illuminate the tension between policies that sound good and have great political appeal (such as free community college) and those that result in improved student outcomes. Additionally, the variation in empirical results across states serves as an important reminder that context matters, and leaders should not assume that an intervention in one place will necessarily play out identically in another. As the authors of chapter 8 demonstrate, variation across states is also an ideal way to study the effects of policy on college choice. Future work should continue to improve our understanding of the conditions that promote or obstruct college match in these different contexts.

Returning to the role of the federal government, Robert Kelchen demonstrates how federal policies interact with many state- and local-level policies—as well as with institutional incentives—most prominently in terms of financial aid. Any discussion of college match must acknowledge the role of federal aid in shaping student behavior and consider how federal policy reforms might improve match rates. To that end, chapter 9 identifies three mechanisms by which the federal government might influence match and suggests concrete options available to federal policy makers. The policy recommendations contained in chapter 9 echo many of the conclusions in the previous chapters, clearly illustrating the significance of the incentives that federal programs and policies create for institutions and for students. What to do about those incentives is somewhat less clear, although Kelchen spells out a number of policy reforms that would give colleges a greater stake in their students' success.

WHERE ARE WE HEADED? UNRESOLVED QUESTIONS

We are confident that the ideas and evidence contained in this volume will spur new research and activity that will move the concept of match forward in broader and more useful directions. At the same time, the volume unearthed some important, unresolved questions that researchers and practitioners will have to grapple with in the years ahead.

Increasing Completion Versus Closing Attainment Gaps

In the rush to improve match rates, some have lost sight of the basic question that underlies the entire endeavor: What problem are we trying to solve? In other words, what does improved match actually achieve? Improving college match alone is probably *not* going to drive us to successfully reach the college completion goals that have gained so much attention nationally over the past decade. As discussed in chapter 1 and elsewhere, simulations of the potential for match to increase degree completion vary in their effects, and that variation is driven almost entirely by different supply-side assumptions about institutional capacity. Researchers who assume institutional capacity is more or less fixed find little effect; others who relax that constraint and assume colleges will make room find a sizable completion effect for low-income students. Even in the latter case, though, the largest estimated positive effects for subgroups of undermatched students suggest a fairly small *overall* effect on US completion rates.[11]

However, improved match could still be a fruitful way to close stubborn socioeconomic gaps in college completion by improving outcomes for those at the bottom of the SES ladder. If match among lower SES students is, in fact, driven by reducing informational asymmetries, eliminating process barriers, and more generous financial aid, then existing solutions to under-match may successfully elevate the postsecondary options and outcomes of low-income and first-generation students. That result is a clear benefit for low-income and first-generation students and for society at large; evidence suggests that these students experience the largest payoff from college completion.[12] The question then becomes whether that benefit must necessarily come at the expense of other students, and how policy reforms and investments can improve college match *and* educational attainment.

Is There a Distinction Between Match and Institutional Quality?

Our focus on the supply side raises an important question about the distinction between match and college quality. In essence, when we discuss and analyze issues of college match, are we really just talking about college quality? And is quality distinct from admissions selectivity? Or is the concept of "match" truly something different entirely?

Much of the existing work on college match translates to advice that many students already hear when it comes to choosing a college: "Go to the best college or university that will admit you." The key question, though, is what "best" means in this context. Is it admissions selectivity? Some measure of student outcomes like graduation rates, student learning, or labor market success? Perhaps it is the actual experience of learning on a given campus—the programs of study and student supports that are available and the quality of teaching? Then there are all the other, non-academic dimensions discussed in chapter 2: Is the school close to home? Does it enroll similar students? Is it in a city or a rural area? and so on. Is the definition of what's "best" highly individualized?

Without a more comprehensive understanding of which institutional characteristics are likely to matter and for which students, the concept of a "best" choice remains largely stuck on the combination of academic background and admissions selectivity. But this approach is fraught with supply-side constraints. It also runs counter to what some researchers have found when they examine overmatching. If there is something truly beneficial about academic match above and beyond college quality, the implication is that overmatch would be as detrimental for student outcomes as undermatch.

Evidence on the asymmetric effect of overmatching may lend support to the notion that we really are just talking about college quality. In order to determine whether overmatching is harmful, one can examine students on the margin of admission—those who just barely squeaked through the admissions process, compared with similar students who narrowly missed receiving an offer of admission. System-specific studies from both Georgia State University and the University of California that take this research approach find that overmatched students are actually better off for having squeaked through the admissions process because they wind up enrolled at higher-quality institutions.[13] Other research reveals that students from wealthier families and more educated neighborhoods are less likely to undermatch, but actually *more* likely to overmatch.[14] This suggests that the affluent students and families whom we typically believe are the most well-informed about their college options behave as though any negatives associated with overmatching are more than offset by the benefits of attending a higher-quality college.

We see this volume as a call to tease apart the various institutional characteristics that influence student success: academic quality (what students learn), student supports and campus climate (what keeps students enrolled), and preparation for life after college (advising and affinity networks). Some of the work in this volume advances this new research agenda by introducing additional variables of "fit" (chapters 2 and 3) and identifying additional student supports (like career and major advising) and data elements (like labor market outcomes by major) necessary to promote more focused decision making about college major (chapter 4). But there is still much more work to be done.

Even with a better understanding of which dimensions of college quality and student characteristics affect a given student's likelihood of success at a certain institution, improving match on these dimensions will require significant change in student advising. Better high school advising would first entail investment in considerable training, information, and skill building of existing counselors and, likely, a broader pipeline of talent into the advising corps. The necessary changes are perhaps more acute at the college level, where students have more independence and autonomy, communication with high schools is ad hoc at best, and academic and career advising is often self-serve. In other words, the research agenda we call for should be used to inform a parallel research and development effort around effective advising, one that takes a broader view of what is important to ensuring student success.

We certainly haven't resolved the issue of college match versus college quality in this volume. Rather, we believe it is important that future work grapple with the question because it has implications for both how we advise students and for our broader approach to reform. Can we make progress through better college choices alone? Or will progress also require that institutions adopt reforms to improve quality and expand access to it?

Improving Colleges Versus Improving College Choice

Better data and advising are worthwhile steps. But if the supply of quality seats is constrained, they will only get us so far. This volume has raised the question of how to improve colleges at various points, but it does not try to answer it. If match and college quality are actually quite closely related, improving the quality of institutions would, by definition, improve the match between them and their students with above-average credentials. However, this is where the deck is stacked against making progress through match-inspired solutions. Most match efforts merely reshuffle students, improving the outcomes for those who respond to interventions and successfully find better universities that willingly make room for them. We might be able to make quick, cheap progress on match by providing students and their families with better information about college options, but solving the overall problem of lackluster college completion requires a broader strategy around improving institutions. This argument is particularly relevant for the thousands of institutions that serve the substantial middle of the academic distribution as well as the majority of students who have been traditionally underserved in US education. We are certainly not the first to make it.[15]

Our stance on this issue is simple but largely unfulfilling. As we collectively labor through other initiatives and efforts to improve the quality of postsecondary institutions in the United States, we must also invest in stopgap measures that help current students navigate this imperfect and often complex higher education world. Efforts to improve match for specific groups are precisely this type of stopgap. We see this volume as a beginning—the start of a new agenda that takes seriously both the demand and supply sides of college match and the implications of existing policy and proposed reforms for making progress. Improving match alone will not solve lagging college completion rates, and it will be unlikely to make a sizable dent in educational equity on its own. But by broadening the lens to include a wider array of institutions, students, and policy makers, this volume should help lay the groundwork for more far-reaching and productive conversations about how college match fits into our national effort to improve educational attainment. From there, we expect a new set of possibilities for change to emerge.

Notes

Introduction

1. National Center for Education Statistics, "Table 236. Percentage of Recent High School Completers Enrolled in 2-Year and 4-Year Colleges, by Income Level: 1975 through 2011," June 2012, https://nces.ed.gov/programs/digest/d12/tables/dt12_236.asp.
2. National Center for Education Statistics, "Table 235. Percentage of Recent High School Completers Enrolled in 2-Year and 4-Year Colleges, by Race/Ethnicity: 1960 through 2011," June 2012, https://nces.ed.gov/programs/digest/d12/tables/dt12_235.asp.
3. National Center for Education Statistics, "Table 303.10. Total Fall Enrollment in Degree-Granting Postsecondary Institutions, by Attendance Status, Sex of Student, and Control of Institution. Selected Years, 1947 through 2023," July 2014, http://nces.ed.gov/programs/digest/d13/tables/dt13_303.10.asp.
4. National Center for Education Statistics, "Table 326.10. Graduation Rate from First Institution Attended for First-Time, Full-Time Bachelor's Degree-Seeking Students at 4-Year Postsecondary Institutions, by Race/Ethnicity, Time to Completion, Sex, Control of Institution, and Acceptance Rate: Selected Cohort Entry Years, 1996 through 2007," November 2014, https://nces.ed.gov/programs/digest/d14/tables/dt14_326.10.asp.
5. Susan Dynarski, "For the Poor, the Graduation Gap Is Even Wider Than the Enrollment Gap," *New York Times*, June 2, 2015, www.nytimes.com/2015/06/02/upshot/for-the-poor-the-graduation-gap-is-even-wider-than-the-enrollment-gap.html?_r=0&abt=0002&abg=1.
6. National Center for Education Statistics, "Table 376. Percentage of First-Time Full-Time Bachelor's Degree-Seeking Students at 4-year Institutions Who Completed a Bachelor's Degree, by Race/Ethnicity, Time to Completion, Sex, and Control of Institution: Selected Cohort Entry Years, 1996 through 2005," November 2012, http://nces.ed.gov/programs/digest/d12/tables/dt12_376.asp.
7. Sandy Baum, Jennifer Ma, and Kathleen Payea, *Education Pays 2013* (New York: The College Board, 2013), http://trends.collegeboard.org/sites/default/files/education-pays-2013-full-report-022714.pdf.
8. US Department of Education, *Better Information for Better College Choice & Institutional Performance*, September 2015, https://collegescorecard.ed.gov/assets/BetterInformationForBetterCollegeChoiceAndInstitutionalPerformance.pdf.
9. Claudio Sanchez, "White House Makes College For Low-Income Students a Priority," NPR, January 16, 2014, www.npr.org/sections/codeswitch/2014/01/16/263128207/white-house-makes-college-for-low-income-students-a-priority.
10. Eleanor Wiske Dillon and Jeffrey Andrew Smith, "The Determinants of Mismatch Between Students and Colleges" (working paper, National Bureau of Economic Research, Cambridge, MA, August 2013), www.nber.org/papers/w19286.pdf; Jonathan Smith, Matea Pender, and

Jessica Howell, "The Full Extent of Student-College Academic Undermatch," *Economics of Education Review* 32 (February 2013): 247–261; Caroline M. Hoxby and Sarah Turner, "Informing Students About Their College Options: A Proposal for Broadening the Expanding College Opportunities Project" (working paper, The Brookings Institution, The Hamilton Project, Washington, DC, June 2013), www.hamiltonproject.org/files/downloads_and_links/THP_HoxbyTurner_FINAL.pdf; D. Crystal Byndloss et al., *In Search of a Match: A Guide for Helping Students Make Informed College Choices* (New York: MDRC, April 2015), www.mdrc.org/sites/default/files/in_search_for_a_match.pdf.

11. Hoxby and Turner, "Informing Students About Their College Options."

12. Matthew M. Chingos, "Graduation Rates at America's Universities: What We Know and What We Need to Know," in *Getting to Graduation: The Completion Agenda in Higher Education*, eds. Andrew P. Kelly and Mark Schneider (Baltimore: Johns Hopkins University Press, 2012): 48–71.

13. Sarah R. Cohodes and Joshua S. Goodman, "First Degree Earns: The Impact of College Quality on College Completion Rates," (working paper, Harvard Kennedy School, Cambridge, MA, 2012), https://dash.harvard.edu/bitstream/handle/1/9396433/RWP12-033_Goodman.pdf?sequence=1; Joshua Goodman, Michael Hurwitz, and Jonathan Smith, "College Access, Initial College Choice and Degree Completion" (working paper, National Bureau of Economic Research, Cambridge, MA, February 2015), www.nber.org/papers/w20996.pdf; Mark Hoekstra, "The Effect of Attending the Flagship State University on Earnings: A Discontinuity-Based Approach," *Review of Economics and Statistics* 91, no. 4 (2009): 717–724; Michal Kurlaender and Eric Grodsky, "Mismatch and the Paternalistic Justification for Selective College Admissions," *Sociology of Education* 86 (2013): 294–310.

14. W. Norton Grubb, "The Decline of Community College Transfer Rates: Evidence from National Longitudinal Surveys," *Journal of Higher Education* 62, no. 2 (March–April 1991): 194–222; Bridget Terry Long and Michal Kurlaender, "Do Community Colleges Provide a Viable Pathway to a Baccalaureate Degree?" *Educational Evaluation and Policy Analysis* 31, no. 1 (March 2009): 30–53.

15. Frederick M. Hess et al., "Diplomas and Dropouts: Which Colleges Graduate Their Students and Which Don't" (Washington, DC: American Enterprise Institute, June 2009), http://static1.squarespace.com/static/5138ee3ee4b0052c92d948f5/t/53d7b653e4b0326a80e199ea/1406645843001/2010-02+Diplomas+and+Dropouts+Study.pdf.

16. Melissa Roderick, Vanessa Coca, and Jenny Nagaoka, "Potholes on the Road to College: High School Effects in Shaping Urban Students' Participation in College Application, Four-Year College Enrollment, and College Match," *Sociology of Education* 84, no. 3 (2011): 178–211.

17. William G. Bowen, Matthew M. Chingos, and Michael S. McPherson, *Crossing the Finish Line: Completing College at America's Public Universities* (Princeton, NJ: Princeton University Press, 2009).

18. Caroline Hoxby and Christopher Avery, *The Missing "One Offs": The Hidden Supply of High-Achieving, Low-Income Students* (Washington, DC: The Brookings Institution, 2013), www.brookings.edu/~/media/projects/bpea/spring-2013/2013a_hoxby.pdf.

19. Smith, Pender, and Howell, "The Full Extent of Student-College Academic Undermatch."

20. Dillon and Smith, "The Determinants of Mismatch Between Students and Colleges."

21. Hoxby and Turner, "Informing Students About Their College Options."

22. College Board, "Realize Your College Potential," http://professionals.collegeboard.com/guidance/access-to-opportunity/realize-your-college-potential.

23. Hess et al., "Diplomas and Dropouts."

24. Susan Scrivener et al., *Doubling Graduation Rates: Three-Year Effects of CUNY's Accelerated Study in Associate Programs (ASAP) for Development Education Students*, MDRC, February 2015, www.mdrc.org/sites/default/files/doubling_graduation_rates_fr.pdf.

25. Sarah R. Cohodes and Joshua S. Goodman, "Merit Aid, College Quality and College Completion: Massachusetts' Adams Scholarship as an In-Kind Subsidy," *American Economic Journal: Applied Economics* 6, no. 4 (2014): 251–284; Goodman, Hurwitz and Smith, "College Access, Initial College Choice and Degree Completion."

Chapter 1

1. Grace Kena et al., *The Condition of Education 2015* (Washington, DC: US Department of Education, National Center for Education Statistics, 2015).

2. D. Crystal Byndloss and Chera Reid, *Promoting College Match for Low-Income Students: Lessons for Practitioners*, MDRC, September 2013, www.mdrc.org/sites/default/files/college_match_brief.pdf.; Eleanor W. Dillon and Jeffrey A. Smith, "The Determinants of Mismatch Between Students and Colleges" (working paper, National Bureau of Economic Research, Cambridge, MA, 2013); Caroline Hoxby and Christopher Avery, *The Missing "One-Offs": The Hidden Supply of High-Achieving, Low-Income Students* (Washington, DC: The Brookings Institution, 2013), www.brookings.edu/~/media/projects/bpea/spring-2013/2013a_hoxby.pdf; Caroline Hoxby and Sarah Turner, "Expanding College Opportunities for High-Achieving, Low-Income Students" (working paper, Stanford Institute for Economic Policy Research, Stanford, CA, 2013); Jonathan Smith, Matea Pender, and Jessica Howell, "The Full Extent of Student-College Academic Undermatch," *Economics of Education Review* 32 (2013): 247–261.

3. Martha J. Bailey and Susan M. Dynarski, "Inequality in Postsecondary Attainment," in *Whither Opportunity? Rising Inequality, Schools, and Children's Life Chances*, ed. Greg Duncan and Richard Murnane (New York: Russell Sage Foundation, 2011), 117–132.

4. Melissa Roderick et al., *From High School to the Future: Potholes on the Road to College*, Consortium on Chicago School Research at University of Chicago, 2008, https://ccsr.uchicago.edu/sites/default/files/publications/CCSR_Potholes_Report.pdf.

5. William G. Bowen, Matthew M. Chingos, and Michael S. McPherson, *Crossing the Finish Line: Completing College at America's Public Universities* (Princeton, NJ: Princeton University Press, 2009); Smith, Pender, and Howell, "The Full Extent of Student-College Academic Undermatch."

6. Smith, Pender, and Howell, "The Full Extent of Student-College Academic Undermatch."

7. Christopher Avery and Thomas K. Kane, "Student Perceptions of College Opportunities: The Boston COACH Program," in *College Choices: The Economics of Where to Go, When to Go, and How to Pay for It*, ed. Caroline M. Hoxby (Chicago: University of Chicago Press, 2004); Mari Luna De La Rosa, "Is Opportunity Knocking? Low-Income Students' Perceptions of College and Financial Aid," *American Behavioral Scientist* 49, no. 12 (2006): 1670–1686; Sandra L. Hanson, "Lost Talent: Unrealized Educational Aspirations and Expectations Among U.S. Youths," *Sociology of Education* 67, no. 3 (1994): 159–183; James C. Hearn, "Academic and Nonacademic Influence on the College Destinations of 1980 High School Graduates," *Sociology of Education* 64, no. 3 (1991): 158–171; Hoxby and Avery, *The Missing "One-Offs"*; Thomas Kane, *The Price of Admission: Rethinking How Americans Pay for College* (Washington, DC: Brookings Institution Press, 1999); Charles F. Manski and David A. Wise, *College Choice in America* (Cambridge, MA: Harvard University Press, 1983); Amanda Pallais and Sarah Turner, "Opportunities for Low-Income Students at Top Colleges and Universities: Policy Initiatives and the Distribution of Students," *National Tax Journal* 59, no. 2 (2006): 357–386.

8. Pallais and Turner, "Opportunities for Low-Income Students."
9. Hanson, "Lost Talent."; Hoxby and Avery, *The Missing "One-Offs"*; Melissa Roderick et al., *From High School to the Future: Making Hard Work Pay Off*, Consortium on Chicago School Research at University of Chicago, 2009, https://ccsr.uchicago.edu/sites/default/files /publications/Making%20Hard%20Work%20Pay%20Off.pdf.
10. Melissa Roderick et al., *From High School to the Future: A First Look at Chicago Public School Graduates' College Enrollment, College Preparation, and Graduation from Four-Year Colleges*, Consortium on Chicago School Research, 2006, https://ccsr.uchicago.edu/sites/default/files /publications/Postsecondary.pdf.
11. George Lowery and Maureen Hoyler, *Expanding College Access and Success: The Chicago Model* (Washington, DC: COE Networks, 2009).
12. Ibid.
13. Jennifer Stephan and James Rosenbaum, *The Post-Secondary Coach Program in Chicago: Does It Affect the College Going Process?* (Washington, DC: Council of the Great City Schools, 2011).
14. Roderick et al., *From High School to the Future* (2006).
15. Ibid.
16. Department of Postsecondary Education and Student Development, Office of High Schools and High School Programs, Chicago Public Schools, "2007 CPS Citywide Final Senior Exit Questionnaire Report for All Graduates," December 3, 2007.
17. Roderick et al., *From High School to the Future* (2006).
18. Roderick et al., *From High School to the Future* (2008).
19. The selectivity categories are based on competitiveness categories from the 2006 *Barron's Profiles of American Colleges*. The *Barron's* college ranking system rates four-year colleges on inputs such as the academic qualifications of the students who attend the college (for instance, college entrance exam scores, GPA, and class rank), as well as the percentage of applicants who are accepted.
20. Bowen, Chingos, and McPherson, *Crossing the Finish Line*.
21. Byndloss and Reid, *Promoting College Match for Low-Income Students*; D. Crystal Byndloss et al., *In Search of a Match: A Guide for Helping Students Make Informed College Choices*, MDRC, April 2015, www.mdrc.org/sites/default/files/in_search_for_a_match.pdf.
22. Caroline Hoxby and Sarah Turner, "Informing Students About Their College Options: A Proposal for Broadening the Expanding College Opportunities Project" (working paper, The Brookings Institution, The Hamilton Project, June 2013); Hoxby and Turner, "Expanding College Opportunities."
23. James C. Hearn, "Academic and Nonacademic Influence on the College Destinations of 1980 High School Graduates," *Sociology of Education* 64, no.3 (1991): 158–171; De La Rosa, "Is Opportunity Knocking?"; Patricia McDonough, *Choosing Colleges: How Social Class and Schools Structure Opportunity* (Albany: State University of New York Press, 1997).
24. Hoxby and Turner, "Expanding College Opportunities."
25. Roderick et al., *From High School to the Future* (2006).
26. Because of data availability, students who graduate from charter or alternative schools and many of those with an Individualized Education Plan are not included in these data.
27. For academic reasons, see: Brian P. An, "The Relations Between Race, Family Characteristics, and Where Students Apply to College," *Social Science Research* 39, no. 2 (2010): 310–323; James Samuel Coleman and Thomas Hoffer, *Public and Private High Schools: The Impact of Communities* (New York: Basic Books, 1987); Barbara Falsey and Barbara Heyns, "The College Channel: Private and Public Schools Reconsidered," *Sociology of Education* 57, no. 2 (1984): 111–122; Sylvia Hurtado et al., "Differences in College Access and Choice Among Racial/

Ethnic Groups: Identifying Continuing Barriers," *Research in Higher Education* 38, no. 1 (1997): 43–75; Laura W. Perna and Marvin A. Titus, "The Relationship Between Parental Involvement as Social Capital and College Enrollment: An Examination of Racial/Ethnic Group Differences," *Journal of Higher Education* 76, no. 5 (2005): 485–518. For financial considerations, see Stephen L. DesJardins and Brian P. McCall, "Simulating the Effects of Financial Aid Packages on College Student Stopout, Reenrollment Spells, and Graduation Chances," *Review of Higher Education* 33, no. 4 (2010): 513–541; Susan M. Dynarski, "Does Aid Matter? Measuring the Effect of Student Aid on College Attendance and Completion" (working paper, National Bureau of Economic Research, 1999); William Elliott and Sondra G. Beverly, "The Role of Savings and Wealth in Reducing 'Wilt' Between Expectations and College Attendance," *Journal of Children and Poverty* 17, no. 2 (2011): 165–185; Thomas J. Kane, "College Entry by Blacks Since 1970: The Role of College Costs, Family Background, and the Returns to Education," *Journal of Political Economy* 102, no. 5 (1994): 878–911; Michael B. Paulsen and Edward P. St. John, "Social Class and College Costs: Examining the Financial Nexus Between College Choice and Persistence," *Journal of Higher Education* 73, no. 2 (2002): 189–236.

28. Graduate rate data reported by the colleges to the Department of Education's Integrated Postsecondary Education Data System and retrieved from US Department of Education, "Integrated Postsecondary Education Data System," https://nces.ed.gov/ipeds/.

29. Roderick et al., *From High School to the Future* (2006).

30. Thomas D. Snyder and Sally A. Dillow, *Digest of Education Statistics 2013*, US Department of Education, National Center for Education Statistics, 2015.

31. For example, Hoxby and colleagues have consistently used the criterion of a student scoring in the ninetieth percentile on the ACT or SAT to be classified as "high-achieving" (e.g., Caroline Hoxby and Sarah Turner, "What High-Achieving Low-Income Students Know About College" [working paper, National Bureau of Economic Research, Cambridge, MA, 2015]; Hoxby and Turner, "Expanding College Opportunities for High-Achieving, Low-Income Students"). Hoxby and Avery in fact, further restrict the classification, including only students who also earn a minimum of an A– high school GPA (*The Missing "One-Offs"*).

32. Matthew Chingos, "Graduation Rates at America's Universities: What We Know and What We Need to Know," in *Getting to Graduation: The Completion Agenda in Higher Education*, ed. Andrew P. Kelly and Mark Schneider (Baltimore: Johns Hopkins University Press, 2012), 48–71.

33. Michael N. Bastedo and Ozan Jacquette, "Running in Place: Low-Income Students and the Dynamics of Higher Education Stratification," *Educational Evaluation and Policy Analysis* 33, no. 3 (2011): 318–339.

34. Jessica Howell and Matea Pender, "The Costs and Benefits of Enrolling in an Academically Matched College," *Economics of Education Review* (forthcoming).

35. Howell and Pender (ibid.) find larger impacts of matching on lower-achieving students than we do, with even students who are simulated to attend a college with a median SAT score below 1000 to see more than a ten-point increase in graduation rate. This may be because of their use of six-year graduation rates compare to our use of four-year rates, suggesting a path for further research in better understanding the trade-offs for researchers—and students— when choosing between these two outcomes.

36. For example, Ruth N. López-Turley, "College Proximity: Mapping Access to Opportunity," *Sociology of Education* 82, no. 2 (2009): 126–146.

37. Awilda Rodriguez and Christian Martell, "A Case for the Study of Average-Performing Students in College Match," in *Matching All Students to Postsecondary Opportunities*,

ed. Andrew P. Kelly, Jessica Howell, and Carolyn Satin-Bajaj (Cambridge, MA: Harvard University Press, forthcoming).

38. Snyder and Dillow, *Digest of Education Statistics 2013*.

Chapter 2

1. For example, see David Leonhardt, "Better Colleges Failing to Lure Talented Poor," *New York Times*, March 16, 2013, www.nytimes.com/2013/03/17/education/scholarly-poor-often-overlook-better-colleges.html; David Leonhardt, "Delaware Seeks to Steer the Poor to Top Colleges," *New York Times*, September 18, 2013, www.nytimes.com/2013/09/19/us/delaware-seeks-to-steer-the-poor-to-top-colleges.html; Paul Tough, "Who Gets to Graduate," *New York Times Magazine*, May 15, 2014, www.nytimes.com/2014/05/18/magazine/who-gets-to-graduate.html; The White House, Executive Office of the President, *Increasing College Opportunity for Low-Income Students: Promising Models and a Call to Action*, 2014, www.whitehouse.gov/sites/default/files/docs/white_house_report_on_increasing_college_opportunity_for_low-income_students_1-16-2014_final.pdf.

2. See Dan A. Black and Jeffrey A. Smith, "Estimating the Returns to College Quality with Multiple Proxies for Quality," *Journal of Labor Economics* 24, no. 3 (2006): 701–728; William G. Bowen, Matthew M. Chingos, and Michael S. McPherson, *Crossing the Finish Line: Completing College at America's Public Universities* (Princeton, NJ: Princeton University Press, 2009); Dominic J. Brewer, Eric R. Eide, and Ronald G. Ehrenberg, "Does It Pay to Attend an Elite Private College? Cross-Cohort Evidence on the Effects of College Type on Earnings," *Journal of Human Resources* 34, no. 1 (1999): 104–123; Stacy B. Dale and Alan B. Krueger, "Estimating the Payoff to Attending a More Selective College: An Application of Selection on Observables and Unobservables," *Quarterly Journal of Economics* 117, no. 4 (2002): 1491–1527; Stacy B. Dale and Alan B. Krueger, "Estimating the Return to College Selectivity over the Career Using Administrative Earnings Data" (working paper, National Bureau of Economic Research, Cambridge, MA, 2011); Eleanor W. Dillon and Jeffrey A. Smith, "The Determinants of Mismatch Between Students and Colleges" (working paper, National Bureau of Economic Research, Cambridge, MA, 2013); Mark Hoekstra, "The Effect of Attending the Flagship State University on Earnings: A Discontinuity-Based Approach," *Review of Economics and Statistics* 91, no. 4 (2009): 717–724; Caroline M. Hoxby, "The Return to Attending a More Selective College: 1960 to the Present" (working paper, Harvard University, Cambridge, MA, 1998); Caroline Hoxby and Sarah Turner, "Expanding College Opportunities for High-Achieving, Low-Income Students" (working paper, Stanford Institute for Economic Policy Research, Stanford, CA, 2013); Mark C. Long, "College Quality and Early Adult Outcomes," *Economics of Education Review* 27, no. 5 (2008): 588–602; Alexandria W. Radford, *Top Student, Top School?: How Social Class Shapes Where Valedictorians Go to College* (Chicago: University of Chicago Press, 2013); Melissa Roderick, Jenny Nagaoka, Vanessa Coca, and Eliza Moeller, *From High School to the Future: Potholes on the Road to College*, Consortium on Chicago School Research at the University of Chicago, March 2008, https://ccsr.uchicago.edu/publications/high-school-future-potholes-road-college; Jonathan Smith, Matea Pender, and Jessica Howell, "The Full Extent of Academic Undermatch," *Economics of Education Review* 32 (2013): 247–261.

3. See Sarah R. Cohodes and Joshua S. Goodman, "First Degree Earns: The Impact of College Quality on College Completion Rates" (working paper, Harvard Kennedy School, Cambridge, MA, August 2012), https://dash.harvard.edu/bitstream/handle/1/9396433/RWP12-033_Goodman.pdf?sequence=1; Joshua Goodman, Michael Hurwitz, and Jonathan Smith, "College Access, Initial College Choice and Degree Completion" (working paper, National

Bureau of Economic Research, Cambridge, MA, 2014); Hoekstra, "The Effect of Attending the Flagship State University on Earnings"; Michal Kurlaender and Eric Grodsky, "Mismatch and the Paternalistic Justification for Selective College Admissions," *Sociology of Education* 86 (2013): 294–310.

4. Kevin Eagan et al., *The American Freshman: National Norms Fall 2014 (Expanded Edition)*, Higher Education Research Institute, 2014, http://heri.ucla.edu/monographs/ TheAmericanFreshman2014.pdf.

5. "Presumptive eligibility" is a phrase used by Bowen, Chingos, and McPherson in determining whether students were undermatched because they presumably were eligible for admission at more selective colleges based on their grades and test scores (see Bowen, Chingos, and McPherson, *Crossing the Finish Line*); The *State of College Admission* publication by the National Association for College Admission Counseling (NACAC) reports the percentage of institutional admissions officers who weight as important various factors in the college admission process (see Melissa Clinedinst, *State of College Admission*, National Association of College Admission Counseling, 2014, www.nxtbook.com/ygsreprints/NACAC/2014SoCA _nxtbk/); Additionally, in a recent survey of senior admissions professionals by the American Council on Education (ACE), 76 percent of surveyed admissions officers report utilizing holistic admissions practices as a strategy for increasing racial/ethnic or socioeconomic diversity (see Lorelle Espinosa, Matthew Gaertner, and Gary Orfield, *Race, Class, and College Access: Achieving Diversity in a Shifting Legal Landscape* [Washington, DC: American Council on Education, July 21, 2015], www.acenet.edu/events/Pages/ADU-Convening.aspx).

6. Yeager and Walton provide an accessible overview of this body of work that suggests college student perceptions of how well they fit in on campus are both malleable and important drivers of college retention and completion (see David S. Yeager and Gregory M. Walton, "Social-Psychological Interventions in Education: They're Not Magic," *Review of Educational Research* 81, no. 2 [2011]: 267–301).

7. These two college exploration/search tools are available at https://nces.ed.gov/collegenavigator/ and https://bigfuture.collegeboard.org/, respectively (see US Department of Education, National Center for Education Statistics, "College Navigator," https://nces.ed.gov /collegenavigator/; College Board, "Big Future," https://bigfuture.collegeboard.org/).

8. For descriptive information on SAT-takers, available annually from 1996 to the present and disaggregated by state and a variety of student demographics, see College Board, "The 2014 SAT Report on College & Career Readiness," http://research.collegeboard.org/programs/sat /data/cb-seniors-2014.

9. Note that the SATQ survey is prepopulated with a student's previous responses, so that senior exam-takers who have previously taken the SAT may update some, none, or all of their previous responses. Detailed data about changes in student responses over time are not currently preserved.

10. Susan M. Dynarski, Steven Hemelt, and Joshua M. Hyman, "The Missing Manual: Using National Student Clearinghouse Data to Track Postsecondary Outcomes" (working paper, National Bureau of Economic Research, Cambridge, MA, 2013).

11. This approach was established in Hoxby and Avery (see Caroline Hoxby and Christopher Avery, *The Missing "One-Offs": The Hidden Supply of High-Achieving, Low Income Students* [Washington, DC: The Brookings Institution, 2013], www.brookings.edu/~/media/projects /bpea/spring-2013/2013a_hoxby.pdf); the approach was utilized in Hoxby and Turner, "Expanding College Opportunities."

12. This definition of academic match encompasses institutions that would be considered safety schools, matches, and reaches. Our analyses are mostly unchanged if we narrow the definition

of match and exclude safety schools (which would allow the percentile differences to be no larger than 5 percentile points rather than the 15 we assume here). Results are robust to alternative definitions of academic match.

13. Previous analyses of the 1999 cohort of SAT-takers' preferences by Mattern et al. included only those SATQ respondents who expressed strong preferences for college attributes by selecting one response on each dimension (see Krista D. Mattern, Sang E. Woo, Don Hossler, and Jeffrey Wyatt, "Use of Student-Institution Fit in College Admissions: Do Applicants Really Know What Is Good for Them?" *College and University* 1 [2010]: 19–28).

14. Similar patterns are evident when the data are segmented by parental education (not reported here).

15. SAT-takers who are not enrolled in a postsecondary institution within one year of high school graduation are excluded from these analyses, but were included in the previous analyses that described SAT-takers' preferences for college attributes. Approximately 10 million SAT-takers across the seven cohorts we examined expressed preferences, and 8.3 million went on to enroll in a postsecondary institution within one year of high school graduation. The descriptive information on student preferences in figures 2.1–2.4 is not sensitive to the exclusion of these 1.7 million eventual delayed or non-enrollees.

16. See Jessica Howell and Matea Pender "The Costs and Benefits of Enrolling in an Academically Matched College," *Economics of Education Review* (forthcoming).

17. Mandy Savitz-Romer and Suzanne M. Bouffard, *Ready, Willing, and Able: A Developmental Approach to College Access and Success* (Cambridge, MA: Harvard Education Press, 2012).

18. Note that policy analyses conducted here are constrained by having only limited information on fit according to questions asked on the SATQ, a point to which we return in the conclusion.

19. See US Department of Education, National Center for Education Statistics, Integrated Postsecondary Education Data System (IPEDS), "Table 326.10. Graduation Rates of First-Time, Full-Time Bachelor's Degree-Seeking Students at Four-Year Postsecondary Institutions, By Race/Ethnicity, Time to Completion, Sex, and Control of Institution: Selected Cohort Entry Years, 1996 Through 2006," https://nces.ed.gov/programs/digest/d13/tables/dt13_326.10 .asp. Our statistics are lower because we include those students who start their postsecondary studies at community colleges.

20. Howell and Pender predict a 13.5 percentage point gain in six-year bachelor's completion using simulation methods that move undermatched low-income students to their least selective safety school ("The Costs and Benefits of Enrolling in an Academically Matched College" [forthcoming]).

21. For a recent overview of research on college counseling, coaching, and mentoring programs, see Christopher Avery, Jessica S. Howell, and Lindsay Page, *A Review of the Role of College Counseling, Coaching, and Mentoring on Students' Postsecondary Outcomes* (New York: College Board, October 2014), http://research.collegeboard.org/sites/default/ files/publications/2015/1/college-board-research-brief-role-college-counseling-coaching-mentoring-postsecondary-outcomes.pdf.

Chapter 3

1. Melissa Roderick, Vanessa Coca, and Jenny Nagaoka, "Potholes on the Road to College: High School Effects in Shaping Urban Students' Participation in College Application, Four-year College Enrollment, and College Match," *Sociology of Education* 84, no. 3 (July 2011): 178–211; Jonathan Smith, Matea Pender, and Jessica Howell, *The Full Extent of Student-College Academic Undermatch* (New York: College Board, 2012), https://aefpweb.org/sites/default/files/

webform/Extent%20of%20Undermatch.pdf; William G. Bowen, Matthew M. Chingos, and Michael S. McPherson, *Crossing the Finish Line: Completing College at America's Public Universities* (Princeton, NJ: Princeton University Press, 2009); Caroline Hoxby and Christopher Avery, *The Missing "One-Offs": The Hidden Supply of High Achieving, Low-Income Students* (Washington, DC: Brookings Institution, 2013), www.brookings.edu/~/media /Projects/BPEA/Spring%202013/2013a_hoxby.pdf; Caroline Hoxby and Sarah Turner, "Expanding College Opportunities for High-Achieving, Low-Income Students" (working paper, Stanford Institute for Economic Policy Research, Stanford, CA, 2013), https://siepr .stanford.edu/?q=/system/files/shared/pubs/papers/12-014paper.pdf.

2. Bowen, Chingos, and McPherson, *Crossing the Finish Line*; Anthony Carnevale and Jeff Strohl, *Separate & Unequal: How Higher Education Reinforces the Intergenerational Reproduction of White Racial Privilege* (Washington, DC: Georgetown Public Policy Institute, 2013), https:// cew.georgetown.edu/wp-content/uploads/2014/11/SeparateUnequal.FR_.pdf.

3. Alexandria Walton Radford, *Top Student, Top School? How Social Class Shapes Where Valedictorians Go to College* (Chicago: University of Chicago Press, 2013); David Leonhardt, "Even for Cashiers, College Pays Off," *New York Times*, June 25, 2011, www.nytimes .com/2011/06/26/sunday-review/26leonhardt.html; Peter Dreier and Richard D. Kahlenberg, "Making Top Colleges Less Aristocratic and More Meritocratic," *New York Times*, September 12, 2014, www.nytimes.com/2014/09/13/upshot/making-top-colleges-less-aristocratic-and-more-meritocratic.html?abt=0002&abg=0; Marian Wang, "Public Colleges' Quest for Revenue and Prestige Squeezes Needy Students," *Chronicle of Higher Education*, September 11, 2013, http://chronicle.com/article/Public-Colleges-Quest-for/141541/; Caroline Hoxby and Sarah Turner, "Expanding College Opportunities," *Education Next* 13, no. 4 (Fall 2013), http:// educationnext.org/expanding-college-opportunities/; College Board, "On the 30th Anniversary of Trends Reports, the College Board Affirms Commitment to Helping Students Prepare for, Access, and Complete College," www.collegeboard.org/releases/2013/30th-anniversary-trends-reports-college-board-affirms-commitment-helping-students; White House, "Fact Sheet: The President and First Lady's Call to Action on College Opportunity," www.whitehouse.gov/the-press-office/2014/01/16/ fact-sheet-president-and-first-lady-s-call-action-college-opportunity.

4. Donna Jones, "Immigrant Brothers Go from Watsonville to Ivy League," *Santa Cruz Sentinel*, January 4, 2015, www.santacruzsentinel.com/social-affairs/20150104/immigrant-brothers-go-from-watsonville-to-ivy-league; Esmerelda Bermudez, "She Finally Has a Home: Harvard," *Los Angeles Times*, June 20, 2009, http://articles.latimes.com/2009/jun/20/local/me-harvard20; Angel Canales, "Gay Marine's Amazing Journey from Homeless Shelter to Ivy League," *ABC News*, March 4, 2014, http://abcnews.go.com/blogs/headlines/2014/03/gay-marines-amazing-journey-from-homeless-shelter-to-ivy-league/; Elisa Crouch, "Normandy High Senior Overcomes Hardships to Land Slot in Ivy League School," *St. Louis Post-Dispatch*, May 10, 2012, www.stltoday.com/news/local/education/normandy-high-senior-overcomes-hardships-to-land-slot-in-ivy/article_d6b9f853-73ad-57af-9d71-6635a9a8b76b.html.

5. Patrick Rooney et al., *The Condition of Education 2006*, US Department of Education, National Center for Education Statistics, June 2006, http://nces.ed.gov/pubs2006/2006071.pdf.

6. However, these definitions are not without debate and can yield varying results—see Michael N. Bastedo and Allyson Flaster, "Conceptual and Methodological Problems in Research on College Undermatch," *Educational Researcher* 43, no. 2 (2014): 93–99; Awilda Rodriguez, "Tradeoffs and Limitations: Understanding the Estimation of College Undermatch," *Research in Higher Education* 56 (2015): 566–594.

7. Carnevale and Strohl, *Separate & Unequal*.

8. Hoxby and Avery, *The Missing "One-Offs."*

9. Michael N. Bastedo and Ozan Jacquette, "Running in Place: Low-income Students and the Dynamics of Higher Education Stratification," *Educational Evaluation and Policy Analysis* 33, no. 3 (2011): 318–339, www.personal.umich.edu/~bastedo/papers/BastedoJaquette2011.pdf; Hoxby and Avery, *The Missing "One-Offs."*

10. John Bound, Brad J. Hershbein, and Bridget T. Long, "Playing the Admissions Game: Student Reactions to Increasing College Competition," *Journal of Economic Perspectives 23*, no. 4 (2009): 119–146.

11. Analysis of NPSAS:12 using AGE, LEVEL and HSGPA for students under the age of 24. Figures weighted by WTA000.

12. William G. Bowen and Derek Bok, *The Shape of the River: Long-term Consequences of Considering Race in College and University Admissions* (Princeton, NJ: Princeton University Press, 1998); Laura Horn and C. Dennis Carroll, *Placing College Graduation Rates in Context: How 4-year College Graduation Rates Vary with Selectivity and the Size of Low-Income Enrollment*, US Department of Education, National Center for Education Statistics, October 2006, http://files.eric.ed.gov/fulltext/ED494020.pdf; Bowen, Chingos, and McPherson, *Crossing the Finish Line.*

13. Melissa Roderick et al., *From High School to the Future: Potholes on the Road to College*, Consortium on Chicago School Research at the University of Chicago, March 2008, https://ccsr.uchicago.edu/sites/default/files/publications/CCSR_Potholes_Report.pdf.

14. Smith, Pender, and Howell, *The Full Extent of Student-College Academic Undermatch.*

15. Rodriguez, "Tradeoffs and Limitations."

16. See Bastedo and Flaster, "Conceptual and Methodological Problems in Research on College Undermatch."

17. Ruth N. López-Turley, "College Proximity: Mapping Access to Opportunity," *Sociology of Education* 82, no. 2 (2009): 126–146.

18. Krista Mattern and Jeffrey Wyatt, "Student Choice of College: How Far Do Students Go for an Education?" *Journal of College Admission*, no. 203 (2009): 18–29; Patricia M. McDonough, *Choosing Colleges: How Social Class and Schools Structure Opportunity* (Albany: State University of New York Press, 1997).

19. Nicholas W. Hillman, "Differential Impacts of College Ratings: The Case of Education Deserts" (working paper, University of Wisconsin, Madison, WI, 2014); Michal Kurlaender, "Choosing Community College: Factors Affecting Latino College Choice," *New Directions for Community Colleges*, no. 133 (2006): 1–84; López-Turley, "College Proximity."

20. *Geography of opportunity* is the extent to which students have postsecondary opportunities based on where they live, given how colleges are not equally distributed. Therefore some students will have more nearby postsecondary options than others (see Hillman, "Differential Impacts of College Ratings"; López-Turley, "College Proximity").

21. Hillman, "Differential Impacts of College Ratings."

22. The NCES collected demographic, academic, and institutional data from a national sample of approximately 16,120 students enrolled in tenth grade in 2002. NCES conducted three follow-ups with students: the first at the end of their twelfth-grade year (2004), the second when many respondents were sophomores in college (2006), and the third eight years after most graduated from high school (2012).

23. As reported in ELS:2002. The resultant sample includes average- and high-performing students for a weighted total of 1,353,889. The data were restricted to students who participated in the base and first two follow-ups; were not enrolled in vocational, alternative, or special education programs; stated the number of colleges they applied to; and had IRT Math

scores of +/– one standard deviation from the mean (average-performing students) or above one standard deviation from the mean (high-performing). There are limitations to this data set. High school GPA was measured in bands (for example, 2.01–2.50) rather than in exact numbers. Students who failed to respond to any of the questions of interest were not included in the sample. The sample was weighted using F2BYWT.

24. Jaekyung Lee, "Multiple Facets of Inequity in Racial and Ethnic Achievement Gaps," *Peabody Journal of Education* 31, no. 1 (2002): 3–12; US Department of Education, National Center for Education Statistics, "Digest of Education Statistics: 2013," https://nces.ed.gov/programs/digest/d13/index.asp.

25. Laura W. Perna, "Studying College Access and Choice: A Proposed Conceptual Model." *Higher Education: Handbook of Theory and Research* 21 (2006): 99–157; McDonough, "Choosing Colleges."

26. McDonough, "Choosing Colleges."

27. Analysis using Beginning Postsecondary Students Survey using PowerStats. Figures were derived for recent high school graduates enrolled in two- and four-year colleges using MAJ09CHG, FLEVEL, and FALLHSFT and were weighted using WTB000.

28. The distance between students' homes and the first college in which they enrolled was calculated by using the "ZIPCITYDISTANCE" command in SAS, which calculates the linear distance between the center of two zip code areas.

29. López-Turley, "College Proximity"; Hillman, "Differential Impacts of College Ratings."

30. Steven J. Ingels, Ben Dalton, and Elise Christopher, *High School Longitudinal Study of 2009 (HSLS:09) First Follow-Up: A First Look at Fall 2009 Ninth-Graders in 2012* (Washington, DC: US Department of Education, National Center for Education Statistics, October 2013), http://nces.ed.gov/pubs2014/2014360.pdf.

31. Roderick, Coca, and Nagaoka, *Potholes on the Road to College*; Smith, Pender, and Howell, "The Full Extent of Student-College Academic Undermatch."

32. While the Obama administration has taken steps to remedy this information gap by requiring all colleges that receive Title IV funding to furnish an online net price calculator on their websites, transparent pricing remains elusive; see *Adding it All Up 2012: Are College Net Price Calculators Easy to Find, Use, and Compare?* (Washington, DC: Institute for College Access and Success, October 2012), http://ticas.org/sites/default/files/pub_files/Adding_It_All_Up_2012.pdf.

33. National Association for College Admission Counseling, "Need-Blind College Admission Still Prevalent, but Enrollment Strategies Increasingly Utilize Merit Aid Targeting Amid Tightening Economy, Rising Costs," news release, November 25, 2008, www.nacacnet.org/media-center/PressRoom/2008PressReleases/Pages/finaidpaper.aspx.

34. Kevin Eagan et al., *The American Freshman: National Norms Fall 2013*, Cooperative Institutional Research Program at the Higher Education Research Institute at UCLA, 2013, www.heri.ucla.edu/monographs/theamericanfreshman2013.pdf.

35. Bowen, Chingos, and McPherson, *Crossing the Finish Line*; Roderick et al., *From High School to the Future*.

36. Roderick et al., *From High School to the Future*.

37. See Hoxby and Turner, "Expanding College Opportunities"; *Chronicle of Higher Education*, "Why Colleges Don't Want to be Judged by Their Graduation Rates," October 17, 2014, http://chronicle.com/article/Why-Colleges-Don-t-Want-to/149435/.

38. Danette Gerald and Kati Haycock, *Engines of Inequality* (Washington, DC: The Education Trust, January 1, 2006), http://1k9gl1yevnfp2lpq1dhrqe17.wpengine.netdna-cdn.com/wp-content/uploads/2013/10/EnginesofInequality.pdf.

39. Rodriguez, "Tradeoffs and Limitations."

40. López-Turley, "College Proximity."

41. For example, one study found that the high school guidance counselors encouraged low-income students in their sample, regardless of ability, to enroll in community college; see Frank Linnehan, Christy H. Weer, and Paul Stonely, "High School Guidance Counselor Recommendations: The Role of Student Race, Socioeconomic Status, and Academic Performance," *Journal of Applied Social Psychology* 41, no. 3 (2011): 536–558.

Chapter 4

1. Joseph G. Altonji, Lisa B. Kahn, and Jamin D. Speer, "Trends in Earnings Differentials Across College Majors and the Changing Task Composition of Jobs," *American Economic Review* 104, no. 5 (2014): 387–393; Douglas A. Webber, "The Lifetime Earnings Premia of Different Majors: Correcting for Selection Based on Cognitive, Noncognitive, and Unobserved Factors," *Labour Economics* 28, issue C (2014): 14–23.

2. David Card, "Using Geographic Variation in College Proximity to Estimate the Return to Schooling" (working paper, National Bureau of Economic Research, Cambridge, MA, 1993); Cecilia E. Rouse, "Democratization or Diversion? The Effect of Community Colleges on Educational Attainment," *Journal of Business and Economic Statistics* 13, no. 2 (1995): 217–224; Jeffrey R. Kling, "Interpreting Instrumental Variables Estimates of the Returns to Schooling," *Journal of Business and Economic Statistics* 19, no. 3 (2001): 358–364; Ruth N. López Turley, "College Proximity: Mapping Access to Opportunity," *Sociology of Education* 82, no. 2 (2009): 126–146.

3. Thomas R. Bailey, D. Timothy Leinbach, and Davis Jenkins, "Is Student Success Labeled Institutional Failure? Student Goals and Graduation Rates in the Accountability Debate at Community Colleges" (working paper, Community College Research Center, Teachers College, Columbia University, New York, 2006).

4. Thomas R. Bailey, Shanna Smith Jaggars, and Davis Jenkins, *Redesigning America's Community Colleges: A Clearer Path to Student Success* (Cambridge, MA: Harvard University Press, 2015).

5. Joseph G. Altonji, Erica Blom, and Costas Meghir, "Heterogeneity in Human Capital Investments: High School Curriculum, College Major, and Careers," *Annual Review of Economics* 4 (2012): 185–223; Peter Arcidiacono, "Ability Sorting and the Returns to College Major," *Journal of Econometrics* 121, no. 1–2 (2003): 343–375; Dan A. Black, Seth Sanders, and Lowell Taylor, "The Economic Reward for Studying Economics," *Economic Inquiry* 41, no. 3 (2003): 365–377.

6. Altonji, Kahn, and Speer, "Trends in Earnings Differentials."

7. Webber, "The Lifetime Earnings Premia of Different Majors."

8. Although college dropouts fail to maximize their returns to postsecondary education, they nonetheless benefit from attending college. Most studies find that credit accumulation in college is positively associated with earnings and that the relationship is approximately linear. Compared with completers, college dropouts are at a disadvantage because they lack the signaling effect of a credential. But the more salient loss occurs because most college dropouts do not accumulate many credits and so are not clearly distinguishable from high school graduates; see Clive Belfield, Yuen Ting Liu, and Madeline Joy Trimble, "The Medium-Term Labor Market Returns to Community College Awards: Evidence from North Carolina" (working paper, Center for Analysis of Postsecondary Education and Employment, New York, 2014); Clive R. Belfield and Thomas Bailey, "The Benefits of Attending Community College: A Review of the Evidence," *Community College Review* 39, no. 1 (2011): 46–68.

9. Belfield, Liu, and Trimble, "The Medium-Term Labor Market Returns."

10. Christopher Jepsen, Kenneth Troske, and Paul Coomes, "The Labor Market Returns to Community College Degrees, Diplomas and Certificates," *Journal of Labor Economics* 32, no. 1 (2012): 95–121; Mina Dadgar and Madeline J. Trimble, "Labor Market Returns to Sub-Baccalaureate Credentials: How Much Does a Community College Degree or Certificate Pay?" *Educational Evaluation and Policy Analysis*, November 5, 2014, http://epa.sagepub.com /content/early/2014/10/21/0162373714553814.full.pdf+html?ijkey=IC4hU3xEM6Gg.&keytype =ref&siteid=spepa.

11. Joseph G. Altonji, Lisa B. Kahn, and Jamin D. Speer, *Cashier or Consultant? Entry Labor Market Conditions, Field of Study, and Career Success* (New Haven, CT: Yale University, 2013); Thomas Bailey and Clive R. Belfield, "Community College Occupational Degrees: Are They Worth It?" in *Preparing Today's Students for Tomorrow's Jobs in Metropolitan America*, ed. Laura W. Perna (Philadelphia: University of Pennsylvania Press, 2012).

12. Madeleine Gelblum, "The Early Impact of Postsecondary Career and Technical Education: Do Workers Earn More in Occupations Related to Their College Major?" (working paper, Center for Analysis of Postsecondary Education and Employment, New York, 2014).

13. John Robst, "Education and Job Match: The Relatedness of College Major and Work," *Economics of Education Review* 26, no. 4 (2007): 397–407.

14. Thomas N. Daymont and Paul J. Andrisani, "Job Preferences, College Major, and the Gender Gap in Earnings," *Journal of Human Resources* 19, no. 3 (1984): 408–428; Matthew Wiswall and Basit Zafar, *Determinants of College Major Choice: Identification Using an Information Experiment* (New York: Federal Reserve Bank of New York, 2011); Demet Yazilitas et al., "Gendered Study Choice: A Literature Review. A Review of Theory and Research into the Unequal Representation of Male and Female Students in Mathematics, Science, and Technology," *Educational Research and Evaluation* 19, no. 6 (2013): 37–41; Basit Zafar, "College Major Choice and the Gender Gap" (working paper, Federal Reserve Bank of New York, New York, 2009).

15. Sarah E. Turner and William G. Bowen, "Choice of Major: The Changing (Unchanging) Gender Gap," *Industrial and Labor Relations Review* 52, no. 2 (1999): 289–313; Tjaša Logaj and Sašo Polanec, "College Major Choice and Ability: Why Is General Ability Not Enough?" (working paper, Institute for Economic Research, Ljubljana, Slovenia, 2011); Todd R. Stinebrickner and Ralph Stinebrickner, "Math or Science? Using Longitudinal Expectations Data to Examine the Process of Choosing a College Major" (working paper, National Bureau of Economic Research, Cambridge, MA, 2011).

16. Lucy W. Sells, *High School Math as the Critical Filter in the Job Market* (Berkeley: University of California, 1973); Jack Florito and Robert C. Dauffenbach, "Market and Nonmarket Influences on Curriculum Choice by College Students," *Industrial and Labor Relations Review* 36, no. 1 (1982): 88–101; Alexander Astin, *What Matters in College: Four Critical Years Revisited* (San Francisco: Jossey-Bass, 1993); Jacqueline C. Simpson, "Segregated by Subject: Racial Differences in the Factors Influencing Academic Major Between European Americans, Asian Americans, and African, Hispanic, and Native Americans," *Journal of Higher Education* 72, no. 1 (2001): 63–100.

17. Sue A. Maple and Frances K. Stage, "Influences on the Choice of Math/Science Major by Gender and Ethnicity," *American Educational Research Journal* 28, no. 1 (1991): 37–60.

18. Karen Leppel, Mary L. Williams, and Charles Waldauer, "The Impact of Parental Occupation and Socioeconomic Status on Choice of College Major," *Journal of Family and Economic Issues* 22, no. 4 (2001): 373–394.

19. Davis Jenkins and Madeline J. Weiss, "Charting Pathways to Completion for Low-Income Community College Students" (working paper, Community College Research Center, Teachers College, Columbia University, New York, NY, 2011).
20. Wiswall and Zafar, "Determinants of College Major Choice."
21. Gary R. Pike, "Students' Personality Types, Intended Majors, and College Expectations: Further Evidence Concerning Psychological and Sociological Interpretations of Holland's Theory," *Research in Higher Education* 47, no. 7 (2006): 801–822; Stephen R. Porter and Paul D. Umbach, "College Major Choice: An Analysis of Person–Environment Fit," *Research in Higher Education* 47, no. 4 (2006): 429–449.
22. Zafar, "College Major Choice and the Gender Gap."
23. Mark Stater, "Financial Aid, Student Background, and the Choice of First-Year College Major," *Eastern Economic Journal* 37 (2011): 321–343.
24. Kevin M. Stange, "Differential Pricing in Undergraduate Education: Effects on Degree Production by Field" (working paper, National Bureau of Economic Research, Cambridge, MA, 2013).
25. Stinebrickner and Stinebrickner, "Math or Science?"
26. Arcidiacono, "Ability Sorting and the Returns to College Major."
27. Matthew J. Foraker, *Does Changing Majors Really Affect the Time to Graduate? The Impact of Changing Majors on Student Retention, Graduation, and Time to Graduate* (Bowling Green: Western Kentucky University, 2012); Krisztina Filep, Edmund Melia, and Marilyn Blaustein, "Is Starting as an Undeclared Major a Bad Thing? A Look at First-Year Undeclared Students' Characteristics, Major Declaration Patterns and Their Influence on Retention and Graduation Rates" (paper presented at the annual meeting of the North East Association for Institutional Research, Newport, RI, November 12, 2013).
28. W. N. Grubb, "'Like, What Do I Do Now?' The Dilemmas of Guidance Counseling," in *Defending the Community College Equity Agenda*, ed. Thomas Bailey and Vanessa Smith Morest (Baltimore: Johns Hopkins University Press, 2006); Foraker, *Does Changing Majors Really Affect the Time to Graduate?*
29. Alissa Gardenhire-Crooks, Herbert Collado, and Barbara Ray, *A Whole 'Nother World: Students Navigating Community College*, MDRC, July 2006, www.mdrc.org/sites/default/files /OD_A_Whole%20_Nother_World_0.pdf.
30. Shanna Smith Jaggars and Jeffrey Fletcher, "Redesigning the Student Intake and Information Provision Process at a Large Comprehensive Community College" (working paper, Community College Research Center, Teachers College, Columbia University, New York, 2014).
31. Melinda M. Karp, "Entering a Program: Helping Students Make Academic and Career Decisions" (working paper, Community College Research Center, Teachers College, Columbia University, New York, 2013).
32. For an in-depth review of research on ways community colleges help students choose programs of study, see Karp, "Entering a Program," 8.
33. Grubb, "'Like, What Do I Do Now?'"
34. Center for Community College Student Engagement, *Benchmarking and Benchmarks: Effective Practice with Entering Students* (Austin: The University of Texas at Austin, Community College Leadership Program, 2010).
35. Karp, "Entering a Program."
36. Melinda M. Karp, Lauren O'Gara, and Katherine L. Hughes, "Do Support Services at Community Colleges Encourage Success or Reproduce Disadvantage? An Exploratory Study of Students in Two Community Colleges" (working paper, Community College Research Center, Teachers College, Columbia University, New York, 2008); Melinda M.

Karp et al., "College 101 Courses for Applied Learning and Student Success" (working paper, Community College Research Center, Teachers College, Columbia University, New York, 2012); *Student Voices on the Higher Education Pathway: Preliminary Insights and Stakeholder Engagement Considerations*, Public Agenda, 2012, www.publicagenda.org/files/student_voices.pdf.

37. Leigh S. Shaffer and Jacqueline M. Zalewski, "A Human Capital Approach to Career Advising," *NACADA Journal* 31, no. 1 (2011): 75–87.

38. Scott Gillie and Meegan G. Isenhour, *The Educational, Social, and Economic Value of Informed and Considered Career Decisions*, America's Career Resource Network Association, 2003, www.careerkey.org/pdf/executiveSummary.pdf; Public Agenda, *Student Voices on the Higher Education Pathway*.

39. Karp, "Entering a Program," 13.

40. Ibid., 15–16.

41. Ibid., 18–19.

42. Melinda M. Karp and Jeffrey Fletcher, *Adopting New Technologies for Student Success: A Readiness for Technology Adoption Framework* (New York: Community College Research Center, Teachers College, Columbia University, 2014).

43. Karp et al., "College 101 Courses for Applied Learning and Student Success."

44. Karp, "Entering a Program," 16–17.

45. James E. Rosenbaum, *Beyond College for All: Career Paths for the Forgotten Half* (New York: Russell Sage Foundation, 2001).

46. Michelle Van Noy et al., "Structure in Community College Career-Technical Programs: A Qualitative Analysis" (working paper, Community College Research Center, Teachers College, Columbia University, New York, 2012).

47. Grubb, "'Like, What Do I Do Now?'"

48. Bailey, Jaggars, and Jenkins, *Redesigning America's Community Colleges*.

49. Karp, O'Gara, and Hughes, "Do Support Services at Community Colleges Encourage Success or Reproduce Disadvantage?"

50. Bailey, Jaggars, and Jenkins, *Redesigning America's Community Colleges*.

51. David B. Monaghan and Paul Attewell, "The Community College Route to the Bachelor's Degree," *Educational Evaluation and Policy Analysis* 37, no. 1 (2015): 70–91.

52. Jaggars and Fletcher, "Redesigning the Student Intake and Information Provision Processes."

53. Judith Scott-Clayton, "The Shapeless River: Does a Lack of Structure Inhibit Students' Progress at Community Colleges?" (working paper, Assessment of Evidence Series, Community College Research Center, Teachers College, Columbia University, New York, 2011).

54. Peter M. Crosta, "Intensity and Attachment: How the Chaotic Enrollment Patterns of Community College Students Affect Educational Outcomes," *Community College Review* 42, no. 2 (2014): 118–142.

55. Public Agenda, *Student Voices*. See also Kathy Booth et al., *What Students Say They Need to Succeed: Key Themes from a Study of Student Support* (Sacramento, CA: The Research and Planning Group for the California Community Colleges, January 2013), www.rpgroup.org/sites/default/files/StudentPerspectivesResearchBriefJan2013.pdf.

56. Bailey, Jaggars, and Jenkins, *Redesigning America's Community Colleges*, 42.

57. Ibid.

58. Jesse Brown and Martin Kurzweil, *Student Success by Design: CUNY's Guttman Community College* (New York: Ithaka S & R, February 2016), www.srithaka.org/publications/student-success-by-design/.

59. The $1 million Aspen Prize for Community College Excellence, awarded every two years, is the nation's signature recognition of high achievement and performance among community colleges and recognizes institutions for exceptional student outcomes in four areas: student learning, certificate and degree completion, employment and earnings, and high levels of access and success for minority and low-income students. For more information, see The Aspen Institute, "College Excellence Program: Aspen Prize for Community College Excellence," www.aspeninstitute.org/policy-work/college-excellence/overview.

60. Philip Regier, "Making the University Student-Centric: eAdvisor at ASU" (paper presented at the annual meeting of Complete College America, New Orleans, LA, December 14, 2013).

61. City Colleges of Chicago, "About City Colleges," www.ccc.edu/menu/Pages/About-City-Colleges.aspx.

62. City Colleges of Chicago, "Kennedy-King College Wins National Award for Rapid Improvement in Completion," news release, March 18, 2015, www.ccc.edu/news/Pages/City-Colleges-of-Chicago%E2%80%99s-Kennedy-King-College-Wins-National-Award-for-Rapid-Improvement-in-Completion.aspx.

63. See Bailey, Jaggars, and Jenkins, *Redesigning America's Community Colleges*, particularly chapter 6 on leadership and management strategies and chapter 7 on the costs of implementing large-scale reforms along these lines at community colleges.

Chapter 5

1. Caroline Hoxby and Christopher Avery, *The Missing "One-Offs": The Hidden Supply of High-Achieving, Low-Income Students* (Washington, DC: The Brookings Institution, 2013), www.brookings.edu/~/media/projects/bpea/spring-2013/2013a_hoxby.pdf. Referenced in Michael Petrilli, "Use Facts, Not Courts, to Fix Affirmative Action," *Bloomberg View*, May 2013, www.bloombergview.com/articles/2013-05-30/use-facts-not-courts-to-fix-affirmative-action.

2. Matthew M. Chingos, "Can We Fix Undermatching in Higher Education? Would It Matter If We Did?" Brookings Institution Chalkboard Series, January 15, 2014, www.brookings.edu/research/papers/2014/01/15-undermatching-higher-ed-chingos; Matthew M. Chingos, "Graduation Rates at America's Universities: What We Know and What We Need to Know," in *Getting to Graduation: The Completion Agenda in Higher Education*, eds. Andrew P. Kelly and Mark Schneider (Baltimore: Johns Hopkins University Press, 2012), 48–71.

3. Ibid.

4. National Center for Education Statistics, "About IPEDS," http://nces.ed.gov/ipeds/about/.

5. As a result, transfer students or students who stop out are not considered in this report.

6. For instance, see National Postsecondary Education Cooperative, *Suggestions for Improving the IPEDS Graduation Rate Survey Data Collection and Reporting*, July 2010, http://nces.ed.gov/pubs2010/2010832.pdf; Jonah Newman, "What Experts on College-Ratings System Mean by 'We Need Better Data,'" *Chronicle of Higher Education*, February 14, 2014, http://chronicle.com/blogs/data/2014/02/14/what-experts-on-college-ratings-system-mean-by-we-need-better-data/; Scott Jaschik, "New Measures of Success," *Inside Higher Ed*, June 24, 2013, www.insidehighered.com/news/2013/06/24/college-associations-introduce-new-ways-measure-student-completion#sthash.KtjOjn5o.dpbs.

7. To account for the volatility of graduation rates over time at smaller institutions, I used a three-year moving average weighted by the size of the cohort. For the data points at ends of the time series (2002 and 2012), I used a two-year weighted moving average (with 2003 and 2011 graduation rates, respectively). Institutions were able to change graduation rate bands over time, capturing the real-time availability of seats in each category in each year.

8. US Department of Education, *Students Attending For-Profit Postsecondary Institutions: Demographics, Enrollment Characteristics, and 6-Year Outcomes*, December 2011, http://nces.ed.gov/pubs2012/2012173.pdf; I also excluded seminaries and other religiously affiliated schools. I considered colleges labeled that IPEDS labels "Associate's-Degree Granting" as two-year colleges for the purposes of this analysis.

9. Note again that throughout this analysis, institutions whose Carnegie classification is "Associate's" or "Primarily Associate's" are categorized as public or nonprofit two-year colleges.

10. Joshua Goodman, Michael Hurwitz, and Jonathan Smith, "College Access, Initial College Choice, and Degree Completion" (working paper, National Bureau of Economic Research, Cambridge, MA, February 2015), http://scholar.harvard.edu/files/joshuagoodman/files/collegetypequality.pdf.

11. Doug Shapiro et al., *Completing College: A National View of Student Attainment Rates—2008 Cohort*, National Student Clearinghouse, 2014, http://nscresearchcenter.org/wp-content/uploads/SignatureReport8.pdf.

12. See Michael Hurwitz and Amal Kumar, *Supply and Demand in the Higher Education Market* (New York: College Board, February 2015), https://research.collegeboard.org/sites/default/files/publications/2015/8/college-board-research-brief-supply-demand-college-admission-college-choice.pdf.

13. For instance, see State Higher Education Executive Officers Association, *Degree Production and Cost Trends*, August 2010, www.sheeo.org/sites/default/files/publications/Degree_Production_and_Cost_Trends.pdf; National Center for Higher Education Management Systems (NCHEMS), "NCHEMS Information Center for Higher Education Policymaking and Analysis," www.higheredinfo.org/dbrowser/index.php?measure=137; and College Measures (www.collegemeasures.org).

14. The Delta Cost Project database includes a variable that measures all entering undergraduates (first-time degree-seeking students and transfers). This variable provides a fuller picture of enrollments at community colleges. The Delta Cost data also groups institutions according to their parent institution, meaning some institutions that appear individually in the graduation rate analysis are grouped together in the Delta Cost data. As a result, the enrollment numbers in table 5.3 are not directly comparable to those in table 5.1, but the trends are still broadly comparable.

15. Sophie Quinton, "Georgia State Improved Its Graduation Rate by 22 Points in 10 Years," *The Atlantic*, September 23, 2013, www.theatlantic.com/education/archive/2013/09/georgia-state-improved-its-graduation-rate-by-22-points-in-10-years/279909/.

16. Susan Scrivener et al., *Doubling Graduation Rates: Three-Year Effects of CUNY's Accelerated Study in Associate Programs (ASAP) for Developmental Education Students* (New York/Oakland, CA: MDRC, February 2015), www.mdrc.org/publication/doubling-graduation-rates.

17. Rita J. Kirshstein and Steven Hurlburt, *Revenues: Where Does the Money Come From? A Delta Data Update, 2000–2010* (Washington, DC: Delta Cost Project at American Institutes for Research, 2012), www.deltacostproject.org/sites/default/files/products/Revenue_Trends_Production.pdf.

18. The Aspen Institute, *The 2015 Aspen Prize for Community College Excellence*, 2015, www.aspeninstitute.org/sites/default/files/content/docs/pubs/2015AspenPrizePublication.pdf.

19. Martha Snyder, *Driving Better Outcomes: Typology and Principles to Inform Outcomes-Based Funding Models*, HCM Strategists, February 2015, http://hcmstrategists.com/drivingoutcomes/wp-content/themes/hcm/pdf/Driving%20Outcomes.pdf.

20. Andrew P. Kelly, "Exploring Institutional Risk-Sharing," testimony before the US Senate Committee on Health, Education, Labor, and Pensions, May 20, 2015, www.aei.org/wp-content/uploads/2015/05/Kelly-Senate-HELP-Risk-Sharing-Testimony.pdf.

Chapter 6

1. David Leonhardt, "'A National Admissions Office' for Low-Income Strivers," *New York Times*, September 16, 2014, www.nytimes.com/2014/09/16/upshot/a-national-admissions-office-for-low-income-strivers.html; Laura Pappano, "First-Generation Students Unite," *New York Times*, April 8, 2015, www.nytimes.com/2015/04/12/education/edlife/first-generation-students-unite.html; Richard Perez-Peña, "Generation Later, Poor Are Still Rare at Elite Colleges," *New York Times*, August 26, 2014, www.nytimes.com/2014/08/26/education/despite-promises-little-progress-in-drawing-poor-to-elite-colleges.html; Michael Stratford, "The White House Summit," *Inside Higher Ed*, January 15, 2014, www.insidehighered.com/news/2014/01/15/president-obama-set-convene-rare-meeting-large-group-college-leaders.

2. Michael N. Bastedo and Ozan Jaquette, "Running in Place: Low-Income Students and the Dynamics of Higher Education Stratification," *Educational Evaluation and Policy Analysis* 33, no. 3 (2011): 318–339.

3. Lorelle L. Espinosa, Matthew N. Gaertner, and Gary Orfield, *Race, Class, and College Access: Achieving Diversity in a Shifting Legal Landscape*, American Council on Education, 2015; Christopher J. Nellum and Terry W. Hartle, *Where Have All the Low-Income Students Gone?* (Washington, DC: American Council on Education, 2015), http://cms.marketplace.org/sites/default/files/Fed%20Watch%20W16_Low-Income%20Students.pdf.

4. Caroline Hoxby and Christopher Avery, *The Missing "One-Offs": The Hidden Supply of High-Achieving, Low-Income Students* (Washington, DC: The Brookings Institution, 2013), www.brookings.edu/~/media/projects/bpea/spring-2013/2013a_hoxby.pdf.

5. Andrew S. Belasco and Michael J. Trivette, "Aiming Low: Estimating the Scope and Predictors of Postsecondary Undermatch," *Journal of Higher Education* 86, no. 2 (2015): 233–263; William G. Bowen, Matthew M. Chingos, and Michael S. McPherson, *Crossing the Finish Line: Completing College at America's Public Universities* (Princeton, NJ: Princeton University Press, 2009); Eleanor W. Dillon and Jeffrey A. Smith, "The Determinants of Mismatch between Students and Colleges" (working paper, National Bureau of Economic Research, Cambridge, MA, 2013); Melissa Roderick, Vanessa Coca, Jenny Nagaoka, "Potholes on the Road to College: High School Effects in Shaping Urban Students' Participation in College Application, Four-Year College Enrollment, and College Match," *Sociology of Education* 84, no. 3 (2011): 178–211; Awilda Rodriguez, "Tradeoffs and Limitations: Understanding the Estimation of College Undermatch," *Research in Higher Education* 56, no. 6 (2015): 566–594; Jonathan Smith, Matea Pender, and Jessica Howell, "The Full Extent of Student-College Academic Undermatch," *Economics of Education Review* 32 (2013): 247–261.

6. Angela D. Bell, Heather T. Rowan-Kenyon, and Laura W. Perna, "College Knowledge of 9th and 11th Grade Students: Variation by School and State Context," *Journal of Higher Education* 80, no. 6 (2009): 663–685.

7. Patricia M. McDonough, *Choosing Colleges: How Social Class and Schools Structure Opportunity* (Albany: SUNY Press, 1997); Laura W. Perna et al., "The Role of College Counseling in Shaping College Opportunity: Variations across High Schools," *Review of Higher Education* 31, no. 2 (2008): 131–159.

8. Caroline Hoxby and Sarah Turner, "Expanding College Opportunities for High-Achieving, Low-Income Students" (working paper, Stanford Institute for Economic Policy Research,

Stanford, CA, 2013); Amanda Pallais, "Small Differences That Matter: Mistakes in Applying to College," *Journal of Labor Economics* 33, no. 2 (2015): 493–520.

9. Stacy Dale and Alan B. Krueger, "Estimating the Return to College Selectivity over the Career Using Administrative Earnings Data" (working paper, National Bureau of Economic Research, Cambridge, MA, 2011).

10. Matthew N. Gaertner and Melissa Hart, "Considering Class: College Access and Diversity," *Harvard Law and Policy Review* 7, no. 2 (2013): 367–387; Matthew N. Gaertner and Melissa Hart, "From Access to Success: Affirmative Action Outcomes in a Class-Based System," *University of Colorado Law Review* 86, no. 2 (2015): 431–475.

11. Vimal Patel, "A Distinction Washington U. Wants to Lose: Least Economically Diverse," *Chronicle of Higher Education*, February 26, 2015, http://chronicle.com/article/A-Distinction-Washington-U/190413/; Richard Perez-Peña, "University of Chicago Acts to Improve Access for Lower-Income Students," *New York Times*, October 1, 2014, www.nytimes.com/2014/10/01/education/university-of-chicago-acts-to-improve-access for-lower-income-students-.html; Rick Fitzgerald, "U-M to Test New Way to Reach High-Achieving, Low-Income Students," *University Record*, August 26, 2015, https://record.umich.edu/articles/u-m-test-new-way-reach-high-achieving-low-income-students.

12. Hoxby and Avery, *The Missing "One-Offs"*; Catharine B. Hill and Gordon C. Winston, "Low-Income Students and Highly Selective Private Colleges: Geography, Searching, and Recruiting," *Economics of Education Review* 29, no. 4 (2010): 495–503.

13. Sean F. Reardon et al., "Simulation Models of the Effects of Race- and Socioeconomic-Based Affirmative Action Policies" (CEPA Working Paper No. 15-04, Stanford University, Stanford, CA, 2015); Espinosa, Gaertner, and Orfield, *Race, Class, and College Access*; Richard D. Kahlenberg, ed., *The Future of Affirmative Action: New Paths to Higher Education Diversity after* Fisher v. University of Texas (Washington, DC: The Century Foundation, 2014).

14. Michael N. Bastedo, "Cognitive Repairs in the Admissions Office" (working paper, University of Michigan, Ann Arbor, MI, 2016).

15. Michael N. Bastedo and Nicholas A. Bowman, "Improving Admission of Low-SES Students at Selective Colleges: A National Experiment" (working paper, University of Michigan, Ann Arbor, MI, 2016).

16. Michael N. Bastedo and Allyson Flaster, "Conceptual and Methodological Problems in Research on College Undermatch," *Educational Researcher* 43, no. 2 (2014): 93–99.

17. Michael N. Bastedo and Ozan Jaquette, "Running in Place"; Rob Bielby et al., "Why Are Women Underrepresented in Elite Colleges and Universities? A Non-Linear Decomposition Analysis," *Research in Higher Education* 55, no. 8 (2014): 735–760; Julie R. Posselt et al., "Access without Equity: Longitudinal Analyses of Institutional Stratification by Race and Ethnicity, 1972–2004," *American Educational Research Journal* 49, no. 6 (2012): 1074–1111.

18. Melissa Clinedinst, *State of College Admission 2014*, National Association for College Admission Counseling, 2015.

19. Michael N. Bastedo, Joseph E. Howard, and Allyson Flaster, "Holistic Admissions after Affirmative Action: Does "Maximizing" the High School Curriculum Matter?" (working paper, University of Michigan, Ann Arbor, MI, 2016).

20. Ibid.

21. Paul Attewell and Thurston Domina, "Raising the Bar: Curricular Intensity and Academic Performance," *Educational Evaluation and Policy Analysis* 30, no. 1 (2008): 51–71; Kristin Klopfenstein, "Advanced Placement: Do Minorities Have Equal Opportunity?" *Economics of Education Review* 23, no. 2 (2004): 115–131. Dylan Conger, Mark C. Long, and Patrice Iatarola,

"Explaining Race, Poverty, and Gender Disparities in Advanced Course-Taking," *Journal of Policy Analysis and Management* 28, no. 4 (2009): 555–576.

22. Attewell and Domina, "Raising The Bar"; Patrice Iatarola, Dylan Conger, Mark C. Long, "Determinants of High Schools' Advanced Course Offerings," *Educational Evaluation and Policy Analysis* 33, no. 3 (2011): 340–359.

23. Iatarola, Conger, and Long, "Determinants of High Schools' Advanced Course Offerings."

24. Mark E. Engberg and Gregory C. Wolniak, "Examining the Effects of High School Contexts on Postsecondary Enrollment," *Research in Higher Education* 51, no. 2 (2010): 132–153; Joshua Klugman, "The Advanced Placement Arms Race and the Reproduction of Educational Inequality," *Teachers College Record* 115, no. 5 (2013): 1–34.

25. Thomas J. Espenshade and Alexandria W. Radford, *No Longer Separate, Not Yet Equal: Race and Class in Elite College Admission and Campus Life* (Princeton, NJ: Princeton University Press, 2009).

26. Bastedo, "Cognitive Repairs in the Admissions Office."

27. Thomas J. Espenshade, Chang Y. Chung, and Joan L. Walling, "Admission Preferences for Minority Students, Athletes, and Legacies at Elite Universities," *Social Science Quarterly* 85, no. 5 (2004): 1422–1446.

28. Pamela R. Bennett, Amy C. Lutz, and Lakshmi Jayaram, "Beyond the Schoolyard: The Role of Parenting Logics, Financial Resources, and Social Institutions in the Social Class Gap in Structured Activity Participation," *Sociology of Education* 85, no. 2 (2012): 131–157; Thomas J. Espenshade, and Chang Y. Chung, "The Opportunity Cost of Admission Preferences at Elite Universities," *Social Science Quarterly* 86, no. 2 (2005): 293–305.

29. Elizabeth Stearns and Elizabeth J. Glennie, "Opportunities to Participate: Extracurricular Activities' Distribution Across Academic Correlates in High Schools," *Social Science Research* 39, no. 2 (2010): 296–309.

30. McDonough, *Choosing Colleges*.

31. Clinedinst, *State of College Admission 2014*.

32. Michael Hurwitz, "The Impact of Legacy Status on Undergraduate Admissions at Elite Colleges and Universities," *Economics of Education Review* 30, no. 3 (2011): 480–492.

33. Cameron Howell and Sarah E. Turner, "Legacies in Black and White: The Racial Composition of the Legacy Pool," *Research in Higher Education* 45, no. 4 (2004): 325–35; Jerome Karabel, *The Chosen: The Hidden History of Admission and Exclusion at Harvard, Yale, and Princeton* (Boston: Houghton Mifflin, 2005).

34. Bastedo and Jaquette, "Running in Place"; Stephen Burd, *Undermining Pell: How Colleges' Pursuit of Prestige and Revenue Is Hurting Low-Income Students*, vol. 2 (Washington, DC: New America, 2015).

35. Klugman, "The Advanced Placement Arms Race."

36. Ozan Jaquette and Bradley R. Curs, "Creating the Out-of-State University: Do Public Universities Increase Nonresident Freshman Enrollment in Response to Declining State Appropriations?," *Research in Higher Education* 56, no. 6 (2015): 535–565; Stephen Burd, *The Out-of-State Student Arms Race: How Public Universities Use Merit Aid to Recruit Nonresident Students*, New America, 2015.

37. Ozan Jaquette, Bradley R. Curs, and Julie R. Posselt, "Tuition Rich, Mission Poor: Nonresident Enrollment Growth and the Socioeconomic and Racial Composition of Public Research Universities," *Journal of Higher Education* (forthcoming).

38. William R. Doyle, "Changes In Institutional Aid, 1992–2003: The Evolving Role of Merit Aid," *Research in Higher Education* 51, no. 8 (2010): 789–810; Nicholas Hillman, "Tuition Discounting for Revenue Management," *Research in Higher Education* 53, no. 1 (2012): 263–281.

39. Susan Dynarski, "Hope for Whom? Financial Aid for the Middle Class and Its Impact on College Attendance," *National Tax Journal* 53 (2000): 629–662; Donald E. Heller, "Is Merit-Based Student Aid Really Trumping Need-Based Aid? Another View," *Change* 34, no. 4 (2002): 6–7.

40. Ronald G. Ehrenberg, Liang Zhang, and Jared M. Levin, "Crafting a Class: The Trade-Off Between Merit Scholarships and Enrolling Lower-Income Students," *Review of Higher Education* 29, no. 2 (2006): 195–211.

41. Christopher Avery, Andrew Fairbanks, and Richard Zeckhauser, *The Early Admissions Game: Joining the Elite* (Cambridge, MA: Harvard University Press, 2003).

42. Christopher Avery and Jonathan D. Levin, "Early Admissions at Selective Colleges" (working paper, National Bureau of Economic Research, Cambridge, MA, 2009).

43. Nicholas A. Bowman and Michael N. Bastedo, "Getting on the Front Page: Organizational Reputation, Status Signals, and the Impact of *U.S. News and World Report* on Student Decisions," *Research in Higher Education* 50, no. 5 (2009): 415–436; Michael Luca and Jonathan Smith, "Salience in Quality Disclosure: Evidence from the *U.S. News* College Rankings," *Journal of Economics & Management Strategy* 22, no. 1 (2013): 58–77.

44. Wendy N. Espeland and Michael Sauder, "Rankings and Reactivity: How Public Measures Recreate Social Worlds," *American Journal of Sociology* 113, no. 1 (2007): 1–40.

45. Michael N. Bastedo and Nicholas A. Bowman, "College Rankings as an Interorganizational Dependency: Establishing the Foundation for Strategic and Institutional Accounts," *Research in Higher Education* 52, no. 1 (2011): 3–23.

46. Shari L. Gnolek, Vincenzo T. Falciano, and Ralph W. Kuncl, "Modeling Change and Variation in *US News & World Report* College Rankings: What Would It Really Take to Be in the Top 20?" *Research in Higher Education* 55, no. 8 (2014): 761–779; Jeongeun Kim, *The Cost of Rankings? The Influence of College Rankings on Institutional Management* (PhD diss., University of Michigan, 2015).

47. Andrew S. Belasco, Kelly O. Rosinger, and James C. Hearn, "The Test-Optional Movement at America's Selective Liberal Arts Colleges: A Boon for Equity or Something Else?" *Educational Evaluation and Policy Analysis* 37, no. 2 (2015): 206–223.

48. Richard C. Atkinson and Saul Geiser, "Reflections on a Century of College Admissions Tests," *Educational Researcher* 38, no. 9 (2009): 665–676.

49. Eric Hoover, "College Admissions, Frozen In Time," *Chronicle of Higher Education*, May 26, 2015, http://chronicle.com/article/College-Admissions-Frozen-in/230363/.

50. Scott Jaschik, "Transcript-Free Admissions," *Inside Higher Ed*, September 4, 2014, www.insidehighered.com/news/2014/09/04/goucher-will-create-new-option-admissions-two-minute-video.

51. Scott Jaschik, "New Ways To Get In," *Inside Higher Ed*, January 13, 2015, www.insidehighered.com/news/2015/01/13/goucher-and-bennington-both-report-success-highly-nontraditional-admissions-options.

52. Eric Hoover, "The Hottest Seat on Campus," *Chronicle of Higher Education*, September 15, 2014, http://chronicle.com/article/The-Hottest-Seat-on-Campus/148777/.

53. Fernando Furquim and Kristen Glasener, "The Effect of QuestBridge on Economic Diversity at Highly Selective Institutions," (working paper, University of Michigan, Ann Arbor, MI, 2015).

54. Emily House, "Exploring Undermatch in Tennessee: An Analysis Using Multiple Definitions of Undermatch" (working paper, University of Michigan, Ann Arbor, MI, 2015). See also Goodman, Hurwitz, and Smith (chapter 8 in this volume).

55. Alicia C. Dowd, John J. Cheslock, and Tatiana Melguizo, "Transfer Access from Community Colleges and the Distribution of Elite Higher Education," *Journal of Higher Education* 79 (2008): 442–472.

56. Sara Goldrick-Rab et al., "Reducing Income Inequality in Educational Attainment: Experimental Evidence on the Impact of Financial Aid on College Completion," *American Journal of Sociology* (forthcoming).

57. Bastedo and Bowman, "Improving Admission of Low-SES Students at Selective Colleges."

58. Bastedo, Howard, and Flaster, "Holistic Admissions After Affirmative Action."

59. Bastedo, "Cognitive Repairs in the Admissions Office."

60. Chip Heath, Richard P. Larrick, and Joshua Klayman, "Cognitive Repairs: How Organizations Compensate for the Shortcomings of Individual Learners," *Research in Organizational Behavior* 20 (1998): 1–37.

61. Bastedo, "Cognitive Repairs in the Admissions Office."

62. Richard D. Kahlenberg, ed., *Rewarding Strivers: Helping Low-Income Students Succeed in College* (Washington, DC: The Century Foundation, 2010); Kahlenberg, ed., *The Future of Affirmative Action*.

63. Bastedo and Jaquette, "Running in Place"; Matthew M. Chingos, "Graduation Rates at America's Universities: What We Know and What We Need To Know," in *Getting to Graduation: The Completion Agenda in Higher Education*, eds. Andrew. P. Kelly and Mark Schneider (Baltimore: Johns Hopkins University Press, 2012).

64. Jessica Howell and Matea Pender, "The Costs and Benefits of Enrolling in an Academically Matched College," *Economics of Education Review* (forthcoming).

65. William G. Bowen and Derek Bok, *The Shape of the River. Long-Term Consequences of Considering Race in College and University Admissions* (Princeton, NJ: Princeton University Press, 1998); Bowen, Chingos, and McPherson, *Crossing the Finish Line*; Jennie E. Brand and Yu Xie, "Who Benefits Most from College? Evidence for Negative Selection in Heterogeneous Economic Returns to Higher Education," *American Sociological Review* 75, no. 2 (2010): 273–302; Stacy Dale and Alan B. Krueger, "Estimating the Return to College Selectivity over the Career Using Administrative Earnings Data" (working paper, National Bureau of Economic Research, Cambridge, MA, 2011).

Chapter 7

1. We are grateful to the Pittsburgh Public Schools and the Pittsburgh Promise for sharing the data needed to complete this work. We thank Aaron Anthony, Emi Iwatani, and Danielle Lowry for exceptional research assistance. We thank Bill Bickel for feedback on early drafts of this chapter.

2. Caroline Hoxby and Christopher Avery, *The Missing "One-Offs": The Hidden Supply of High-Achieving, Low-Income Students* (Washington, DC: The Brookings Institution, 2013), www.brookings.edu/~/media/projects/bpea/spring-2013/2013a_hoxby.pdf; Caroline Hoxby and Sarah Turner, *Expanding College Opportunities for High-Achieving, Low Income Students* (working paper, Stanford Institute for Economic Policy Research, 2013), https://siepr.stanford.edu/?q=/system/files/shared/pubs/papers/12-014paper.pdf.

3. Hoxby and Turner, *Expanding College Opportunities*.

4. See figure 1 of Caroline Hoxby and Sarah Turner, "Expanding College Opportunities," *Education Next* 13, no. 4 (Fall 2013): 67–73.

5. Low-income (high-income) students here are defined as those with annual household incomes of 40,000 or below ($100,000 or above), see Jessica Howell and Matea Pender, "The Costs and

Benefits of Enrolling in an Academically Matched College," *Economics of Education Review* (forthcoming).

6. The reader should note that the Pittsburgh Promise recently announced program changes that include a reduction in the annual award to a maximum of $7,500 beginning with the class of 2017 along with a narrowing to cover only tuition and fees (previously room, board, and books were also included). Details of the program changes can be found in Marcie Cipriani, "Changes Made to Pittsburgh Promise College Scholarship Amounts," WTAE, July 14, 2015, www.wtae.com/news/changes-made-to-pittsburgh-promise-college-scholarship-amounts /34161870.

7. We limit our examination here to two years of college-going outcomes.

8. Lindsay Page and Judith Scott-Clayton, "College Access in the United States: A Comprehensive Review," *Economics of Education Review* (forthcoming).

9. Suzanne Mettler, *How U.S. Higher Education Promotes Inequality—and What Can Be Done to Broaden Access and Graduation*, Harvard University, Scholars Strategy Network, 2014, www .scholarsstrategynetwork.org/brief/how-us-education-promotes-inequality-%E2%80%93-and- what-can-be-done-broaden-access-and-graduation.

10. Ibid.

11. Ibid.

12. For a recent review of the literature on barriers to college access, including those related to financial aid, see Page and Scott-Clayton, "College Access in the United States."

13. Advisory Committee on Student Financial Assistance, *The Student Aid Gauntlet: Making Access to College Simple and Certain* (Washington, DC: US Department of Education, January 23, 2005), https://www2.ed.gov/about/bdscomm/list/acsfa/edlite-gauntlet.html; Benjamin L. Castleman and Lindsay Page, *Summer Melt: Supporting Low-Income Students Through the Transition to College* (Cambridge, MA: Harvard Education Press, 2014); Eric Grodsky and Melanie T. Jones, "Real and Imagined Barriers to College Entry: Perceptions of Cost," *Social Science Research* 36, no. 2 (2007): 745–766.

14. Hoxby and Turner, "Expanding College Opportunities."

15. John Bound, Michael Lovenheim, and Sarah Turner, "Why Have College Completion Rates Declined? An Analysis of Changing Student Preparation and Collegiate Resources," *American Economic Journal: Applied Economics* 2, no. 3 (2010): 129–157.

16. Howell and Pender, "The Costs and Benefits of Enrolling in an Academically Matched College."

17. Jonathan Smith, Matea Pender, and Jessica Howell, "The Full Extent of Student-College Academic Undermatch," *Economics of Education Review* 32 (2013): 247–261.

18. Hoxby and Avery, *The Missing "One-Offs."*

19. Estimates of grant-based aid provided by net price calculators can still differ substantially from the grant aid students actually receive in their financial aid packages, see Aaron M. Anthony, Lindsay C. Page, and Abigail Seldin, "In the Right Ballpark? Assessing the Accuracy of Net Price Calculators," *Social Science Research Network*, January 2015, http://ssrn.com /abstract=2555051.

20. The Pittsburgh Promise, "About Us," http://pittsburghpromise.org/about_whoweare.php.

21. The Pittsburgh Promise, "Our Partners and Investors," April 2014, www.pittsburghpromise. org/give_partners.php.

22. The Pittsburgh Promise very recently announced a scaling back of the maximum generosity of the scholarship in order to support longer-run viability of the fund. For more information, see The Pittsburgh Promise, "Pittsburgh Promise Adjusts Program to Benefit More Pittsburgh

Students," news release, July 14, 2015, http://pittsburghpromise.org/assets/documents/
news_7_14.pdf.

23. Pennsylvania Higher Education Assistance Agency, "Pennsylvania State Grant 2014–15
Program Manual," www.pheaa.org/funding-opportunities/state-grant-program/pdf/2014-
2015/Program-Manual.pdf.

24. Although the maximum Promise benefit was $5,000 in the first three years of the program.
See Jeff Baker, "2014–2015 Federal Pell Grant Payment and Disbursement Schedules," January
31, 2014, http://ifap.ed.gov/dpcletters/attachments/GEN1401.pdf.

25. For complete discussion, see Page and Scott-Clayton, "College Access in the United States."

26. During the period of our investigation, two PPS high schools shuttered their doors and
non-senior students served by these schools transferred to other high school settings in
the community. We observe a gap in our data, whereby we do not have college enrollment
data for those students who were part of the final graduating cohorts from these schools.
Therefore, we exclude these school-cohort-specific groups of students from our analytic
sample.

27. Community-level measures include unemployment rate, share of the population living
in poverty and median household income. Data obtained from American Fact Finder,
"Download Center," http://factfinder.census.gov/faces/nav/jsf/pages/download_center.xhtml.

28. The neighborhood socioeconomic characteristics differ substantially for the students we
do and do not identify as low income. Low-income students live in communities with, on
average, an 11 percent unemployment rate, a median household income of $32,000 (ranging
from $18,000 to $37,000) and where a quarter of the population lives below the poverty line
(ranging from 19 to 45 percent). This is compared with students in non-low income settings,
where the typical unemployment rate is 7 percent, median income is $49,000 and 14 percent
of the population lives below the poverty line. Thus, students we designate as low-income and
non-low-income live in very different community settings and likely face different personal
socioeconomic circumstances themselves.

29. While not shown, it is worth noting that, among those who actually sat for the exam, the
corresponding average math and critical reading scores are 469 and 460, respectively. Among
those students who did not sit for the SAT, imputed scores were approximately 400 for both
the math and critical reading sections of the exam, on average. In short, those students who sit
for the exam are higher performing than those who do not.

30. Joshua Goodman, Michael Hurwitz, and Jonathan Smith, "College Access, Initial College
Choice and Degree Completion" (working paper, National Bureau of Economic Research,
Cambridge, MA, February 2015).

31. Hoxby and Turner, *Expanding College Opportunities.*

32. Hoxby and Avery, *The Missing "One-Offs"*; Howell and Pender, "The Costs and Benefits of
Enrolling in an Academically Matched College."

33. We determined this threshold empirically. While a score of 1000 is used by some as a
benchmark for college readiness, we observe that many PPS students with SAT scores below
this threshold are nevertheless enrolling in four-year postsecondary institutions, with a
score of 800 representing a natural breaking point in our data, see Jeffrey Wyatt et al., *SAT
Benchmarks: Development of a College Readiness Benchmark and its Relationship to Secondary
and Postsecondary School Performance* (New York: College Board, 2011), https://research.
collegeboard.org/sites/default/files/publications/2012/7/researchreport-2011-5-sat-college-
readiness-benchmark-secondary-performance.pdf.

34. In this analysis, we exclude a small number of students (n=112) who continue to postsecondary institutions for which we cannot assess match. These include "specialized" schools
such as culinary institutes, art institutes, and music conservatories.

35. Smith, Pender and Howell, "The Full Extent of Student-College Academic Undermatch."

36. We do so by including fixed effects for high school of graduation. In addition, we include a fixed effect to differentiate between students in the graduating classes of 2010 and 2011.

37. We do not control for high school GPA, SAT-taking or SAT scores, as these factors themselves may have been impacted by the implementation of the Promise. In fact, these measures of academic achievement do trend over time in a direction that points to the Promise as motivation for high levels of academic performance in high school. Given the focus of this chapter, however, we refrain from examining these outcomes further here.

38. Sarah R. Cohodes and Joshua S. Goodman, "Merit Aid, College Quality, and College Completion: Massachusetts' Adams Scholarship as an In-Kind Subsidy," *American Economic Journal: Applied Economics* 6, no. 4 (2014): 251–285. The focal students in the analysis by Cohodes and Goodman (2014) were quite high performing relative to all high school graduates in Massachusetts. In our analysis of the Pittsburgh Promise, the typical student is quite different academically. In addition, the Promise in its full implementation allows students to utilize scholarship funds at both public and private institutions in the state. Therefore, Pittsburgh students are able to use Promise funds to access institutions of a wide range of selectivity.

39. Howell and Pender, "The Costs and Benefits of Enrolling in an Academically Matched College."

40. This hypothesis is consistent with Judith Scott-Clayton's examination of the West Virginia Promise program, see Judith Scott-Clayton, "On Money and Motivation: A Quasi-Experimental Analysis of Financial Incentives for College Achievement." *Journal of Human Resources* 46, no. 3 (2011): 614–646.

41. We conducted a number of sensitivity checks for these results, including fitting models with and within school and year fixed effects, with and without covariate controls, and with narrower bandwidths. For full technical details, see Lindsay C. Page, Jennifer E. Iriti, Danielle J. Lowry, and Aaron M. Anthony, "The Promise of Place-Based Investment in College Access and Success: Investigating the Impact of the Pittsburgh Promise" (working paper, University of Pittsburgh, 2015).

42. Michael Mitchell and Michael Leachman, *Years of Cuts Threaten to Put College out of Reach for More Students* (Washington, DC: Center for Budget and Policy Priorities, May 13, 2015), www.cbpp.org/research/years-of-cuts-threaten-to-put-college-out-of-reach-for-more-students.

43. Smith, Pender and Howell, "The Full Extent of Student-College Academic Undermatch."

44. Adam M. Lavecchia, Heidi Liu, and Philip Oreopoulos. "Behavioral Economics of Education: Progress and Possibilities" (working paper, National Bureau of Economic Research, Cambridge, MA, 2014).

45. Amanda Pallais, "Small Differences That Matter: Mistakes in Applying to College," *Journal of Labor Economics* 33, no. 2 (2015): 493–520; Michael Hurwitz, Preeya P. Mbekeani, Margaret Nipson, and Lindsay C. Page, *Surprising Ripple Effects: How Changing the SAT Score-Sending Policy for Low-Income Students Impacts College Access and Success* (Cambridge, MA: Center for Education Policy Research, Harvard University, January 31, 2016), http://cepr.harvard.edu/files/cepr/files/surprising_ripple_effects.pdf?m=1454689016.

Chapter 8

1. This research reflects the views of the authors and not their corresponding institutions.

2. We frequently refer to college "quality" in this chapter. There are many ways to measure quality but we have a particular metric in mind, namely the institution's track record of successfully graduating students. Many other measures of quality are highly correlated with

this, but institutional graduation rates seem most directly relevant to the question of whether choosing a given college will improve a student's labor market prospects.

3. See Table 1 of State Higher Education Executive Officers Association, *State Higher Education Finance FY2013*, 2014, www.sheeo.org/sites/default/files/publications/SHEF_FY13_04292014. pdf.

4. See Table 2 of State Higher Education Executive Officers Association, *State Higher Education Finance FY2013*, 2014, www.sheeo.org/sites/default/files/publications/SHEF_FY13_04292014. pdf.

5. Sam Peltzman, The Case of Higher Education," *Journal of Political Economy* 81, no. 1 (1973): 1–27.

6. Philip T. Ganderton, "The Effect of Subsidies in Kind on the Choice of a College," *Journal of Public Economics* 48, no. 3 (1992): 269–292.

7. Bridget T. Long, "Does the Format of a Financial Aid Program Matter? The Effect of State In-Kind Tuition Subsidies," *Review of Economics and Statistics* 86, no. 3 (2004): 767–782.

   Peltzman, Ganderton, and Long's estimates are generated by regression analyses that include controls for potentially confounding factors (see, respectively, "The Effect of Government Subsidies-in-Kind on Private Expenditures"), Ganderton ("The Effect of Subsidies in Kind on the Choice of a College"), and Long. More recent studies, including those by Cellini (Stephanie R. Cellini, "Crowded Colleges and College Crowd-Out: The Impact of Public Subsidies on the Two-Year College Market," *American Economic Journal: Economic Policy* 1, no. 2 [2009]: 1–30) and Bound and Turner (John Bound and Sarah Turner, "Cohort Crowding: How Resources Affect Collegiate Attainment," *Journal of Public Economics* 91, nos. 5–6 [2007]: 877–899), have exploited natural experiments to try to identify the impact of changes in in-kind spending on student outcomes.

8. Cellini, "Crowded Colleges and College Crowd-Out."

9. Bound and Turner, "Cohort Crowding."

10. John Kennan, "Spatial Variation in Higher Education Financing and the Supply of College Graduates" (working paper, National Bureau of Economic Research, Cambridge, MA, 2015).

11. National Association of State Student Grant and Aid Programs, *44th Annual Survey Report on State-Sponsored Student Financial Aid*, 2013, www.nassgap.org/viewrepository.aspx.

12. See Table 12 of National Association of State Student Grant and Aid Programs, *44th Annual Survey Report on State-Sponsored Student Financial Aid*, 2013, www.nassgap.org /viewrepository.aspx.

13. Susan Dynarksi, "Hope for Whom? Financial Aid for the Middle Class and Its Impact on College Attendance," *National Tax Journal* 53, no. 3, part 2 (September 2000): 629–662.

14. Thomas J. Kane, "A Quasi-Experimental Estimate of the Impact of Financial Aid on College-Going" (working paper, National Bureau of Economic Research, Cambridge, MA, May 2003).

15. Thomas J. Kane, "Evaluating the Impact of the D.C. Tuition Assistance Grant Program," *Journal of Human Resources* 42, no. 3 (Summer 2007): 555–582.

16. Susan Dynarski, "Building the Stock of College-Education Labor" (working paper, National Bureau of Economic Research, Cambridge, MA, September 2005).

17. Benjamin L. Castleman and Bridget Terry Long, "Looking Beyond Enrollment: The Causal Effect of Need-Based Grants on College Access, Persistence, and Graduation" (working paper, National Bureau of Economic Research, Cambridge, MA, August 2012).

18. Jeffrey T. Denning, "College on the Cheap: Costs and Benefits of Community College" (Job Market paper, University of Texas at Austin, 2014).

19. Sarah Cohodes and Joshua Goodman, "Merit Aid, College Quality and College Completion:

Massachusetts' Adams Scholarship as an In-Kind Subsidy," *American Economic Journal: Applied Economics* 6, no. 4 (2014): 251–285.

20. Rajashri Chakrabarti and Joydeep Roy, *Merit Aid, Student Mobility, and the Role of College Selectivity* (New York: Federal Reserve Bank of New York, 2013), www.newyorkfed.org /research/staff_reports/sr641.pdf.

21. Jonathan Smith, Matea Pender, and Jessica Howell, "The Full Extent of Undermatch," *Economics of Education Review* 32 (2013): 247–261.

22. These include Colorado (2002, ACT); Illinois (2002, ACT); Maine (2006, SAT); Michigan (2008, ACT); Kentucky (2009, ACT); Delaware (2010, SAT); Idaho (2010, SAT); Tennessee (2010, ACT); and New Hampshire and Delaware (2015, SAT). Michigan switched to require the SAT in 2014, as did Illinois in 2015.

23. Michael Hurwitz, Jonathan Smith, Jessica Howell, and Matea Pender, *The Role of High Schools in Students' Postsecondary Choices* (New York: College Board, 2012), http://media.collegeboard .com/digitalServices/pdf/nosca/research-role-high-schools-students-postsecondary-choices .pdf.

24. Sarena F. Goodman, "Learning from the Test: Raising Selective College Enrollment by Providing Information" (working paper, Finance and Economics Discussion Series, Washington, DC, 2013).

25. George Bulman, "The Effects of Access to College Assessments on Enrollment and Attainment," *American Economic Journal: Applied Economics* 7, no. 4 (2015): 1–36.

26. Christopher Avery and Thomas J. Kane, "Student Perceptions of College Opportunities: The Boston COACH Program," in *College Choices: The Economics of Where to Go, When to Go, and How to Pay For It*, ed. Caroline Hoxby (Chicago: University of Chicago Press, 2004), 355–394.

27. Eleanor W. Dillon and Jeffrey A. Smith, "The Determinants of Mismatch Between Students and Colleges" (working paper, National Bureau of Economic Research, Cambridge, MA, 2013); Caroline Hoxby and Christopher Avery, *The Missing "One-Offs": The Hidden Supply of High-Achieving, Low-Income Students* (Washington, DC: The Brookings Institution, 2013), www .brookings.edu/~/media/projects/bpea/spring-2013/2013a_hoxby.pdf; Smith, Pender, and Howell, "The Full Extent of Undermatch."

28. Caroline Hoxby and Sarah Turner, "Expanding College Opportunities for High-Achieving, Low Income Students" (working paper, Stanford Institute for Economic Policy Research, Stanford, CA, 2013).

29. Michael Hurwitz et al., "The Maine Question: How Is 4-Year College Enrollment Affected by Mandatory College Entrance Exams?," *Educational Evaluation and Policy Analysis* 37, no. 1 (2014): 138–159; Strategic Data Project, *Do College Enrollment Rates Differ Across High Schools?*, Center for Education and Policy Research, Harvard University, 2012, www .strivetogether.org/sites/default/files/images/The%20Strategic%20Data%20Project- Analytics%20that%20Impact%20Student%20Outcomes1.pdf.

30. Hurwitz et al., "The Maine Question."

31. Daniel Klasik, "The ACT of Enrollment: The College Enrollment Effects of Required College Entrance Exam Taking," *Educational Researcher* 42, no. 3 (2013): 151–160.

32. Goodman, "Learning from the Test."

33. Joshua Hyman, "ACT for All: The Effect of Mandatory College Entrance Exams on Postsecondary Attainment and Choice" (working paper, University of Connecticut, Mansfield, CT, 2014).

34. Klasik, "The ACT of Enrollment."

35. Ibid.; Hyman, "ACT for All."

36. Goodman, "Learning from the Test."

37. Klasik, "The ACT of Enrollment."

38. Dillon and Smith, "The Determinants of Mismatch Between Students and Colleges"; Hoxby and Avery, "The Missing 'One-Offs.'"

39. Hurwitz et al., "The Maine Question."

40. Hyman, "ACT for All."

41. Ibid.; Goodman, "Learning from the Test."

42. Ibid.

43. William G. Bowen and Derek Bok, *The Shape of the River: Long-Term Consequences of Considering Race in College and University Admissions* (Princeton, NJ: Princeton University Press, 1998).

44. Peter Arcidiacono et al., "Does Affirmative Action Lead to Mismatch? A New Test and Evidence," *Quantitative Economics* 2, no. 3 (2011): 303–333.

45. Richard H. Sander, "A Systemic Analysis of Affirmative Action in American Law Schools," *Stanford Law Review* 57, no. 2 (2004): 367–483.

46. Daniel E. Ho, "Why Affirmative Action Does Not Cause Black Students to Fail the Bar," *Yale Law Journal* 114, no. 8 (2005): 1997–2004.

47. Jesse Rothstein and Albert H. Yoon, "Affirmative Action in Law School Admissions: What Do Racial Preferences Do?" (working paper, National Bureau of Economic Research, Cambridge, MA, 2008).

48. Peter Arcidiacono and Michael Lovenheim, "Affirmative Action and the Quality-Fit Tradeoff," *Journal of Economic Literature* (forthcoming).

49. Liliana M. Garces, "Understanding the Impact of Affirmative Action Bans in Different Graduate Fields of Study," *American Educational Research Journal* 50, no. 2 (2013): 251–284.

50. Marta Tienda et al., "Closing the Gap? Admissions & Enrollments at the Texas Public Flagships Before and After Affirmative Action" (working paper, Woodrow Wilson School of Public and International Affairs, Princeton, NJ, 2003).

51. Peter Hinrichs, "The Effects of Affirmative Action Bans on College Enrollment, Educational Attainment, and the Demographic Composition of Universities," *Review of Economics and Statistics* 94, no. 3 (2012): 712–722.

52. Marta Tienda and Sunny Xinchun Niu, "Flagships, Feeders, and the Texas Top 10% Law: A Test of the 'Brain Drain' Hypothesis," *Journal of Higher Education* 77, no. 4 (2006): 712–739.

53. Mark C. Long and Marta Tienda, "Winners and Losers: Changes in Texas University Admissions post-*Hopwood*," *Educational Evaluation and Policy Analysis* 30, no. 3 (2008): 255–280.

54. Sunny X. Niu and Marta Tienda, "The Impact of the Texas Top Ten Percent Law on College Enrollment: A Regression Discontinuity Approach," *Journal of Policy Analysis and Management* 29, no. 1 (2010): 84–110.

55. Eric Furstenberg, "Academic Outcomes and Texas's Top Ten Percent Law," *Annals of the American Academy of Political and Social Science* 627, no. 1 (2010): 167–183.

56. Lindsay Daugherty, Paco Martorell, and Isaac McFarlin Jr., "Percent Plans, Automatic Admissions, and College Outcomes," *IZA Journal of Labor Economics* 3, no. 10 (2014): 1–29.

57. National Association for College Admission Counseling, *2009 State of College Admission*, 2009, www.nacacnet.org/research/PublicationsResources/Marketplace/Documents/2009SOCA.pdf.

58. Joshua Goodman, Michael Hurwitz and Jonathan Smith, "College Access, Initial College Choice and Degree Completion" (working paper, National Bureau of Economic Research, Cambridge, MA, 2015).

59. Goodman, Hurwitz, and Smith, "College Access, Initial College Choice and Degree Completion."

60. Seth Zimmerman, "The Returns to College Admission for Academically Marginal Studies," *Journal of Labor Economics* 32, no. 4 (2014): 711–754.

61. Ibid.

62. Michael N. Bastedo, "Conceptual and Methodological Problems in Research on College Undermatch," *Educational Researcher* 43, no. 2 (2014): 93–99.

Chapter 9

1. Amanda Pallais, "Small Differences That Matter: Mistakes in Applying to College" (working paper, National Bureau of Economic Research, Cambridge, MA, 2013), www.nber.org/papers/ w19480.pdf; Eric P. Bettinger et al., "The Role of Application Assistance and Information in College Decisions: Results from the H&R Block FAFSA Experiment" (working paper, National Bureau of Economic Research, Cambridge, MA, 2009), www.nber.org/papers/w15361.pdf; Benjamin L. Castleman and Lindsay C. Page, "Summer Nudging: Can Personalized Text Messages and Peer Mentor Outreach Increase College Going Among Low-Income High School Graduates?" *Journal of Economic Behavior & Organization* 115 (2015): 144–160; Scott E. Carrell and Bruce Sacerdote, "Why Do College Going Interventions Work?" (working paper, National Bureau of Economic Research, Cambridge, MA, 2013), www.nber.org/papers/w19031. pdf.; Benjamin L. Castleman, Lindsay C. Page, and Korynn Schooley, "The Forgotten Summer: Does the Offer of College Counseling After High School Mitigate Summer Melt Among College-Intending, Low-Income High School Graduates?" *Journal of Policy Analysis and Management* 33, no. 2 (2014): 320–344.

2. Barack Obama, "Remarks of President Barack Obama—As Prepared for Delivery: Address to Joint Session of Congress," The White House, February 24, 2009, www.whitehouse.gov/ the_press_office/remarks-of-president-barack-obama-address-to-joint-session-of-congress/.

3. Executive Office of the President, "Commitments to Action on College Opportunity," December 15, 2014, www.whitehouse.gov/sites/default/files/docs/121514_college_opportunity_commitment_report.pdf.

4. The College Board, "Total Undergraduate Student Aid by Source and Type, 2013–14," http://trends.collegeboard.org/student-aid/figures-tables/ total-undergraduate-student-aid-source-type-2013-14.

5. National Center for Education Statistics, *Integrated Postsecondary Education Data System (IPEDS) 2014–2016 and 2013 Carry Over: Supporting Statement Part A—OMB Paperwork Reduction Act Submission*, U.S. Department of Education, 2013, http://nces.ed.gov/ipeds/.

6. US Department of Education, "College Navigator," https://nces.ed.gov/collegenavigator/.

7. US Department of Education, "College Affordability and Transparency Explanation Form: Summary Guide to College Costs for the 2012–13 Collection Year," http://collegecost.ed.gov /catc/resources/2012-13%20CATEF%20Summary%20Guide%20to%20College%20Costs.pdf.

8. US Department of Education, "College Affordability and Transparency Center," http:// collegecost.ed.gov/catc/Default.aspx.

9. US Department of Education, "College Scorecard," https://collegescorecard.ed.gov/.

10. Carol Fuller and Carlo Salerno, *Information Required to be Disclosed Under the Higher Education Act of 1965: Suggestions for Dissemination (updated)*, National Postsecondary Education Cooperative, 2009, http://nces.ed.gov/pubs2010/2010831rev.pdf.

11. Kevin Carey and Andrew P. Kelly, *The Truth Behind Higher Education Disclosure Laws* (Washington, DC: Education Sector and American Enterprise Institute, 2011), www .thecollegesolution.com/wp-content/uploads/2011/11/HigherEdDisclosure_RELEASE.pdf; Andrew H. Nichols, *The Pell Partnership: Ensuring a Shared Responsibility for Low-Income*

Student Success (Washington, DC: The Education Trust, 2015), https://edtrust.org/wp-content/
uploads/2014/09/ThePellPartnership_EdTrust_2015.pdf.

12. College Board and Art & Science Group, LLC, *A Majority of Students Rule Out Colleges Based on Sticker Price*, 2012, www.artsci.com/studentpoll/v9n1/index.html.

13. Libby A. Nelson, "No Magic Bullet," *Inside Higher Ed*, June 12, 2013, www.insidehigh-ered.com/news/2013/06/12/first-year-shopping-sheet-doesnt-make-big-splash; Ben Miller, "No One's Watching the Watch List," New America, June 12, 2013, https://web.archive.org/web/20130914111010/http://higheredwatch.newamerica.net/blogposts/2013/the_failed_tuition_watch_lists-86916.

14. Carolin Hagelskamp, David Schleifer, and Christopher DiStasi, *Is College Worth It for Me? How Adults Without Degrees Think About Going (Back) to School*, Public Agenda, 2013, www.publicagenda.org/files/IsCollegeWorthItForMe_PublicAgenda_2013.pdf; Carey and Kelly, *The Truth Behind Higher Education Disclosure Laws*; Andrea Sykes, *Information Required to Be Disclosed Under the Higher Education Act of 1965: Suggestions for Dissemination—A Supplemental Report* (Washington, DC: National Postsecondary Education Cooperative, 2011), http://nces.ed.gov/pubs2012/2012831.pdf.

15. Eric Grodsky and Melanie T. Jones, "Real and Imagined Barriers to College Entry: Perceptions of Cost," *Social Science Research* 36, no. 2 (June 2007): 745–766.

16. Kelly Field, "Company Selling Net-Price Calculators Stymies Efforts to Compare College Costs," *Chronicle of Higher Education*, October 29, 2013, http://chronicle.com/article/Company-Selling-Net-Price/142671/.

17. Kevin Eagan et al., *The American Freshman: National Norms Fall 2014* (Washington, DC: Higher Education Research Institute, 2014), www.heri.ucla.edu/monographs/theamerican-freshman2014.pdf.

18. Clare McCann and Amy Laitinen, *College Blackout: How the Higher Education Lobby Fought to Keep Students in the Dark*, New America, 2014, www.newamerica.org/downloads/CollegeBlackoutFINAL.pdf.

19. For more details on College Measures, see College Measures, "Economic Success Metrics (ESM) Program," www.collegemeasures.org/esm/; For more details on Virginia data, see State Council of Higher Education for Virginia, "Student Outcomes: Reports and Resources," http://research.schev.edu/.

20. PayScale, "2014–2015 PayScale College Salary Report," www.payscale.com/college-salary-report; Jonathan Rothwell and Siddharth Kulkarni, *Beyond College Rankings: A Value-Added Approach to Assessing Two- and Four-Year Schools* (Washington, DC: The Brookings Institution, 2015), www.brookings.edu/~/media/Research/Files/Reports/2015/04/29-college-value-add/BMPP_CollegeValueAdded.pdf?la=en.

21. The same is also true in K–12 education, see Jon Valant, *Better Data, Better Decisions: Informing School Choosers to Improve Education Markets*, (Washington, DC: American Enterprise Institute, 2014), www.aei.org/wp-content/uploads/2014/11/Better-Data-Better-Decisions-4.pdf.

22. Amanda Pallais and Sarah Turner, "Opportunities for Low-Income Students at Top Colleges and Universities: Policy Initiatives and the Distribution of Students," *National Tax Journal* 59, no. 2 (June 2006): 357–386; Melissa Roderick, Jenny Nagaoka, and Vanessa Coca, "Potholes on the Road to College: High School Effects in Shaping Urban Students' Participation in College Application, Four-Year College Enrollment, and College Match," *Sociology of Education* 84, no. 3 (2011): 178–211.

23. Art & Science Group, LLC, *Influence of the Rankings on College Choice*, 2013, www.artsci.com/studentpoll/october/index.aspx.

24. Ben Miller, *Colleges Are Supposed to Report Pell Graduation Rates—Here's How to Make Them Actually Do It*, New America Foundation, 2013, www.edcentral.org/colleges-are-supposed-to-report-pell-graduation-rates-heres-how-to-make-them-actually-do-it/.

25. For a summary of the act, see Office of Senator Ron Wyden, *The Student Right to Know Before You Go Act*, www.wyden.senate.gov/download/?id=a50c8905-64f7-4b6c-b32a-e57ce619c818&download=1.

26. Andrew Gillen, *In Debt and in the Dark: It's Time for Better Information on Student Loan Default* (Washington, DC: American Institutes for Research, 2013), www.educationsector.org/sites/default/files/publications/Defaults_CYCT-F_JULY.pdf.

27. Debbie Cochrane, *Where More Default Than Graduate: Career Education Program Parasites*, The Institute for College Access and Success, 2014, http://ticas.org/blog/where-more-default-graduate-career-education-program-parasites.

28. Andrea Fuller and Douglas Belkin, "The Watchdogs of College Education Rarely Bite," *Wall Street Journal*, June 17, 2015, www.wsj.com/articles/the-watchdogs-of-college-education-rarely-bite-1434594602.

29. Mamie Lynch and Jennifer Engle, *Big Gaps, Small Gaps: Some Colleges and Universities Do Better Than Others in Graduating African American Students* (Washington, DC: The Education Trust, 2010), http://1k9gl1yevnfp2lpq1dhrqe17.wpengine.netdna-cdn.com/wp-content/uploads/2013/10/CRO-Brief-AfricanAmerican.pdf.

30. Caroline M. Hoxby and Sarah Turner, "Expanding College Opportunities for High-Achieving, Low-Income Students" (working paper, Stanford Institute for Economic Policy, Stanford, CA, 2013).

31. Melissa Roderick et al., *From High School to the Future: A First Look at Chicago Public School Graduates' College Enrollment, College Preparation, and Graduation from Four-Year Colleges* (Chicago: Consortium on Chicago School Research, 2006), https://ccsr.uchicago.edu/sites/default/files/publications/Postsecondary.pdf.

32. Andrew P. Kelly and Mark Schneider, *Filling in the Blanks: How Information Can Affect Choice in Higher Education* (Washington, DC: American Enterprise Institute, 2011), http://www.aei.org/wp-content/uploads/2011/01/fillingintheblanks.pdf.

33. John R. Thelin and Marybeth Gasman, "Historical Overview of American Higher Education," in *The Student Services Handbook*, 5th ed., eds. John H. Schuh, Susan R. Jones, and Shaun R. Harper (San Francisco: Jossey-Bass, 2010).

34. Sara Goldrick-Rab, Lauren Schudde, and Jacob Stampen, "Economic Diversity for Cost Containment," in *Reinventing Student Aid for the 21st Century*, eds. Andrew P. Kelly and Sara Goldrick-Rab (Cambridge, MA: Harvard University Press, 2014).

35. Federal Student Aid, "Title IV Program Volume Reports," http://studentaid.ed.gov/about/data-center/student/title-iv.

36. Robert Kelchen, "Campus-Based Financial Aid Programs: Trends and Alternative Allocation Strategies," *Educational Policy* (forthcoming).

37. Lauren Schudde and Judith Scott-Clayton, "Pell Grants as Performance-Based Aid? An Examination of Satisfactory Academic Progress Requirements in the Nation's Largest Need-Based Aid Program" (working paper, Center for Analysis of Post-Secondary Education and Employment, New York, NY, 2014).

38. Martha J. Bailey and Susan M. Dynarski, "Inequality in Postsecondary Education," in *Whither Opportunity?* eds. Greg J. Duncan and Richard J. Murnane (New York: Russell Sage, 2011).

39. Josh Logue, "Next Steps on FAFSA," *Inside Higher Ed*, September 15, 2015, https://www.insidehighered.com/news/2015/09/15/excitement-and-concern-about-prior-prior-year-fafsa-changes/.

40. Timothy J. Bartik, Brad J. Hershbein, and Marta Lachowska, "The Effects of the Kalamazoo Promise Scholarship on College Enrollment, Persistence, and Completion" (working paper, Upjohn Institute, Kalamazoo, MI, 2015); Robert K. Toutkoushian et al., "Effect of Twenty-First Century Scholars Program on College Aspirations and Completion" (working paper, Association for Education Finance and Policy, Columbia, MO, March 2013).

41. Chad Adelman, "On College Signing Day, a Look at FAFSA Completion Rates," *Ahead of the Heard* (blog), May 1, 2015, http://aheadoftheheard.org/on-college-signing-day-a-look-at-fafsa-completion-rates/.

42. Robert Kelchen and Sara Goldrick-Rab, "Accelerating College Knowledge: A Fiscal Analysis of a Targeted Early Commitment Pell Grant Program," *Journal of Higher Education* 86, no. 2 (2015): 199–232.

43. Douglas N. Harris, Alan Nathan, and Ryne Marksteiner, "The Upward Bound College Access Program 50 Years Later: Evidence from a National Randomized Trial" (working paper, Institute for Research on Poverty, Madison, WI, December 2014).

44. Office of Postsecondary Education, "Academic Competitiveness and National SMART Grants," www2.ed.gov/about/offices/list/ope/ac-smart.html.

45. US Department of Education, "Academic Competitiveness Grants and National Science and Mathematics Access to Retain Talent (SMART) Grants," www2.ed.gov/programs/smart/funding.html.

46. For the sake of brevity, I exclude discussions of the "90/10 rule," an additional federal accountability policy that requires for-profit colleges to get at least 10 percent of total tuition revenue from sources other than federal grants and loans (veterans' benefits excluded) in order to receive student financial aid dollars.

47. Federal Student Aid, "Three-Year Official Cohort Default Rates for Schools," www2.ed.gov/offices/OSFAP/defaultmanagement/cdr.html.

48. US Senate Committee on Health, Education, Labor and Pensions, "Risk-Sharing/Skin-in-the-Game Concepts and Proposals," www.help.senate.gov/imo/media/Risk_Sharing.pdf.

49. Debbie Cochrane and Laura Szabo-Kubitz, *At What Cost? How Community Colleges That Do Not Offer Federal Loans Put Students at Risk* (Washington, DC: The Institute for College Access and Success, 2014), http://ticas.org/sites/default/files/pub_files/At_What_Cost.pdf.

50. Federal Student Aid, "Heightened Cash Monitoring," http://studentaid.ed.gov/sa/about/data-center/school/hcm.

51. Goldie Blumenstyk, "Education Department Didn't Set Out to Shut Down Corinthian," *Chronicle of Higher Education*, July 8, 2014, http://chronicle.com/article/Education-Department-Didn-t/147533/.

52. Michael Stratford, "Cash Monitoring List Unveiled," *Inside Higher Ed*, March 31, 2015, www.insidehighered.com/news/2015/03/31/education-department-names-most-colleges-facing-heightened-scrutiny-federal.

53. Office of Postsecondary Education, "The Database of Accredited Postsecondary Institutions and Programs," http://ope.ed.gov/accreditation/.

54. *Bloomberg BusinessWeek*, "How Colleges are Buying Respect," March 4, 2010, www.bloomberg.com/bw/magazine/content/10_11/b4170050344129.htm.

55. Fuller and Belkin, "The Watchdogs of College Education Rarely Bite."

56. US Government Accountability Office, *Education Should Strengthen Oversight of Schools and Accreditors*, 2014, www.gao.gov/assets/670/667690.pdf.

57. Andy Thomason, "Gainful-Employment Rule Survives For-Profit Group's Court Challenge," *Chronicle of Higher Education*, June 23, 2015, http://chronicle.com/blogs/ticker/gainful-employment-rule-survives-for-profit-groups-court-challenge/101079.

58. Michal Stratford, "Obama Seeks Funding Boost," *Inside Higher Ed*, February 3, 2015, www.insidehighered.com/news/2015/02/03/ obama-seeks-boost-higher-education-spending-and-proposes-some-loan-reforms-have.

59. Anya Kamenetz, "New Federal College Ratings Will Consider Aid, Total Cost, Employment," National Public Radio, December 19, 2014, www.npr.org/sections/ed/2014/12/19/371705270/ details-on-the-administrations-new-college-ratings-system.

60. Robert Kelchen, "Proposing a Federal Risk-Sharing Policy," (Indianapolis, IN: Lumina Foundation, 2015).

61. Eagan et al., *The American Freshman.*

62. Tami Strang, "Students' Top Reasons for Choosing Community College," Cengage Learning, April 28, 2015, http://blog.cengage.com/students-top-reasons-for-choosing-community-college/; Joshua Goodman, Michael Hurwitz, and Jonathan Smith, "College Access, Initial College Choice and Degree Completion" (working paper, National Bureau of Economic Research, Cambridge, MA, 2015); Bridget Terry Long and Michael Kurlaender, "Do Community Colleges Provide a Viable Pathway to a Baccalaureate Degree?" *Educational Evaluation and Policy Analysis* 31, no. 1 (2009): 30–53.

63. Peter M. Kinsley, "The Pull of Home: Family Dynamics and the Initial College Experiences of Low-Income Undergraduates" (PhD diss., University of Wisconsin-Madison, 2014), http:// gradworks.umi.com/36/43/3643032.html.

64. Nicholas W. Hillman, *Differential Impacts of College Ratings: The Case of Education Deserts,* Civil Rights Project Research and Policy Briefing, 2014, http://news.education.wisc.edu/docs/ WebDispenser/news-connections-pdf/crp---hillman---draft.pdf?sfvrsn=6.

65. David Leonhardt, "A Nudge to Poorer Students to Aim High on Colleges," *New York Times*, September 25, 2013, www.nytimes.com/2013/09/26/education/for-low-income-students-considering-college-a-nudge-to-aim-high.html.

66. Audrey Light and Wayne Strayer, "Determinants of College Completion: School Quality or Student Ability?" *Journal of Human Resources* 35, no. 2 (2000): 299–332; Stacy Dale and Alan B. Krueger, "Estimating the Return to College Selectivity over the Career Using Administrative Earnings Data," (working paper, National Bureau of Economic Research, Cambridge, MA, 2011); Jennie E. Brand and Yu Xie, "Who Benefits Most from College? Evidence for Negative Selection in Heterogeneous Economic Returns to Higher Education," *American Sociological Review* 75, no. 2 (2010): 273–302.

67. Dale and Krueger, "Estimating the Return to College Selectivity."

68. Michael Bastedo and Allyson Flaster, "Conceptual and Methodological Problems in Research on College Undermatch," *Educational Researcher* 43, no. 2 (2015): 93–99.

69. Robert Kelchen, "Are 'Affordable Elite' Colleges Growing in Size, or Just Selectivity?" *Washington Monthly*, August 29, 2014, www.washingtonmonthly.com/college_guide/blog /are_affordable_elite_colleges.php.

70. Michael N. Bastedo and Ozan Jaquette, "Running in Place: Low-Income Students and the Dynamics of Higher Education Stratification," *Educational Evaluation and Policy Analysis* 33, no. 3 (2011): 318–339.

71. Matthew M. Chingos, "Graduation Rates at America's Universities: What We Know Now and What We Need to Know," in *Getting to Graduation: The Completion Agenda in Higher Education*, ed. Andrew P. Kelly and Mark S. Schneider (Baltimore: Johns Hopkins Press, 2012).

72. Jeff Selingo et al., *The Next Generation University* (Washington, DC: New America, 2013), http://static.newamerica.org/attachments/2318-the-next-generation-university/Next_ Generation_University_FINAL_FOR_RELEASE.8897220087ff4bd6afe8f6682594e3b0.pdf.

73. Scott E. Carrell, Richard L. Fullerton, and James E. West, "Does Your Cohort Matter? Measuring Peer Effects in College Achievement," *Journal of Labor Economics* 27, no. 3 (2009): 439–464; Ralph Stinebrickner and Todd R. Stinebrickner, "What Can Be Learned About Peer Effects Using College Roommates? Evidence from New Survey Data and Students from Disadvantaged Backgrounds," *Journal of Public Economics* 90, no. 8–9 (2006): 1435–1454.

74. Donna M. Desrochers and Steven Hurlburt, *Trends in College Spending: 2001–2011: A Delta Data Update* (Washington, DC: American Institutes for Research, 2014), www.deltacostproject .org/sites/default/files/products/Delta%20Cost_Trends%20College%20Spending%202001-2011 _071414_rev.pdf.

75. Andrew P. Kelly, "The Thorny Politics of Higher Education Reform," *Forbes*, March 31, 2014, www.forbes.com/sites/akelly/2014/03/31/the-thorny-politics-of-higher-education-reform/.

Conclusion

1. Scott Jaschik, "Admissions Revolution," *Inside Higher Ed*, September 29, 2015, www.inside-highered.com/news/2015/09/29/80-colleges-and-universities-announce-plan-new-applicat-ion-and-new-approach.

2. Jonathan Smith, Matea Pender, and Jessica Howell, "The Full Extent of Student-College Academic Undermatch," *Economics of Education Review* 32 (February 2013): 247–261.

3. Caroline Hoxby and Christopher Avery, *The Missing "One-Offs": The Hidden Supply of High-Achieving, Low-Income Students* (Washington, DC: The Brookings Institution, Spring 2013), www.brookings.edu/~/media/projects/bpea/spring-2013/2013a_hoxby.pdf.

4. See Michael Hurwitz and Amal Kumar, *Supply and Demand in the Higher Education Market* (New York: College Board, February 2015), https://research.collegeboard.org/sites/default/ files/publications/2015/8/college-board-research-brief-supply-demand-college-admission-college-choice.pdf. Figures 5a and 5b demonstrate that competitive colleges both have the most seats and the strongest growth over time.

5. See Figure 5b in Hurwitz and Kumar, *Supply and Demand in the Higher Education Market*.

6. Nick Anderson, "Princeton President Says Elite School Is 'Inclined' to Expand Undergrad Enrollment," *Washington Post*, August 4, 2015, www.washingtonpost.com/news/grade-point/wp/2015/08/04/ princeton-president-says-elite-school-is-inclined-to-expand-undergrad-enrollment/.

7. Mamie Voight and Colleen Campbell, "A Bitter Pell," *Washington Monthly*, September/ October 2015, www.washingtonmonthly.com/magazine/septemberoctober_2015/features/a _bitter_pell057181.php; Andrew Howard Nichols, *The Pell Partnership: Ensuring a Shared Responsibility for Low-Income Student Success*, The Education Trust, September 2015, https:// edtrust.org/wp-content/uploads/2014/09/ThePellPartnership_EdTrust_20152.pdf; For a list of commitments by roughly 250 institutions and organizations who pledged in late 2014 to increase student opportunities by improving counseling, K–16 partnerships, STEM, and degree completion, see The White House, *Commitments to Action on College Opportunity*, December 2014, www.whitehouse.gov/sites/default/files/docs/121514_college_opportunity _commitment_report.pdf.

8. For more information, see National Association for College Admission Counseling, "Prior-Prior Year Income Data for the FAFSA," www.nacacnet.org/issues-action/LegislativeNews /Pages/PPY.aspx.

9. John Bound and Sarah Turner, "Cohort Crowding: How Resources Affect Collegiate Attainment," *Journal of Public Economics* 91, nos. 5–6 (2007): 877–899; Susan Dynarski, "Building the Stock of College-Education Labor" (working paper, National Bureau of Economic Research, Cambridge, MA, September 2005); Benjamin L. Castleman and Bridget

Terry Long, "Looking Beyond Enrollment: The Causal Effect of Need-Based Grants on College Access, Persistence, and Graduation" (working paper, National Bureau of Economic Research, Cambridge, MA, August 2012).

10. Adam Looney and Constantine Yannelis, "A Crisis in Student Loans? How Changes in the Characteristics of Borrowers and in the Institutions They Attended Contributed to Rising Loan Defaults," (working paper, The Brookings Institution, September 10, 2015), www .brookings.edu/about/projects/bpea/papers/2015/looney-yannelis-student-loan-defaults.

11. Matthew M. Chingos, "Graduation Rates at America's Universities: What We Know and What We Need to Know," in *Getting to Graduation: The Completion Agenda in Higher Education,* eds. Andrew P. Kelly and Mark Schneider (Baltimore: Johns Hopkins University Press, 2012), 48–71; Jessica Howell and Matea Pender "The Costs and Benefits of Enrolling in an Academically Matched College," *Economics of Education Review* (forthcoming).

12. Jennie E. Brand and Yu Xie, "Who Benefits Most from College? Evidence for Negative Selection in Heterogeneous Economic Returns to Higher Education," *American Sociological Review* 75, no. 2 (2010): 273–302.

13. Joshua Goodman, Michael Hurwitz and Jonathan Smith, "College Access, Initial College Choice and Degree Completion" (working paper, National Bureau of Economic Research, Cambridge, MA, February 2015), www.nber.org/papers/w20996.pdf; Michal Kurlaender and Eric Grodsky, "Mismatch and the Paternalistic Justification for Selective College Admissions," *Sociology of Education* 86 (2013): 294–310.

14. Eleanor Wiske Dillon and Jeffrey Smith, "The Determinants of Mismatch Between Students and Colleges," (working paper, National Bureau of Economic Research, Cambridge, MA, August 2013).

15. Thomas R. Bailey, Shanna Smith Jaggars, and Davis Jenkins, *Redesigning America's Community Colleges: A Clearer Path to Student Success* (Cambridge, MA: Harvard University Press, 2015); Mark Schneider and KC Deane, eds., *The University Next Door: What Is a Comprehensive University, Who Does It Educate, and Can It Survive?* (New York: Teachers College Press, 2014); Andrew P. Kelly and Mark Schneider, eds., *Getting to Graduation: The Completion Agenda in Higher Education* (Baltimore: Johns Hopkins University Press, 2012).

Acknowledgments

For half a century, American higher education policy has sought to expand postsecondary access. While more students than ever are heading to college after high school, college completion outcomes unfortunately have been stuck in first gear. Many education scholars have thus inquired about how to improve postsecondary outcomes, particularly for disadvantaged students, and recent research has homed in on the college choice process as key to student success. A number of studies have found that students often enroll at institutions that are a poor "match" for their academic qualifications, noting that mismatching lowers the probability of completing a degree. Some scholars have observed that high-achieving, low-income students are particularly inclined to "undermatch," attending a school that is less selective than they are probably academically qualified to attend. In all, this body of research has emerged quickly, garnering national attention from media and policymakers along the way. It is not without certain limitations, however. Our volume originated from this robust collection of scholarly work and its blind spots alike.

Many of the initial conversations that led to this volume's development took place at a small invitational conference on college match hosted by the Center for College Readiness at Seton Hall University in June 2012. We are grateful for the support provided by Felice Levine and the American Educational Research Association's Education Research Conference Grant program and The College Board for this first conference. Over the course of many months that followed, we continued these and other conversations about college match—in meetings and at conferences as well as over phone calls, e-mail, and Twitter—and eventually commissioned nine new pieces of research to explore some of the important yet understudied questions surrounding college choice and match, and the relevant policy implications of this work. In August 2015, the authors came together to present early drafts of their work at a public research conference at the American Enterprise Institute, and subsequently wove new insights and feedback garnered from the audience and fellow panelists to produce the final versions included in this book.

We express our sincerest thanks to the authors for their important contributions as well as for their patience throughout the editing process. We are grateful for the following discussants who provided insightful feedback at the 2015 conference: Jon Boeckenstedt of DePaul University, Crystal Byndloss of MDRC, Harry J. Holzer of Georgetown University, Nicole Farmer Hurd of College Advising Corps, Scott Jenkins of the Lumina Foundation, Bridget Terry Long of the Harvard Graduate School of Education, Michael S. McPherson of the Spencer Foundation, Marsha Silverberg of the US Department of Education, and Lesley J. Turner of the University of Maryland.

We are also indebted to the steadfast support provided by AEI and its president, Arthur Brooks. The Bill & Melinda Gates Foundation generously provided financial support for this project as well. This book would not exist without the tireless efforts of the terrific staff at AEI, in particularly Rooney Columbus for his work managing and overseeing this project and coordinating the conference, and Sarah DuPre, Max Eden, Elizabeth English, Jenn Hatfield, and Kelsey Hamilton for their vital assistance along the way. Finally, we express our gratitude to the Harvard Education Press team, specifically executive director Douglas Clayton and editor-in-chief Caroline Chauncey, who, as always, provided skillful and timely guidance throughout the life of this project.

About the Editors

Andrew P. Kelly is the director of the Center on Higher Education Reform and a resident scholar in education policy studies at the American Enterprise Institute. His research focuses on higher education policy, innovation, financial aid reform, and the politics of education policy. Previously, he held a National Science Foundation research training fellowship at the University of California, Berkeley, and served as a research assistant at AEI. His scholarly work has appeared in the *American Journal of Education, Teachers College Record, Educational Policy, Policy Studies Journal,* and *Education Next,* and he has also published in popular outlets such as the *New York Times,* the *Wall Street Journal, The Atlantic, National Review, Education Week,* and *Inside Higher Education.* He writes a regular column on higher education reform on *Forbes* Opinion. He is coeditor of multiple edited volumes, including *Reinventing Financial Aid: Charting a New Course to College Affordability* (Harvard Education Press, 2014), *Stretching the Higher Education Dollar: How Innovation Can Improve Access, Equity, and Affordability* (Harvard Education Press, 2013), and *Getting to Graduation: The Completion Agenda in Higher Education* (Johns Hopkins University Press, 2012). In 2011, Kelly was named one of "16 Next Generation Leaders" in education policy by the *Policy Notebook* blog on *Education Week.*

Jessica S. Howell is executive director of policy research at the College Board, which conducts rigorous quantitative research on a variety of topics related to college readiness, access, affordability, admissions, and collegiate outcomes. Before joining the College Board in 2011, Howell was an associate professor of economics at California State University, Sacramento. Engaged in quantitative research on pressing education policy issues, she focuses on access and success throughout the educational pipeline for different socioeconomic and racial groups. Her current research projects focus on the match between students and colleges, the role of community colleges in achieving national degree-completion goals, and higher education policy levers for improving student outcomes.

Carolyn Sattin-Bajaj is an assistant professor in the Department of Education Leadership, Management, and Policy and codirector of the Center for College Readiness at Seton Hall University. Her research focuses on school choice and issues of educational equity and access for Latino, immigrant-origin students and families across the preK–20 educational spectrum. Sattin-Bajaj's work has appeared in a variety of academic journals and popular media outlets including the *Peabody Journal of Education*, *Journal of School Choice*, *American Journal of Education*, the *Huffington Post*, and *SchoolBook*. Her most recent book is *Unaccompanied Minors: Immigrant Youth, School Choice, and the Pursuit of Equity* (Harvard Education Press, 2014). Previously, Sattin-Bajaj worked on secondary school reform at the New York City Department of Education.

About the Contributors

Thomas R. Bailey is the George and Abby O'Neill Professor of Economics and Education at Teachers College, Columbia University. He is also director of the Community College Research Center and two national centers funded by the Institute of Education Sciences: the Center for Analysis of Postsecondary Education and Employment, established in 2011, and the Center for the Analysis of Postsecondary Readiness, established in 2014. Along with Shanna Smith Jaggars and Davis Jenkins, he wrote *Redesigning America's Community Colleges: A Clearer Path to Student Success* (Harvard University Press, 2015). Bailey is an American Educational Research Association fellow and a member of the National Academy of Education.

Michael N. Bastedo is a professor at the University of Michigan and director of the Center for the Study of Higher and Postsecondary Education. His scholarly interests focus on higher education decision making, particularly college admissions; stratification; and rankings. In 2013, he received the Early Career Award from the American Educational Research Association. Bastedo has been a Fulbright Scholar in the Netherlands and a visiting scholar at the Bellagio Center, Stanford University, and Sciences Po. His latest book is *The Organization of Higher Education: Managing Colleges for a New Era* (Johns Hopkins, 2012). Bastedo's most recent research has been reported in the *New York Times*, the *New Yorker*, the *Washington Post*, *Slate*, and the *Chronicle of Higher Education*, among others.

Clive R. Belfield is an associate professor in the department of economics at Queens College, City University of New York. He is the project lead for the Community College Research Center's assessment measures in college systems project and the Center for Analysis of Postsecondary Education and Employment's North Carolina study. His most recent book is *The Price*

We Pay: The Economic and Social Costs of Inadequate Education (Brookings Institution Press, 2007). Belfield has authored numerous articles on the economics of education and has served as a consultant to the World Bank, the US Department of Education, and the British government, as well as nonprofit foundations and education think tanks.

Joshua S. Goodman is an associate professor of public policy at the Harvard Kennedy School of Government and studies the economics of education. He has explored the impacts of merit aid on college choice, college quality on degree completion, and various math coursework interventions on the long-term success of students.

Matthew A. Holsapple is an associate program officer at the Spencer Foundation and an affiliated researcher with the University of Chicago Consortium on School Research. His research focuses on the relationship between student experiences and institutional practices and characteristics in predicting college outcomes, the effects of college choice on outcomes, college student learning and development, and moral and ethical education in colleges and universities. In addition, he teaches courses on data use and analysis at the University of Chicago's School of Social Service Administration.

Michael Hurwitz is a policy research scientist at the College Board. His research has been published in scholarly journals including the *Journal of Policy Analysis and Management, Educational Evaluation and Policy Analysis*, and *Economics of Education Review*, and he has been featured in numerous media outlets, such as the *New York Times* and the *Chronicle of Higher Education*. Previously, Hurwitz was a research analyst at the Consortium on Financing Higher Education and the American Institutes for Research.

Jennifer E. Iriti is the director of the Evaluation for Learning Group at the University of Pittsburgh's Learning Research and Development Center. She designs, manages, and implements evaluations of education programs and organizations in preK–16 settings. Iriti applies improvement science, utilization-focused evaluation, and developmental evaluation to support organizations in continuous improvement. Recently, she has focused on organizations and programs that support college attendance and success in urban education settings, such as The Pittsburgh Promise and other public school initiatives. In addition to her evaluation work, Iriti is a faculty fellow of the Center for Urban Education and an adjunct assistant professor in the Learning Sciences and Policy Program. She has published articles in the *American Journal of Evaluation* and *Educational Technology Research and Development*, is co-author of a chapter in the *International Handbook of Educational Evaluation*, and regularly presents at peer-reviewed conferences such as the American Evaluation Association, the American Educational Research Association, and PromiseNet.

Davis Jenkins is a senior research associate at the Community College Research Center (CCRC) at Columbia University's Teachers College. His research has informed the development and spread of innovative approaches to improve college performance and student outcomes, including career pathways, adult technical bridge programs (such as Washington State's I-BEST), and guided pathways to success. Together with Thomas Bailey and Shanna Smith Jaggars, Jenkins is the author of *Redesigning America's Community Colleges: A Clearer Path to Student Success* (Harvard University Press, 2015), which is based on CCRC's research on strategies for improving student completion and learning. His current research focuses on strategies for helping students choose a program of study, improving community college baccalaureate transfer outcomes, and understanding the costs of large-scale institutional reforms.

Robert Kelchen is an assistant professor of higher education at Seton Hall University. His research interests include higher-education finance, student financial aid, and accountability policies. He has recent articles published in the *Journal of Higher Education*, *Journal of Education Finance*, and *Journal of Student Financial Aid*. His work as a methodologist for *Washington Monthly* magazine's annual college rankings won an award for best data journalism from the Education Writers Association. Kelchen is frequently quoted in the media, including the *Washington Post*, National Public Radio, the *Chronicle of Higher Education*, and *Politico*. He has also appeared on *Marketplace*, KABC radio, and MSNBC.

Elizabeth Kopko is a senior research assistant at the Community College Research Center (CCRC) at Columbia University's Teachers College. Kopko is also a doctoral candidate in economics and education at Teachers College. She conducts both quantitative and qualitative research on a variety of topics surrounding student decision-making processes. Kopko's current research interests include higher-education policy and student choice, particularly the relationships between college choice, academic focus, and student success.

Amal Kumar is a senior policy research analyst at the College Board, where he researches college enrollment, match, transfer, and persistence. Before joining the College Board, Kumar was a research analyst at the Center for Education Policy Research at Harvard University, where he worked closely with school districts and state education agencies to research high school graduation, college enrollment, transfer, and persistence. Kumar's research focuses on identifying actionable policy levers and metrics that can drive evidence-based decision making in K–12 and higher education.

Christian Martell is a doctoral student in the Center for the Study of Higher and Postsecondary Education at the University of Michigan. Her current research interests include college access and choice for underrepresented students, and the governance and strategy of educational institutions. Christian's professional background is in teaching and overseeing preK–12 academic and enrichment programs at independent schools.

Jenny Nagaoka is the deputy director of the University of Chicago Consortium on School Research. Her research interests focus on policy and practice in urban education reform, particularly developing school environments and instructional practices that promote college readiness and success. She has coauthored numerous journal articles and reports, including studies of college readiness, noncognitive factors, the transition from high school to postsecondary education, authentic intellectual instruction, and Chicago's initiative to end social promotion. Nagaoka's current work includes developing a framework of the foundational factors for young adult success and how students can be supported through developmental experiences and relationships; documenting models of school networks to build the capacity of practitioners to use data and support student performance; a project examining how to design effective high school graduation and college readiness indicator systems; and leading the Consortium's efforts to translate its research findings into school-level data reports.

Lindsay C. Page is an assistant professor of education and a research scientist for the Learning Research and Development Center at the University of Pittsburgh. Her work focuses on quantitative methods and their application to questions regarding the effectiveness of educational policies and programs across the preschool to postsecondary spectrum. Much of her recent work involves the implementation of large-scale randomized trials to investigate innovative strategies for improving students' transition to and through postsecondary education. A key area of focus in this domain is Page's work on strategies to mitigate summer melt, the phenomenon where students fail to transition successfully from high school to college. She has coauthored a book on this topic and has published her work in journals including the *Journal of Human Resources, Journal of Policy Analysis and Management, Economics of Education Review*, and *Educational Evaluation and Policy Analysis*.

Matea Pender is an associate policy research scientist in the College Board's policy research division. She conducts research on college access, college choice, and retention. Pender also focuses on financial aid policy and provides research support for the College Board's annual publications *Trends in Student Aid* and *Trends in College Pricing*.

Melissa Roderick is the Hermon Dunlap Smith Professor at the University of Chicago School of Social Service Administration, a Senior Director at the Consortium on School Research, and the codirector of the Network for College Success. She is an expert in urban school reform, high-stakes testing, minority adolescent development, and school transitions. Her areas of research have focused on the transition to high school, school dropout, grade retention, and the effects of summer programs. Roderick is an expert in mixing qualitative and quantitative methods in evaluation, and her new work links quantitative and qualitative research to explore the relationship between students' high school careers and preparation, their college selection choices, and their postsecondary outcomes. From 2001 to 2003, Roderick joined the administration of the Chicago Public Schools to establish a new department of planning and development. In 2004, Roderick was honored by the *Chicago Sun-Times* as one of "Chicago's 100 Most Powerful Women." She is a founding board member and chair of the board of North Lawndale College Preparatory Charter High School. Nationally, she serves on the Carnegie Council for Advancing Adolescent Literacy and on MDRC's Education Studies Committee.

Awilda Rodriguez is an assistant professor in the Center for the Study of Higher and Postsecondary Education. Her research is at the intersection of higher education policy; college access and choice; and the representation of black, Latino, low-income, and first-generation students in post-secondary education. Her most recent project examines issues of equity in access to rigorous high school coursework. Along with policy reports and contributions to edited volumes, Rodriguez's work has been published in *Research in Higher Education, Educational Policy, Diverse Issues in Higher Education*, and the *Chronicle of Higher Education*. She previously worked as a research fellow at American Enterprise Institute's Center on Higher Education Reform and as a research associate at the National Center for Public Policy and Higher Education.

Jonathan Smith is a policy research scientist at the College Board. His research focuses on the behavioral and institutional factors that determine how students choose colleges and the consequences of those decisions. His research is published in leading economics, policy, and education journals. Smith teaches at the Trachtenberg School of Public Policy and Public Administration at George Washington University.

Index